HAMLIN GARLAND's

Observations
on the

AMERICAN INDIAN

1895–1905

HAMLIN GARLAND's

Observations on the

The University of Arizona Press

Tucson, Arizona

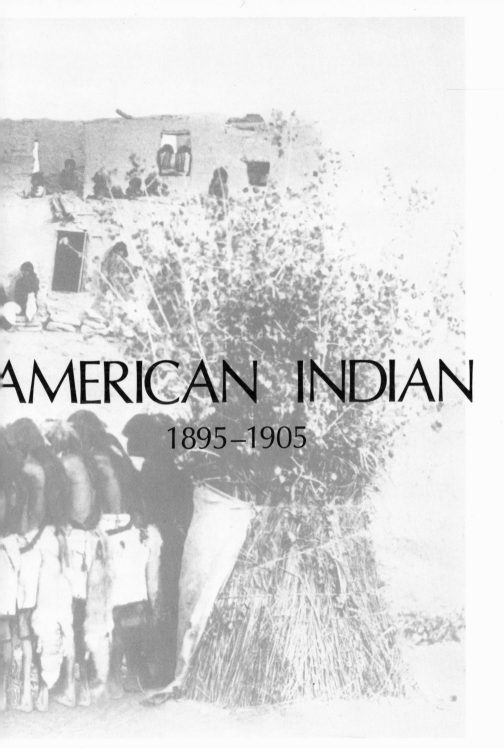

AMERICAN INDIAN
1895–1905

Compiled and Edited by

LONNIE E. UNDERHILL and DANIEL F. LITTLEFIELD, Jr.

About the Editors . . .

LONNIE E. UNDERHILL has supplemented his background in American literature with doctoral work at the University of Arizona in western U.S. history. An English instructor since 1965, he is the author and editor of several articles concerning Western and native American history.

DANIEL F. LITTLEFIELD, JR., taught at several colleges and universities in the Midwest and South before becoming associate professor of American literature at the University of Arkansas at Little Rock. The author of a number of articles dealing with the Trans-Mississippi West and the American Indian, he holds a Ph.D. in American literature from Oklahoma State University.

In 1975 the editors shared the Forest History Society's Frederick K. Weyerhaeuser Award for their article entitled "Timber Depredations and Cherokee Legislation, 1869–1881."

THE UNIVERSITY OF ARIZONA PRESS

Copyright © 1976
The Arizona Board of Regents
All Rights Reserved
Manufactured in the U.S.A.

I.S.B.N.-0-8165-0485-7 cloth
I.S.B.N.-0-8165-0505-5 paper
L.C. No. 75-19863

To Hamlin Garland,
Friend to the American Indian

Contents

III. Reference Materials

Illustrations

Maps

Preface

HAMLIN GARLAND'S nonfictional writings about the American Indian
provide a fresh, first-hand view of native Americans during a critical period
of their history. When Garland traveled among the Indians during the two
decades following 1895, he found many in the process of giving up the modified life styles of the reservation and adopting those of the Anglo-dominated
culture. Garland's sensitive portrayals of these often-painful transitions offer
new insights to the general reader as well as to scholars in anthropology, history, sociology, and literature.

These nonfiction pieces will be a refreshing surprise to those familiar only
with Hamlin Garland's fiction, which often has inherent weaknesses. Throughout his career, Garland was best at writing realistic description. The word pictures painted in his Indian essays are especially enthusiastic and accurate, since
most of them were written directly from field notes.

The works in this volume cover the period from 1895 through 1905, the
time of Garland's greatest interest in the American Indian. Much of the material
has previously been unpublished. Both literary appeal and ethnographic significance were factors considered in selecting the thirteen essays presented here.

Each work is preceded by a brief historical sketch of the pertinent tribe
and a statement of its condition at the time of Garland's visit. In the works
themselves, clarifying annotation has been provided. No substantive changes
have been made in the essays, but the editors have supplied punctuation where
a lack of it would make reading more difficult.

The writings are arranged in chronological order, according to the dates
of Garland's travels which produced the relevant notes. Thus the collection
begins with the author's first visit to an Indian reservation ("Among the Southern Utes") and ends with the dissolution of the tribal governments of the Five
Civilized Tribes ("The Final Council of the Creek Nation"). Through the
essays, the reader can trace Garland's developing attitude toward native
Americans.

Preceding the edited works is a general Introduction, which provides the
biographical and historical background of Garland's interest in the American
Indian. It surveys the greater part of his work on the Indian, including poetry,
fiction, and nonfiction — both published and unpublished.

Acknowledgments

The production of this volume has been the result of the efforts and kind-
nesses of many. Our appreciation goes especially to the officers, directors, and
board members of the Rockefeller Foundation for the grant which defrayed

the greatest part of the expense of the project. We also thank Professors Harwood P. Hinton, Richard Hosley, Byrd H. Granger, Frederick R. Rebsamen, and John H. McElroy of the University of Arizona and Clinton C. Keeler of Oklahoma State University for recommending us to the foundation. We are also indebted for further financial assistance to the Faculty Research Committee and the administration of the University of Arkansas at Little Rock.

Others we wish to thank include the following: Richard A. Kassander, Jr., vice president for research at the University of Arizona; Warren V. Ford, Kenneth J. Hayes, and Mrs. Dorothy Willison of the University of Arizona for administering the Rockefeller funds; Mrs. Kathy Essary and Steve Parker, reference librarians at the library of the University of Arkansas at Little Rock; John C. McKay and his staff of the University of Arizona Library, who gave interlibrary loan assistance; Glenn W. Bunday, curator of the American Literature Collection at the University of Southern California, for his assistance in making the Garland papers available to us; Garland's daughters, Mrs. Constance Garland Doyle and Mrs. Isabel Garland Lord, who have granted permission to quote from their father's work; and Miss Ruth N. Knittel for careful typing and proofreading of the manuscript.

We are particularly grateful to the University of Southern California Library for permitting us to use extensively materials in the Hamlin Garland Collection. We would also like to thank director Marshall Townsend, editor Karen Thure, and the rest of the staff of the University of Arizona Press for their skill and cooperation in projecting the manuscript into published form. For their encouragement, we offer a special thanks to our wives, Carolyn G. Underhill and Mary Ann Littlefield. Our appreciation likewise goes to all others whom we have failed to mention, but who played some part in the production of this volume.

LONNIE E. UNDERHILL
DANIEL F. LITTLEFIELD, JR.

HAMLIN GARLAND's

Observations
on the

AMERICAN INDIAN

1895–1905

Reservations Visited by Garland, 1895–1905

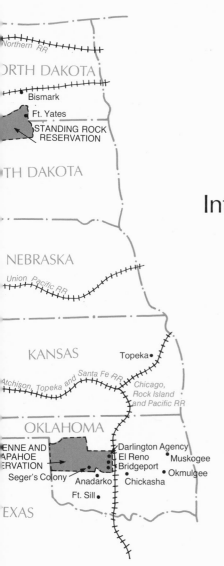

PART I

Introductory Survey of Garland's Writings on the American Indian

Introductory Survey

In the fall of 1884, twenty-three-year-old Hamlin Garland packed his imitation leather valise, donned his broad-brimmed black hat, and left the little town of Ordway, South Dakota, on a train bound for glamorous Boston. Envisioning a distinguished career as a professor of literature and oratory, he felt no regret as he watched the bleak midwestern prairie lands pass by the dirty window.

As the eldest of three children of a pioneer farmer, this brown-bearded young man well knew the repetitious drudgery of farm work. Born in West Salem, Wisconsin, on September 14, 1860, he had moved with his family to a farm near Osage, Iowa, in 1869. Twelve years later, Garland, already disenchanted with country life, graduated from Cedar Valley Seminary. That year his parents selected a homestead at Ordway, but their eldest son stayed behind. He worked at odd jobs for a year, taught a year in Ohio, then decided at least to try the vocation of his father. He took up a homestead near his parents' place in South Dakota in 1883.

Garland was predictably discontented as a farmer. In the summer of 1884 he told the Reverend James W. Bashford, a visiting Methodist from Maine, that he was "sick of the country and in despair of its future"; that he was thinking of selling his homestead and attending an Illinois normal school. Bashford, sympathetic toward Garland's malaise, urged the bright youth to go instead to Boston University and gave him letters of introduction to the faculty there.

Garland excitedly arrived in Boston in late October, only to meet disappointment. Despite his letters of introduction, the young man was refused entrance to both Boston University and Harvard. He remained in the city, however, studying on his own, living on the dwindling proceeds from the sale of his homestead.

The Prairie: A Place to Reform

Fortunately, in 1885 Garland met William Dean Howells, perhaps the most noted man of letters in America at the time. Howells urged his young friend to write about the manners and customs of the people of the Midwest. Encouraged by Howells and with the assistance of Charles Hurd, literary editor of the *Boston Evening Transcript,* Garland began his writing career.

During the next few years, the young man drew on his memories of prairie life and on first-hand experiences acquired during visits to his family in South Dakota. In June, 1887, after observing the situations of many of the farmers, he decided to write a story about the hard conditions of rural people in the Midwest. His mother told of a neighbor in Iowa, who, after many years of border life, had gone back to New York for a visit. Garland transformed the story into "Mrs. Ripley's Trip," published by *Harper's Weekly* in 1888. To earn train fare back to Boston, the writer worked for his father in the wheat harvest, and he became aware, first-hand, of the physical drag of the work.

Garland returned to the Midwest in 1888 and found the people despondent because of their hard labor and poor economic condition. He was especially moved by the condition of women on the farms. Their loneliness and drudgery led him to write "A Prairie Heroine" (1890).

The new writer sent the piece to Benjamin O. Flower, editor of *The Arena* magazine, a periodical devoted to protest. Flower accepted the story, and with that acceptance, Garland established one of the most significant relationships of his literary career. The editor collected six of the young man's short stories and published them under the title of *Main-Travelled Roads* in 1891. This work, dealing with rural life in the Midwest, firmly established Garland as a writer, mainly because of the literary furor it created.

While his work was praised by Howells and others, Garland was accused by some of being disloyal to the West, for the pictures of drudgery he drew did not agree with the pastoral images of rural life previously presented in fiction. But Flower was delighted. He had asked Garland to write a serial novel based on the Farmers' Alliance and sent the author to the South and Midwest to talk to leaders of the farmers' movement. The novel, *A Spoil of Office* (1892), was not successful.

At the time the book appeared, Garland's interests began to shift to new subjects. To broaden the young writer's experiences, Flower sent him to Colorado in the summer of 1892 and to the West Coast that fall. Garland's purpose in going to Colorado was to see Louis Ehrich, a fellow reformer who had gone west for his health, in an effort to solicit financial aid for *The Arena*.

The West: A New Enthusiasm

When Garland returned to Boston, he was excited over what he had seen in the West. He later wrote of the experience in *Roadside Meetings* (1930):

I had entered a fresh scene — discovered a new enthusiasm. . . . Thereafter neither the coulee country nor the prairie served exclusively as material for my books. From the plains, which were becoming each year more crowded, more prosaic, I fled in imagination as in fact to the looming silver-and-purple summits of the Continental Divide, while in my mind an ambition to embody, as no one at that time had done, the spirit and the purpose of the Rocky Mountain trailer was vaguely forming in my mind.

Garland had entered an experimental period, one of "vascillation between social reform and fictive art." He had no irking sense of responsibility for the social conditions of the West, and he reacted to the area enthusiastically. He returned to Boston with "a new scale of values." With these values, the destruction of the People's Party, which Garland had supported through his political writing, and the failure of *A Spoil of Office,* he gave up political fiction and retreated, as he said, "from the ethic to the esthetic."

His reactions to his trip to the West Coast appear in "Western Landscapes," published in *The Atlantic Monthly* in December, 1893. It is an ununified collection of short descriptive pieces variously titled "Arizona," "Santa Barbara," "Oakland Ferry," "San Francisco Bay (December)," "Sunset at San José (Christmas)," "An Oregon Landscape," "Washington State," and "A Dakota Landscape."

The work is interesting mainly as a transitional piece. In his new-found enthusiasm for the Far West, Garland often seems to give in to the excesses of language, appearing at times to be doing little more than going through exercises in alliteration, exclamation, and the making of similes. However, the reader notes a change in tone in the final section. There the language is more subdued as Garland returns, somewhat, to his old attitude about the upper Midwest.

The Dakota landscape is beautiful and alluring, yet it destroys man by enslaving him "to wind and sky and the unspeakable domination of space" — space, which reduced him to "a speck in the measureless prairie" and "made his motions the crawling of an ant, his house a withered leaf, and his arm an infinitesimal thread." The idea of space also is inherent in "Arizona," although Garland does not discuss it philosophically. Yet it is not oppressive there. Garland knew the Dakota landscapes too well to react to them as freshly and simply aesthetically as he did to those he had just discovered in the West. Thus he demonstrates early his "reaction from the drab life of the plain."

These travels in the West, and another trip to Colorado in the summer of 1894, marked the end of one stage in Garland's literary career. The writer's discovery of the West caused his writing to take a different turn, of which he was most conscious. He wrote:

If any of my critics wish to call this a confused, wavering, experimental period, I shall not dispute their statement. I was a boy let loose to play. I could go where I wished, and I particularly wished to go into every Western state and territory. I wanted to know as much about the Rocky Mountains as any other writer. Unfortunately, I could not write and travel at the same time. The concentration which I had enjoyed in Boston for seven years now gave way to a period of casual composition, writing which was perilously journalistic in nature.

The result of his "experimentation" was a large body of writing — articles, stories, and poems — written between 1892 and 1916, which had as its subject matter the American West. Many aspects of the West interested Garland, but he found the American Indian most fascinating, and much of his material during those two and one-half decades dealt with that subject. The writer's treatment of the Indian was sympathetic from the start, and that sympathy caused him to expend much of his energy on works that were as much sociological as literary and more reformist than aesthetic.

The result, so far as Garland's fiction is concerned, was unfortunate, for few pieces have been judged successful. These novels and short stories focusing on the American Indian have been adequately dealt with by scholars. Outstanding among these works are studies by Owen J. Reamer and Roy W. Meyer,[1] the latter being the most thorough. Both writers point out the weaknesses of Garland's Indian fiction. Reamer says, "Whatever their artistic merit, his stories are still worth reading for their historical and sociological values." He feels that Garland was "the pioneer in this matter of the handling of the reservation Indian, and that by his true and sympathetic portraits he made a contribution of lasting importance to American literature." Finally, Reamer describes Garland as a "diligent" reformer of more success, in respect to the American Indian, than Meyer will admit.

Meyer feels that "Garland's position was not only enlightened for the time but more sympathetic toward the Indian than typical American public opinion in any period of our national history." But he adds that Garland failed "to think through the implications of his theories on the Indian question" and that Garland "was not artist enough to embody his conceptions in consistently satisfying literary form." Meyer concludes that Garland is most effective in an article entitled "The Red Man's Present Needs," published in *North American Review* in 1902.

With the exception of that article and "The Red Man as Material" (1903), Garland's Indian essays have received little attention. Few of this writer's nonfiction pieces were published during his lifetime, despite the fact that they often contain a charm and intrinsic interest superior to that of the fiction.

It is astonishing that these nonfiction pieces have remained so long neglected. Hamlin Garland was a first-rate man of letters, a very meticulous observer, and a talented writer, who, in all of his associations with the American Indian, was an active and careful note-taker. His notebooks contain great quantities of raw materials relating to the American Indian during the period 1895 through 1905.[2] Some of these notes were later worked into a more coherent form and constitute substantial sections of his autobiographical works such as *A Daughter of the Middle Border* (1921), *Roadside Meetings* (1930), and *Companions on the Trail* (1931). Others found more immediate use as germs of stories, poems, sketches, articles, and essays.

---

[1] Owen J. Reamer, "Garland and the Indians," pp. 257–280; and Roy W. Meyer, "Hamlin Garland and the American Indian," pp. 109–125.

[2] Hamlin Garland's papers are in the Library of the University of Southern California, Los Angeles. All unpublished materials cited in the following pages are from the Hamlin Garland Collection there.

Garland takes early morning field notes in camp, 1898. His heavy indelible pencil and habit of writing on his knee resulted in the scrawled manuscripts pictured on pages 10 and 11.

Garland daughters

These latter nonfiction pieces are, for the most part, first-hand observations of and about the American Indian in a period of transition, on the very verge of assimilation into Anglo-dominated society on terms dictated by the white man. The body of this writer's material on the Indian is an early link in a long chain of sympathetic accounts of native life which led up to the vast amount of pro-Indian writing in the 1960s and 1970s. The following survey of the literary, historical, and personal milieu which produced Garland's works on the American Indian — both fiction and nonfiction — will put his writings into perspective.[3]

---

[3] This survey is based on a close reading of Garland's notebooks, correspondence, and published works, specifically *Roadside Meetings, Companions on the Trail, A Daughter of the Middle Border,* and *Back-Trailers from the Middle Border.* All Garland quotations contained in the survey can be found in these basic sources. The notebooks were particularly useful in dating much of the unpublished material and in determining the source of most of the essays. However, two works were the ultimate authority in some difficult bibliographic matters. For problems relating to Garland's published works, Jean Holloway's *Hamlin Garland: A Biography* and Lloyd A. Arvidson's "A Bibliography of the Published Writings of Hamlin Garland" were consulted, and for problems relating to manuscript materials, the editors turned to Lloyd A. Arvidson's compilation entitled *Hamlin Garland: Centennial Tributes and a Checklist of the Hamlin Garland Papers in the University of Southern California Library.*

line — all time holler
He rode ~~Chestnut~~ horse
with white face and
~~white~~ forelegs. Indian
keep swirling around the
man — shoot, shoot, shoot.
once in a while
~~~~ a man
would break toward
the ~~~~ — # Custer's
Colored interpreter was killed
by horse fallen here.
Gray horse Co — Some
of soldiers fall and
horses fall on him.
on horses and about
few men ~~~~ breastwork,
made funeral breast
men
down the hill, led by
the man in Buckskin shirt.
All killed near river ~~~~
all clothes
~~~~ everywhere. While
dusk + — that night
the men were stripped

This typical page from Garland's Indian field notes shows how he penciled rough impressions on location as he interviewed and observed. The editing in ink was done later in the day as the author began to develop a story around the raw field material.

A Typical Indian Scare

The Cheyenne Trouble.

Hamlin Garland's Letter from Lame Deer.

The Cheyenne reservation is in Custer County, Montana and adjoins the eastern line of the Crow lands. It is a dry county — pitilessly dry. It is watered by small streams, the Rosebud River, the Lame Deer and Big Muddy Creek, all else is dry. These streams can be made to irrigate a few small patches of bottom land — no more. It must forever remain... the whole tract... is from four to five thousand feet above the sea and is composed for the most part of hills covered with scattering pines.

On the East is a strip of land several miles in width which... has been withdrawn from settlement by the department but which has not been added to the actual reservation. The eastern line of the acknowledged Indian lands has not been accurately surveyed and out of this... much of the trouble of recent years has arisen. Another and fruitful source of trouble is the presence of white settlers on the... by the Indians... These ranchers came into the... country before the land was set aside for the Cheyennes and they held

This manuscript page for Essay 9, "A Typical Indian Scare," shows Garland's idiosyncratic handwriting, from which most of the essays in this book were transcribed. Until 1900, when he began to employ a typist, this was the sort of copy the author submitted for publication.

[11]

Indian Tour of 1895: A Profound Influence

Garland had seen Indians in passing during his travels in 1892 and 1894, but his first-hand experience with them did not begin until 1895. In the summer of 1893, he had moved to Chicago, where he lectured and established new and valuable acquaintances with several artists including Lorado Taft, Edward Kemeys, Oliver D. Grover, Ralph Clarkson, Charles Francis Browne, and Hermon Atkins MacNeil. With Browne and MacNeil, Garland planned a trip to the West in the summer of 1895. Neither of the artists had been west of the Mississippi River, and both were anxious to know more about the region. Garland described them as Easterners who were anxious to "see the red people" and to "collect 'Wild West' material." Garland, himself a novice at "seeing the red people," was to be their guide.

It is true that in May, 1890, Garland had published a story titled "Drifting Crane" in *Harper's Weekly,* and it had been reprinted in the first edition of *Prairie Folks* in 1893. But since the substance of the story is a philosophical debate over Indian-white relations, Garland had little need for first-hand knowledge of the Indians.

The debate is between Henry Wilson, a cattleman, and Drifting Crane, a chief of the Sisseton Sioux. When Wilson drives his herd onto lands claimed by the Indians, he is welcomed on the assumption that he will leave in the winter. However, Wilson sees himself as the vanguard of advancing American civilization and refuses to leave. When Drifting Crane confronts him, Wilson convinces the chief of the futility of driving him away because of the thousands of whites who would follow. He says, "It ain't no use, Drifting Crane; it's *got* to be. You an' I can't help n'r hinder it." However, in the process of convincing the chief, Wilson realizes the despair the Indians feel, and he becomes confused. He realizes the injustice of the situation, on the one hand, but feels, on the other, that there is enough land for both. "Drifting Crane" was reprinted again in the 1899 edition of *Prairie Folks.*

The basic underlying deterministic philosophy presented in the story is understandable. With *Main-Travelled Roads* in 1891, Garland put himself clearly in the camp of the later realists, commonly called "literary naturalists," by means of his pessimistic world view and his determinism. In "Drifting Crane" it appears that he simply attempted to use determinism in a different type of social situation in an effort to explain the eventual outcome of "the meeting of the modern vidette of civilization with one of the rear guard of retreating barbarism." As Garland gained first-hand knowledge of the American Indian during the next few years, the explanation became more complex to him. However, for the better part of the decade, determinism dominated his feelings toward the American Indian. The first inroads on this early attitude came during the trip of 1895.

When Garland, Browne, and MacNeil went west, they stopped first at Colorado Springs and then went to Cripple Creek, which was at its height of notoriety as a mining camp. For a week they absorbed life and scenery. The artists painted and sketched, while Garland took notes of his observations. Then, in an effort to learn about the American Indian, the group went to Ignacio, the agency for the Southern Utes, whose lands lay in southwestern Colorado.

Garland was struck by the vast changes which were taking place in the life style of these Indians. Thus, he carefully noted their curious, and sometimes grotesque, adoption of Anglo- and Mexican-American customs into their own modes of dress, speech, naming practices, and amusements. Through interviews with the reservation trader he learned of the Ute customs concerning birth, death, burial, and religion. Everywhere was evident to him the bastardization of the Ute culture. From his notes he wrote a piece titled "Among the Southern Utes." Mounted proofsheets in Garland's papers indicate that the essay was published in a syndicated newspaper series called "Over Indian Trails." In the essay, the writer touches on most of the matters discussed in his interviews.

The piece demonstrates further development in Garland's thinking about the American Indian. The rhetoric of a deterministic philosophy is still there. Part of the Utes' condition, he says, results from their being "suddenly forced out of their own environment and exposed to totally new conditions." He sets the following criteria for comprehending the Indian: "First, his inherited habits of thought must be understood and, second, the power, the almost infrangible power of his environment. He must be considered as a man born of a certain race, and situated in a certain environment — he must be considered relatively in all questions of morality."

That was certainly one way of looking at the Indian's situation, but it did little to better his condition. However, Garland goes beyond determinism. He knows the absurdity of applying "the measures of Saxon virtues" to the native; yet he criticizes the Department of the Interior for forcing "civilization" on the Indian and for failing to meet his needs by sending him ill-fitting clothes, the wrong kind of farming equipment, and missionaries rather than practical teachers. Thus, early in his association with the Indian, Garland saw the necessity of utilitarian reforms, but several years were to pass before he would give a full-blown argument for them.

In "Among the Southern Utes," Garland commented upon a young Ute he had observed, playing what Garland took to be a love song on a flute: "The Ute lover no longer sings to his sweetheart, but, no doubt, this fluted strain has been used for ages to express the lover's longing and despair." Garland amplified the scene into a poem, "The Ute Lover," published in *Century,* in June, 1899, and reprinted in *The Trail of the Goldseekers* later that year. In this poem, Garland makes an ominous prophecy about the Indians', particularly the Utes', future:

> Flute on, O lithe and tuneful Utah,
>   Pipe from the shade;
> There are no other joys to secure to either
>   Man or maid.
> Soon you shall know the tribal sorrow,
>   Untouched of mirth,
> For on you lies the white man's gory
>   Greed of earth.

Among Garland's writings and notes on the Utes is the first substantial evidence of his interest in the naming systems of the American Indian. Like many Indians of the time, the Utes had adopted names from their English- and Spanish-speaking neighbors, sometimes to their own degradation. In "Among the Southern Utes" Garland noted one "very dignified and splendid" Ute who went by the name of "Biscuits," and in his papers are several pages from the ration books of the Southern Ute Agency which illustrate the mixture of Anglo-American and Ute naming practices.

From Ignacio, Garland, Browne, and MacNeil went to New Mexico, where they visited the Isleta pueblo near Albuquerque. They were there for only one day, but Garland recorded his observations of the inhabitants in an essay titled "A Day at Isleta," apparently written for the "Over Indian Trails" series. Like the Southern Utes, the Isletans were experiencing the encroachment of the Anglo and Mexican society upon their own. For that reason, Garland found refreshing the primitive threshing method still practiced at the pueblo and devoted a large portion of his essay to describing it. It is interesting to compare Garland's attitude toward these primitive modes of agriculture with those demonstrated in scenes of farm labor in *Main-Travelled Roads*. In the latter work, he had often presented themes of the degradation of "civilized" man by the grind of physical labor, despite his labor-saving machinery. In the former, Garland found the primitive agricultural practices and the manual labor refreshing.

The threshing scene served to remind Garland of the richness of the Indian culture, much of which was, even then, forever lost. He asks a number of pertinent questions: "Why disturb this peace — why 'civilize' these kindly folk?" and "Why disturb them? Why harass them with our problems?" Unable to see anything positive the white man can give the pueblans, Garland makes another ominous prediction: "The Pueblo is undoubtedly beginning to feel the terrible solvent power of the white man. That which neither the Navajo nor the Ute, nor the Comanche could do, this restless, relentless wonder-working white man is doing. In the mighty solvent of his passion all the old things give way."

Garland and his friends went from Albuquerque to Winslow, Arizona, and from there, by horseback, north toward the Hopi Reservation, where they planned to attend the snake dance at Walpi on First Mesa. Garland had read of the strange ceremony, and it promised to be of great interest. From Holbrook, the group rode north toward Keams Canyon, where they hoped to find shelter. At La Rue Wash they were detained by a heavy rain and were forced to take shelter under one of the wagons of several freighters they met there.

One of the freighters was a young Navajo named Carlo, who caught Garland's attention and became the central character in his story "Joe, the Navajo Teamster," published in *The Youth's Companion* in November, 1897. In the story, Joe and a fellow teamster are forced to camp, like Garland and his companions, because of a heavy rain and flash flood. The other teamster and a companion who joins them steal a mule and supplies from the wagon and go on a prospecting venture, leaving Joe in the desert with the two wagons. Joe's honesty and sense of duty make him try to get the wagons through to the trading post for which the goods are intended. He is finally helped by three Navajos, who find him stranded. The trader rewards them all with guns and meat and hires another Navajo to help Joe. He knows that the Navajo can be trusted.

When the rain stopped, Garland and his companions rode on toward Mormon Ranch, where they stayed for a few days of rest. They observed the Navajos at the small trading post at the ranch and again when they resumed their trip to Walpi. From his notes on the Navajo, Garland wrote an essay, "Glimpses of the Navajo Indians," apparently published in the "Over Indian Trails" series. This piece gives a clearer expression of Garland's attitude toward the American Indian's condition than any previous statement. Whereas he had doubted the wisdom of the agent's attempts to dissuade the Utes from traditional burial practices and had advocated a "hands off" policy with the pueblans, Garland said of the Navajo, "He should be taken for what he is, and little by little helped to a secure life, and then to a better life."

From Mormon Ranch, Garland and his friends continued to Walpi near Keams Canyon. Camped near the base of the mesa was a group of government ethnologists under the charge of Dr. Jesse W. Fewkes and his assistant, Frederick W. Hodge. Garland's party were invited to camp with them, but Browne and MacNeil wanted to camp on the mesa so they could be closer to the action of the snake dance ceremony. They stayed at Hano, a Tewa village on First Mesa.

The rite lasted ten days. Garland arrived on the second day. He watched with interest those parts of the ceremony that the whites were allowed to see. With the aid of Fewkes, Garland was permitted to keep "close to the elbow of the snake priests, seeing and hearing everything." His notes on Walpi cover twenty-three pages. Part of his understanding of the ritual was due to Fewkes' explanations. To Garland the effect of the ritual was hypnotic: "For an hour I had been carried out of myself, and I set to work at once to record what I had seen, not as a scientist but as a writer of stories, a singer of songs." His description of the ceremony appears in "Among the Moki Indians," published in *Harper's Weekly* in August, 1896.

Garland found the ceremony impressive and exciting but not revolting as he had evidently been led to expect. It was certainly a rite left over from more savage days, but now it had intensely religious overtones. Garland's ultimate opinion was that the ceremony should not be interfered with or condemned. Here is an early statement of a theme that runs throughout this writer's works on the Indian: the Indian should not be "civilized" at the expense of his native rituals, ceremonies, and amusements. Garland argued constantly against the idea held by most missionaries and many governmental agents that such practices were barbaric, immoral, and degrading.

After Garland had completed his description of the snake dance, he sent the manuscript to Fewkes, who was delighted with it. He made a few suggestions aimed at clarifying certain descriptions and at improving the spelling of names, but for the most part, the ethnologist had nothing but praise for the essay. On November 19, 1895, he wrote to Garland: "I like most of all the sympathetic way in which you treat this, to the Mokis, religious ceremony, and hope it will give a new meaning to this weird ceremonial in the minds of your readers. . . . I think your presentation of the subject admirable and the account of the public dance the best I have ever read. There are several novel observations in it which suggest points for me to 'look up' the next time I see it." Fewkes concluded by saying that the ethnologists — the "dry as dust recorders of facts," as he called them — owed Garland much for the "attractive literary form" he had given his description. What a sense of success Garland must have felt in having made his writing on his new-found subject palatable to one of America's foremost authorities on the Indian!

In "Among the Moki Indians" Garland writes, "At the foot of the mesa we came upon many little adobe houses with red roofs. They were the houses given by the government to entice the Mokis down from the rocks." These houses and the government school at Keams Canyon evidently served as a basis for his story "The Iron Khiva," published in *Harper's Weekly* in August, 1903. It is the story of a pueblan people, presumably Hopi, who through threats of destruction are forced to send their children to the white missionary's school (called the iron kiva because of its iron roof similar to the ones Garland had seen). After two years the missionary wants to send six children to the East for schooling. The people refuse and prepare for war. Soldiers come and make demonstrations of their force, and once more the people give in, a father and grandfather volunteering their son and grandson to be sacrificed. The Anglos are satisfied, but when they come for the boys, they have run away. Indians and whites pursue the youngsters into the desert and find them dead, killed by their own hands. The army retreats, and the missionary flees with them. The commander of the troops promises he will plead against the missionary on behalf of the Indians.

The story, with the tone and quality of a parable, tells of the means by which the Anglo made inroads into the Indian's society. By forcing him to make one concession at a time, through superior numbers or military strength, the white man changed the Indian's language, religion, and way of living. Although the natives of "The Iron Khiva" dreaded the coming of the whites, as they had previously dreaded the return of the Spanish, they were powerless to thwart that coming. The story was reprinted in Garland's *The Book of the American Indian* in 1923 and appeared in translation as "La Maison d'Ecole des Hommes Blancs" in *Revue Politique et Littéraire* in February, 1939.

At Walpi, Garland met Dr. Theophil Mitchell Prudden, head of the Department of Bacteriology at Columbia University. They became friends and made plans to go to the Little Colorado River and then to the pueblos of New Mexico, while Browne and MacNeil remained at Walpi to paint and sketch the Hopi and Hano people before returning to Chicago.

Garland and Prudden spent one day at Zuni pueblo. From his five pages of notes, the author developed an unpublished essay titled "A Day at Zuni," which records his observations at the pueblo. Most of its occupants were at their summer camps, giving Garland little opportunity to observe the people. Therefore, much of his essay deals with the extreme poverty of the Zuni as a result of the drought of the previous year. Their condition was made worse by the whites to whom the Indians had to sell, at nominal prices, most of their possessions in order to survive. As a reformist, Garland could hardly pass up an opportunity to make a commentary on such a situation. Much of what he records of the Zuni's life style was received second-hand from the trader, Douglas D. Graham.

From Zuni, Garland and Prudden went to Laguna, where the writer noted that the pueblo was falling into ruin because the people were slowly leaving the mesa and making permanent homes in their summer villages, where they farmed. Garland felt that the change was coming in "a perfectly natural way": "The change comes gradually. When the old people pass away, the pueblo will be deserted. The young people want to be like Americans." Garland left only three pages of notes taken at this pueblo.

At Laguna, he and Prudden learned of the harvest dance at Acoma, eighteen miles to the south. They stayed at Acoma for two days, and Garland took some twenty-four pages of notes, including careful and close descriptions of the people and the pageantry and ritual of the harvest dance. From his experiences at Acoma, Garland wrote a sketch, "The Harvest Dance among the Accomans," apparently for the "Over Indian Trails" series. Too brief to be of much value, this essay simply records the writer's emotional response to the dance. The notes, however, are graphic and informative.

Garland set down some of his observations at Acoma, as well as at the other pueblos, in an article entitled "The Most Mysterious People in America: The Cliff Dwellers and Pueblo People of Arizona," published in *Ladies' Home Journal* in October, 1896. The article serves as a summary piece for his 1895 trip in more ways than one. Garland covers a wide range of topics: architecture, modes of dress, occupations, hair styles, and demeanor. He often points out similarities and differences among the pueblans in regard to these aspects of life.

As usual, Garland is concerned with the influence of whites on the Indians, and he seems to have arrived at a conclusion which, for the time being, apparently guided his thinking. He says that these people were driven to the high reaches of the mesas by the warring Navajo and Apache. There, they developed a rich culture, and their isolation made them mysterious. But Garland knows that the white man will lure the Indians down from the mesas and destroy their culture. In answer to those who say that such destruction is the price of progress, Garland answers that progress is possibly worth the price to the white man but that it is not likely to be so for the Indian. Thus, Garland winds up his essay on a pessimistic note.

Garland's 1895 tour among the Indians ended at Acoma. It had been a significant one which he said "profoundly influenced" his life and his writing. "Aside from its esthetic delight," he wrote in *A Daughter of the Middle Border* (1921), "this summer turned out to be the most profitable season of my whole career. It marks a complete 'bout face in my march. Coming just after *Rose of Dutcher's Cooly* [1895], it dates the close of my prairie tales and the beginning of a long series of mountain stories. . . . In truth every page of my work there-

after was colored by the expressions of this glorious, savage, splendid summer."
The reasons for this turn were easy for him to define: his emotional relationships with the West were pleasant, engendering none of the resentment he had
expressed for unjust social conditions in his earlier works.

More Indian Visits: A Developing Sympathy

The fall of 1895 was spent in writing articles based on his experiences in
the West, trying to depict the West as it had appeared to him, "verifying every
experience." Some of these highly descriptive Western articles were sold for
newspaper syndication and were illustrated by H. T. Carpenter. Garland's
writing and thinking about his new subject were interrupted in January, 1896,
when the editor of *McClure's* commissioned him to write a biography of Ulysses
S. Grant. That effort occupied him during the better part of 1896. However,
Garland took time from the project to return to the Southwest in the summer
of that year.

He went first to see Ehrich in Colorado Springs and then went for a
second time to the Southern Ute Reservation. He took almost forty pages of
notes in which he recorded interviews at Durango with a man called Navajo
Bill, as well as observations on the moon dance, Chief Charley and his family,
game laws, and the Indians' attitudes toward children and education. In addition there are lists of Ute words, a brief sketch of the life of the black interpreter
at the agency, and notes on a Ute dance. Most of what Garland had seen the
year before he saw again on this visit. He also had opportunity to visit with
the trader George H. Kraus and Indian Agent David F. Day.

In the notes Garland took on the Southern Ute Reservation appears the
name "Cap-pe-a-witz, or wich, 'sun-flowers gatherer.' " This became the name
of the central character in a very short story "The Stony Knoll," which appeared
in *The Youth's Companion* in December, 1897. Capeawitz is an old woman,
once "called 'the sunflower-gatherer' because of her girlish lightness and grace,
and her love of flowers," who appears before the "rough but kindly" agent to
receive her allotment. It was the agent's practice to settle the Indians on the
best land along the streams, but Capeawitz wants a stony knoll.

The agent tries to dissuade the woman, stressing the impossibility of irrigating the rocky hill. When she still insists upon the knoll, the agent agrees
on the condition that she tell him why she selected that spot. She finally, but
reluctantly, reveals through the interpreter that it was the burial place of her
husband and son, whose bodies had been hidden in the crevices of the rocks.

Garland introduces the simple story with an attack on the theory of allotment, resenting "that the beautiful sentiment which had considered the earth
as common property should give way to the system of the white man." In like
fashion, he attacks the white settlers, "hard, eager and greedy," who wait to
enter and occupy the surplus Indian lands and in whose eyes "the red man
was a pest to be exterminated like the tarantula."

From the Southern Ute Reservation, Garland traveled south to Dulce,
New Mexico, a sub-agency of the Pueblo Agency for the Jicarilla Apaches.
He was given a tour of the reservation by John Gaylord, the agency clerk,

who spoke the native language and was therefore able to give Garland much information about the Jicarilla Apaches. The fourteen pages of notes the writer left contain information on Jicarilla medicine, magic, and taboos as well as their economic condition and demeanor.

In his unpublished account of the visit, "The Jicarilla Apaches," Garland is sympathetic to the Indians in their state of poverty as a result of the drought in 1896 and in their extreme isolation. Here the author demonstrates more control in regard to Indian-white relations than he had been able to maintain during his 1895 visit to the West. He limits himself to only a few caustic remarks and devotes most space to the spiritual beliefs of the Indians. "The Jicarilla Apaches" also contains criticism of allotment, which Garland blamed for the isolation and the loneliness of the Indians who, traditionally, were extremely gregarious. As his reformist attitude in regard to the Indian gained momentum, his attacks on allotment became more frequent.

One other piece of writing grew out of Garland's trip of 1896. It is a long, unpublished poem titled "The Indian," in which Garland expounds on the injustice the Native Americans had received at the hands of the whites. The lines, which are often prosaic, were never revised. Garland also made notes for a play titled "The Daughter of Rushing Bear," in which a sculptor at an Indian agency finds himself in difficulties when he falls in love with a young Indian maiden.

When Garland left the West after his 1896 tour, he was not in as high spirits as he had been in after his trip the year before. An awareness of the unjust social conditions, of which he thought he was free, had begun to creep into his thoughts. In his notes he wrote:

I left Ouray with a disgust of the men who were connected with the service. They are not able to comprehend the real state of the Indian's mind. The trader is more nearly just. He finds it to his interest and also he naturally inclines to being fair and just to them, and they trust him. The deep-seated distrust of the whiteman yields only after the severest test. It does not do to *say* "I am your friend" — it must be demonstrated. He must be tried, tried hard. His words must be studied. A man who is good today and swears at the "damn Indian" tomorrow may win the silent toleration of the Indian but not his confidence.

Here are the beginnings of another reformist theme in Garland's writing about the American Indian. His reformism continued to grow until it reached its height with the publication of "The Red Man's Present Needs" in 1902. Always inherent in that reformism was an insistence that the Anglo recognize the point of view of the Indian or, as he put it here, "comprehend the real state of the Indian's mind."

By the end of 1896, Garland had published a number of stories and essays based on his travels in the West, including "Among the Moki Indians" and "The Most Mysterious People in America." He found magazine editors more hospitable because his "tales of the Indian and the miner had created a friendlier spirit among their readers." He wrote in *A Daughter of the Middle Border:*

"My later themes were, happily, quite outside the controversial belt. Concerned less with the hopeless drudgery, and more with the epic side of western life, I found myself almost popular."

Garland traveled in the West again in the summer of 1897. His purpose was two-fold: to study the Sioux and to get to know the Northwest. He had a letter of introduction from General Nelson A. Miles, who recommended him to all Indian agents and military personnel in the West. In company with his brother Franklin, an aspiring actor who had performed in several minor New York City plays, he arrived at Bismarck, North Dakota, on July 1 on his way to the Standing Rock Reservation. At Fort Yates, they took lodging at a boardinghouse near the post's store and, with an interpreter, spent every waking moment observing the Sioux, interviewing the headmen concerning their history, and examining the agency records for material concerning Sitting Bull.

Garland interviewed, among others, Crazy Dog, Slohan, and Bull Head. From Louis Primeau, his interpreter, he learned more of Sitting Bull, and from Captain W. J. Turner, who had seen much service in the West, he obtained the views of a sympathetic Anglo. In speaking of the Indians, Turner told Garland:

They are forced to surrender the spontaneously picturesque and take up the cheap and prosaic, to leave the eagle feather for the strip of flannel, the fringed buckskin for the blue denim over-all. In these things the whole change is summed up. They must leave the characteristic and the significant and take up the unpoetic and the cheap.

Along these lines, Garland also learned of the speech of Umapine, who refused to come before Sherman and his commission until he chose. When he did appear, the chief made a speech in which he weighed the Indian against the white man, saying, "I have looked long to see the kind of man you will make of my sons and I have found him. There he is." The chief pointed at a tramp in the street, adding, "This strange thing I have seen. It is hard for the Indian to become civilized but it is very easy for the whiteman to become uncivilized." Garland expanded this anecdote into an unpublished story called "Rushing Bear and the Commission" in which Rushing Bear delivers an eloquent speech, at the end pointing to a swamper across the street and saying that the Anglos would make his children swampers "to clean the spittoons of the white man's civilization."

Although little writing came directly from Garland's stay at Standing Rock, the efforts he made there formed the basic groundwork for his extensive research and writing on Sioux matters during the next five years. From the pages of the agency records, the writer took material which began to separate Sitting Bull the man from Sitting Bull the legend. Garland began to form a sympathetic opinion of the man whom he came to admire as a great leader and to whom he was to devote much time. Beyond this, Garland left some thirty-five pages of notes containing observations of the Sioux, records of interviews with Indians and post officials, anecdotal matter, ideas for stories, and a short poem. This latter, a quatrain titled "Sioux Reservation," addresses itself to the dreary nature of the land.

Montana: A Rich Source of Material

Garland was diverted from his primary purpose in coming West by news that trouble had broken out between whites and the Northern Cheyenne on the Tongue River Reservation in Montana. He and Franklin left immediately for Fort Custer, where they were put in the charge of Lieutenant George P. Aherne, meat inspector at the Crow Agency. Garland accompanied him on his rounds the next day.

The first night, however, Garland talked with Aherne concerning Indian matters. Among the stories the inspector told was that of two young Cheyenne boys who wanted to fight to the death instead of being imprisoned. While the whole tribe watched, they charged down a hill into the waiting soldiers, firing as they came. After his notes on the story, Garland wrote the following fragment: "The man Stanly of the. . . ." Here is evidence that the writer had a preview of the incident he was on his way to investigate at the Tongue River Agency, for Stanley was a principal character in that event. The episode Aherne described had occurred in 1891 on the Tongue River Reservation, and Stanley had attempted to follow those youths' example. Garland evidently found the event intriguing, for he soon began considering it as the basis for a story. It was finally worked into *The Captain of the Gray-Horse Troop* (1902), along with other Cheyenne materials.

Garland also continued his research on Sitting Bull. Aherne talked with him at length about the chief from the army's point of view and told what he knew of the events surrounding the Custer fight. Garland then obtained from the Crows what knowledge they had of the event. Finally, he interviewed R. W. Cummings, a trader at the Crow Agency, who had been long among the Indians and who talked to him at length about the Custer battle as well as of Sioux and Crow social conventions. Later Cummings would prove to be a valuable source of information.

Garland spent only one day at the Crow Agency. However, his notes cover about seventy pages, including an extended description of the pageantry of a dance he attended on July 12 and what appears to be the idea for a play concerning a man who marries an Indian, leaves her, marries again, becomes a successful governmental official, and is, at last, confronted by his Indian wife.

The Garland brothers rode from Fort Custer to Lame Deer, also in Montana. Enroute, they spent the night at a ranch and heard, with disgust, the ranchers' talk of exterminating the Cheyenne. The details of this event found their way into *The Captain of the Gray-Horse Troop*. Garland described the ride to Lame Deer in an unpublished essay, "Notes on the Cheyenne Country and Lame Deer." He was impressed by the barrenness of the land and, as was his usual method, recorded his first impressions of the Cheyenne, comparing them with other Indians he had observed. He found them "eager to learn the best that the Whiteman can teach them." Here the writer has somewhat tempered his earlier stance promoting the retention of native cultures, for he called the Cheyenne "progressive" because of their eagerness to adopt white ways.

On the second day of his visit at Lame Deer, Garland attended a dance at the agency given in honor of some visiting Crows. The writer's account of this experience in "Notes on the Cheyenne Country and Lame Deer" offers a detailed and graphic description of the color and pageantry of the dance as well as of the traditional ceremonies which accompanied it. Garland found nothing in the dance or the speeches of the old men that could be called "ferocious or demoralizing," as proponents of Indian assimilation were charging. To him it was a "social" gathering: "In the olden time they had many such social gatherings, many feasts, many festivities. It would be cruel to cut them off from this, their principal way of meeting in harmless amusement. The story-telling of the old men is no longer an incitement to daring deeds. There is no danger in the talk of the old-timer."

Garland is repeating here, in part, something which Cummings had said about the Crows. Cummings found no immorality in their dancing but feared that the speeches of the old men might inspire the young men to raid the livestock of neighboring ranches. Garland doubted the old men's influence because the young men referred to them as "old-timers."

The dance was the source of a poem which Garland later wrote and revised at different times until 1903, but never published. It was variously titled "The Cheyenne Dance," "Indian Dance," and "Cheyennes Dancing." Its theme is the value of the dance to the Indian as a way of momentarily sloughing off the white man's trappings and recapturing the sense of freedom and pride that was his before he was "Americanized":

> Only in dance the white man's curse
> Is lifted. Only in dreams his weapons fail.
> Only in song the redman's heart awakens
> And swells in joy of sky and plain.
>
> *   *   *
>
> The old ignore their age, the lame
> Forget their stiffened limbs and leap
> As the wolf leaps, tireless and glad.

Garland had come to Lame Deer with a letter of introduction to the agent, Captain George W. H. Stouch, who was to become his good friend. Garland was also introduced to the commanding officers of soldiers stationed temporarily near the agency and to the principal Cheyenne chiefs. Troops had been ordered to Camp Merritt near the agency to restore peace in a dispute wherein white settlers who lived on land bordering the reservation were blaming the Indians for the death of a sheep-herder. Several settlers lived on land claimed by the Indians, and when they drove their herds too close to land used by the natives or when the Indians raided the settlers' livestock, tempers flared. Such was the case during May, 1897, when the body of the sheep-herder was found just off the reservation.

Garland spent much of his time interviewing Stouch, the Indians, and army officers concerning the incident. With Wolf Voice as interpreter, he talked with White Bull, Spotted Elk, Bull Thigh, White Shield, Spotted Hawk, and White Hawk. On July 20, the day murder charges were filed against six accused Cheyenne, Garland drafted an account of the affair, which he titled "A Typical Indian Scare: The Cheyenne Trouble."

This unpublished piece is very dramatic. Garland records the capture of the young Cheyenne, David Stanley, who for some time was thought to be the only one involved in the killing. The writer describes Stanley's attempt to fight the cowboys to the death and the confrontation between Stouch and a posse of white ranchers who invade the reservation and demand deliverance of the killer. Garland's notes indicate that he considered these two incidents the central moments of "the whole controversy." Although Garland made no literal use of the account, it was later to serve as the germ for his most successful novel, *The Captain of the Gray-Horse Troop* (1902).

In this novel, Captain George Curtis, Stouch's equivalent, is the sympathetic agent to the fictional Tetong Indians, the Northern Cheyenne's counterpart. He is unpopular with the whites surrounding the reservation, whose cattle and sheep graze on Indian land, representing a constant cause of conflict. The whites, led by ex-Senator Brisbane, want to get the Indians removed and look for reasons to give them bad publicity. The situation becomes grave when a sheep-herder is killed and a mob of whites invade the reservation to find the killer. Curtis calls out the troops, who rout the cowboys, but he allows the sheriff and three deputies to remain as a compromise (similar to the one Stouch made) and promises to find and deliver the killer to the white authorities.

Word comes that a young brave named Cut Finger, Stanley's equivalent, did the killing. He, like Stanley, wants to die fighting the cowboys, but Curtis captures him and delivers him to white authorities after having escaped a lynch mob waiting at the edge of the reservation. The persistent mob comes to town, takes Cut Finger from the jail, then shoots and drags him to death. (Stanley and his accomplices were tried and sentenced.) The whites become ashamed and go home, and the tension dies down.

When peace comes, the Indians take to farming with some enthusiasm, and the novel ends with a harvest dance in which the Indians carry agricultural implements and stalks of grain instead of their traditional weapons. To this story is added that of Curtis's love for Elsie Brisbane, the ex-senator's daughter, who comes to the reservation to paint the Indians. Not only does he win her love, but he also converts her from the bigot her father has made her to a humanist who shares her sweetheart's enthusiasm for his job. Though the novel has been judged a weak piece of literature, Garland claimed it sold more copies than any other of his works.

Garland did not devote all of his time to the Cheyenne "outbreak." He continued his research on Sitting Bull by interviewing Two Moon, who had been the guest of honor at the Crow dance he attended and who Garland knew had been in the Custer fight. An account of the interview was published as "General Custer's Last Fight as Seen by Two Moon" in *McClure's* in September, 1898. Two Moon told Garland how his Cheyenne had encamped with the Sioux beyond what they thought was the white soldiers' reach. However, they were surprised by Custer, and though they were disorganized and confused, they defeated him. His story refutes the accounts which present Custer's defeat in terms of an organized and intentional war effort on the part of the allied Sioux and Cheyenne. Garland used Two Moon's story as the basis for the chapter dealing with the fight in his major work on Sitting Bull, "The Silent Eaters," discussed later in this introduction.

Apparently from Stouch, Garland got the idea for the story of Howling Wolf, who appeared as Hakonuse in "The Outlaw," published in *Harper's Weekly* in June, 1903. Garland used as background for the narrative the enmity which existed between the Cheyenne and the cowboys around the reservation. A young Indian named Hakonuse is bitter because some cowboys have used his brother for target practice and killed him. Through the efforts of the agent, the Indian is reconciled and vows to take up the white man's ways.

One day Hakonuse and some other Indians drive several freight wagons to town. There, a cowboy gets drunk and approaches Hakonuse, who holds out his hand in friendship. The cowboy spits on it, and Hakonuse slaps him. The cowboy then draws his gun, and Hakonuse runs.

In the affray, a man is shot, and the Indian is put in jail. Prejudice thwarts the agent's attempts to get him released. Later the whole town turns out for a baseball game, and rather than miss it, the sheriff takes his prisoner with him. When Hakonuse sees the crowd, he thinks he is to be tortured and killed, so he tries to escape. The cowboys ride him down, shooting, stabbing, and kicking him. He lives, but he is disfigured and becomes embittered against the white man once more. With revisions, this story appeared as "The Story of Howling Wolf" in *The Book of the American Indian* (1923) and as "Histoire de l'Indian Loup Hulant" in *Revue Politique et Littéraire* in February and March, 1933.

Garland's story of Rising Wolf also had its inception during his stay at Lame Deer. An Indian named Porcupine was his model. His wife was killed by lightning, and he angrily fired his rifle into the sky as Rising Wolf does. Like Rising Wolf, Porcupine brought the ghost dance to his people. "Rising Wolf — Ghost Dancer" was published in *McClure's* in January, 1899. In it, Rising Wolf tells the story of his life. As a young man he was a successful and wealthy medicine man. But the death of his wife and the placing of his people on the poor reservation land had reduced him to poverty.

One night a Snake messenger came and said that a wonderful white man who had once been nailed to a tree by other whites had come among his people. He had called a meeting of headmen of surrounding tribes to teach them a new dance and magic that would bring back the buffalo and drive away the white man. Rising Wolf went to the meeting and there saw the wonderful man. The Messiah taught them the dance, instructed them to go home and dance for four days, and then disappeared. They did as he said, expecting the whites to disappear at the end of the dance.

The agent and the soldiers at the reservation laughed at the Indians for being so foolish. Rising Wolf was humiliated, but he learned:

I will follow the white man's trail. I will make him my friend, but I will not bend my neck to his burdens. I will be cunning as the coyote. I will ask him to help me to understand his ways, and then I will prepare the way for my children. Maybe they will outrun the white man in his own shoes. Anyhow, there are but two ways. One leads to hunger and death, the other leads where the poor white man lives. Beyond is the happy hunting-ground, where the white man cannot go.

There are obvious parallels between the arrival of word about the Messiah in this story and that in Garland's later work "The Silent Eaters." Here the ghost dance is the last hope of bringing back the old days, just as it is to Sitting Bull in the later story.

Garland took 110 pages of notes during his two-week stay at Lame Deer. In them are to be found his interviews with Porcupine and White Bull on Cheyenne "medicine," notes on courtship and burial practices, observations and anecdotes of personalities such as American Horse, Two Moon, and Wolf Voice, and notes for three stories which he never developed. One called "Story of Crazy Mule and Head Chief" was to deal with the last heroic fight of two young Indians who had killed a white youth. This material later was worked into *The Captain of the Gray-Horse Troop*. Garland probably got the idea for "Killing of the Dogs" from Stouch, and his notes indicate that "Story of Lone Dog" came from Wolf Voice.

When Garland left the Northern Cheyenne Reservation, he went back to Fort Custer to catch a train west. Wolf Voice, whom he had grown to like and admire, rode with him and his brother and showed them a rock about thirty inches high, decorated with beads, ribbons, and shells. The Indians thought the rock looked like an old man in a blanket, and they came there to pray for a long and more prosperous life. This was the Cheyenne's equivalent of the Sioux's Standing Rock at Fort Yates. Garland describes the stone and explains the lore surrounding it in an unpublished essay, "The Sacred Rock of the Cheyennes." Later, Garland wrote of Wolf Voice and the Cheyenne trouble: "He, Two Moon, American Horse, and Porcupine were of incalculable value to me in composing *The Captain of the Gray-Horse Troop*, which was based upon this little war."

At the Crow Agency in southern Montana, Garland had opportunity to talk once more with R. W. Cummings, who had married a niece of Sitting Bull. He told the writer of an experience of his which, he said, involved a "scheme of men in Montana" to defraud the government. According to Cummings, Congress had appropriated ninety thousand dollars to negotiate a treaty with the Teton Sioux. There was no such tribe, but the commissioner sent was determined to negotiate with someone. So he decided to treat with the Hunkpapas, camped under the leadership of Black Moon, Gall, and Sitting Bull on the other side of a river.

The Indians were hostile, and the commissioner could get no one to cross the river and ask the Indians to come for a talk. He finally convinced Cummings to go. Loaded with gifts, he crossed the water and convinced Black Moon, his son, and Gall to return with him. They talked of a treaty with the commissioner, but Black Moon had to go back to his camp for a council. Cummings and others took the chiefs back across the river in several boats filled with goods. After they had unloaded and were halfway across the river, they looked back to see the Indians slitting the sacks and cutting the blankets. Sitting Bull called after them: "This is the way I make a treaty with you, white dogs!" With only minor changes, Garland published the story as "Sitting Bull's Defiance" in *McClure's* in November, 1902.

Cummings told Garland two more stories, one called "Wrap Up His Tail" and another about Spotted Tail, who had once killed a cousin who had tried to undermine his authority and had called him a squaw. In a fit of rage, Spotted Tail killed his cousin with a knife and then immediately covered his face with his blanket, went out on the plain, flung himself down, and cried in remorse and agony. Garland expanded this anecdote into "The Remorse of Waumdisapa," which was not published until its inclusion in *The Book of the American Indian* in 1923.

The story, which Garland noted as a "substantially true account of an incident well known to border men," is about the great chief of the Tetons who has a reputation as a good warrior and an honorable and fair man. He is envied by his cousin Mattowan, who is more warlike than Waumdisapa and wants to be chief. When the leader hears of Mattowan's talk against him, he calls a council. All smoke the pipe and praise Waumdisapa but Mattowan, who calls them squaws. In a moment of anger, Waumdisapa leaps on Mattowan and stabs him to death. As a result of the act, Waumdisapa declares himself no longer fit to lead his people. When the council meets again, he appears dressed in rags, with dust on his head, and sits outside the circle of the council.

From the Crow Reservation, the Garland brothers went by train to the Flathead Reservation. Garland apparently found time to reflect on his experiences at Lame Deer before striking out for the Flathead country from Missoula. Such entries as "Stanley on the Hill" and "Lame Deer Matters" and a ten-page draft of a story about Crazy Mule indicate that the idea of a fight to the death as an alternative to imprisonment or capital punishment was still intriguing him. And his extensive sketch of a projected play indicates that *The Captain of the Gray-Horse Troop* had already begun to take shape in his mind. The play was to deal with a young lieutenant who was made Indian agent, then found himself at odds with the local authorities in the matter of a murder committed by an Indian. The sheriff was to be the villain, and the daughter of a senator was to be interested in the agent. Other characters included the agent's sister, the senator, Chief White Shield, and the interpreter Wolf Voice, most of whose equivalents appear in the novel.

At the Flathead Reservation, Garland talked with George Carter, the agent. He found the Flatheads plagued by some of the same problems as the other tribes he had visited. They were losing their arts. He wrote, "There will now ensue a dreary time when they will have lost the old and will have failed to take on the new." White ranchers were poised on the boundaries of the reservation, ready at the first opportunity to enter Indian land. Garland took nearly forty pages of notes in which he recorded his observations of the condition of the Indians, their population, dress, and racial make-up, the agency, and the mission at Saint Ignatius. He also described a herd of buffalo which grazed on the open range of the reservation.

These notes bear witness to Garland's sensitivity to and his concern for the American Indian's condition. "It is not a question," he writes, "of ceasing to be an Indian and becoming a banker, a political leader, a merchant. It is a question of ceasing to be a free man, equal to any in privileges, in order to become poor cowboys, ranchers, eating at the third table of the white men — hired men and renters. So it is that many of them persist in being Indians in rags rather than cowhands in denims." In another instance he writes, "The Flathead reservation is a sort of corral into which the Government has from time to time driven various tribes of the northwest."

Here, too, are to be found Garland's thoughts concerning the rights of the Indians as human beings, rights all but uniformly ignored in the West at the time. "It is not enough," he wrote, "to say that the Indians are criminal. They have rights as human beings. Would we apply the same reasoning to dealing with the Italians or Polanders because they are dirty or quarrelsome?" Here is an early statement of an argument Garland was to put forth in years to come: that the Indian could be dealt with in the same manner as immigrants, whose cultures differed greatly from that of native born white Americans. Unfortunately, Garland failed to take into account the fact that in those dealings the immigrants' rights as human beings were also often ignored.

The Far West: Cradle of A New Reformism

From the Flathead Reservation, the two Garlands returned to Missoula, where they parted, Franklin going back East and Hamlin continuing west into Idaho to the Nez Percé Reservation. Lands had been allotted to this tribe; thus Garland devoted most of his time to investigating the economic condition of the Indians and the attempts by whites to make them over in their image. He hit again upon a theme that he often propounded: that the process of acculturation was a reduction of the Indian to the lowest Anglo denominator, the poor white. Garland wrote, "They have an ideal to which they wish the Indian to conform. This is the poor farmer. Nothing that does not work toward this end is estimated good."

Garland also tried to get into the psychology of the land speculator, who seemed to find something intriguing about the Indian's land and something glorious in defrauding him of it. He attacked the reservations as "mere corrals," which are destructive to the native's morale and culture. The condition is worsened by those "semi-savage" whites who gather around the reservations and serve as models for the natives: "Their savagery is worse than the Indian's for it has in it Saxon greed." Garland was critical of the missionary who "seeks to destroy all the native man's habit, songs, traditions and arts." He wrote, "Their bigotry and narrowness is the motive power which keeps them employed. . . . People of full and rounded education are seldom found in the remote places. It takes religious zeal to carry them."

Garland left only a dozen pages of notes on the Nez Percé. More significant than the notes is the equal amount of reformist outpourings. At the Nez Percé Reservation, Garland had seen the government's Indian policy of allotment, aimed at assimilation, in a more advanced stage than any he had witnessed heretofore, and he did not like the product of that policy. Thus, in his hastily jotted thoughts are the seeds of the reformist ideas to which he later gave fuller expression, particularly in "The Red Man's Present Needs."

From the Nez Percé Reservation, Garland went to the Yakima Reservation in Washington. In the interim, however, he sketched out a poem titled "Signal Fires," which told of the arrival of the Spanish among the pueblans of the Southwest, and made notes for a description called "The Cheyenne War

Dance." This latter appears to be the germ of the dance scene in *The Captain of the Gray-Horse Troop*. Garland later wrote a more complete version of "Signal Fires" in which the Tewan people — men, women, and children — stop their work and play to look with awe and fear at the fires which signal the coming of the "iron men."

At the reservation, the writer interviewed J. L. Banks, the agent, and made notes on the tribal make-up of the Yakima reservation, the Indians' mode of dress, their social conventions, and their superstitions. These notes cover sixteen pages.

From the Yakima country, Garland traveled to Anacortes, arriving there on August 22. He visited briefly with his old childhood friend Burton Babcock, setting plans for their 1898 prospecting trip to the Yukon. Then he turned back east to Lake McDonald and the Blackfoot Indian Reservation. In some twenty pages of notes taken there, Garland made observations of the physical features of the reservation, the Indians' taboos, and their religion and medicine. He heard much talk of George Bird Grinnell, who had lived among the Blackfeet and was an authority on their history and lore. Garland jotted down several messages from the Indians to Grinnell and took a letter to him, which White Calf had dictated.

Garland continued east to the Fort Belknap Reservation for the Assiniboin and the Gros Ventre. He left only a few pages of notes containing the usual entries on the aspects of the Indians' condition which interested him. As summary to his visit to Fort Belknap, he gave vent to further reformist outpourings. He had found the clerks at the agency "all strong with whiskey" and concluded that the pay was too small to get good men to remain in the service. If one did decide to stay, he was ruined by politics, or the monotony and isolation of the job caused him to get tired of the Indians and his associates, making him irritable and lax in his habits, a bad example for the Indians. These observations and those he had made at the Nez Percé Reservation later formed a major part of his argument in "The Red Man's Present Needs."

Garland traveled on to the Fort Peck Reservation, where he took more extensive notes. He met John Brugiere, who served as an interpreter and guide and from whom Garland obtained an account of the surrender of Gall and Sitting Bull. From the superintendent of schools, he learned the problems that the educator faced in preparing his students to face the white world. And, finally, he made more observations about the Indian service, concluding that "Civil service should either cover all the helpers in the Indian service or the agent should be an army officer and kept in during good service." The latter alternative was to be propounded in *The Captain of the Gray-Horse Troop*.

At Fergus Falls, Minnesota, on his homeward journey, Garland hit upon an idea for a story. It was to be about a young man named Mose who was reared in the farm country of the Midwest. He has heard tales of the adventurous life to be had in the West, and when his sweetheart dies, he leaves for the West to become a part of that wild land. This character appears in a number of Garland's later Indian stories.

At home once more in West Salem, Wisconsin, Garland wrote of the Indians: "How far away they seem — how helpless and how miserable. They look out at the whiteman with eyes that dream tragic dreams. The old suffer the most. The boys and girls born in the prison land are ignorant of the wild free life of the olden time. They are rapidly becoming commonplace. They will end by becoming supine and stupid toilers."

The trip had been the most productive of the author's travels among the Indians. He had gathered vast amounts of materials; he had come back with ideas for poems, plays, and stories; and he had formed new attitudes about the natives and the government's policy toward them. He was enthusiastic, later describing the trip as a turning point in his career. In his words, "This trip completed my conversion." He concluded that he would devote his creative energies thereafter to writing about the mountain West. However, use of the Indian materials he had gathered had to wait.

Wide Traveling: A Time of Transition

In the Northwest, Garland had heard much of the Klondike and had wanted to go there, but his biography of Grant was yet unfinished. He completed it in the fall and winter of 1897, and in the spring of 1898, with Burton Babcock as a traveling companion, he went to Alaska, returning home in the autumn. The Grant biography and the Alaskan trip arrested, to a large extent, his writing on the American Indian until 1900. He published only one piece on the subject in 1898 and two in 1899 — "General Custer's Last Fight As Seen by Two Moon," "Rising Wolf — Ghost Dancer," and "The Ute Lover" — two of which resulted from his travels in 1897.

Upon his return from the Klondike, Garland found himself caught in "a time of halting, of transition." For six years he had been absorbing impressions of the West; now he had gathered a vast amount of information on the Klondike. In order to utilize some of this material, he went to New York in December, 1898, to write.

The author wanted to improve his financial status in order to propose marriage to Zulime Taft, the sister of his sculptor friend Lorado Taft. He had met Zulime a few years earlier, just before she had left for Paris to study art. Garland returned to Chicago in March, 1899, and hearing that Zulime was engaged, he went on a tour of England. Upon his return from abroad, the writer found that she was not in fact engaged, and during the fall he courted her. They planned to marry just before Thanksgiving.

Shortly before his marriage, Garland suddenly made a trip to the Navajo country. Later, he could not completely explain why he went at that particular time, but he speculated that he needed something to offset his impressions of his recent trip abroad and that to lose touch with his material "even for twelve months was to be cheated." Garland was sure, however, that he wanted to buy some Navajo art work for his new home. His destination was the trading house of Lorenzo Hubbell at Ganado, Arizona.

He spent several days at Ganado, making notes on the post and the Navajos who came to it. Entries such as "The Navajo Country" and "Condition of the Navajoes" in his notebook give an indication of the content of them. Besides fifteen pages of jottings on Navajo matters, there are the notes and plans for two stories, presumably suggested by Hubbell.

"The Bad Medicine Man" is the story of the Indian policeman Aglar, who, with two companions, reports that the medicine man Gray Eagle kills people by shooting pellets of poison into their bodies. The agent asks them to bring Gray Eagle in, and the policemen ask what will be done to him. When the agent jokingly says he will hang the medicine man, the Indians take him seriously. He tries to correct his mistake but fails to convince the natives that Gray Eagle does not deserve to die.

Later, word comes that Aglar has killed Gray Eagle for poisoning his sister. The agent feels that Gray Eagle probably deserved killing but for the sake of "law and order" he "must give somebody a big scare about this." Therefore, he strips Aglar of uniform, badge, and revolver until he receives instructions in the matter. Aglar then denounces the agent as a liar with two faces, "one toward Washington, one toward the red man." The people are glad, for Aglar is no longer an agent of the white man. The story was published in *The Independent* in December, 1900.

Notes for "Lost His Moggasens" became "Big Moggasen," which appeared in *The Independent* in November, 1900. It is the story of an old Navajo headman whose people lived far away from the agency, "independent of the white man's bounty." They followed their herds and suffered the many hardships of a remote, primitive life until the people began to complain that their neighbors to the south had tools to work with and proper clothing. Big Moggasen, doubting the white man's motives for giving these things, agrees to go to the agency to see if he can secure them for his people. As he travels south, he sees more and more evidence of the white man's presence, a presence which is tolerated and even accepted by many of the Navajos. At the agency, the agent names the price Big Moggasen must pay for the white man's gifts: he must send the children in to be schooled. The old man angrily rejects the bargain and returns to his people to follow the ways of his fathers.

After two weeks among the Navajo Indians, Garland returned to Topeka, where he joined Zulime, who was on her way to Hanover, Kansas, to visit her father. Together they went to her father's home and were married.

The couple spent the winter in New York, where Garland had long conversations with Dr. Mitchell Prudden, whom he had met at Walpi in 1895, and Ernest Thompson Seton, the painter and naturalist, short story writer, and lecturer, whom he had met in 1896. His talk with the latter often turned to the American Indian, about whom they shared similar views:

We both saw the red man as Catlin saw him, an animal adapted to a certain environment. Biologically he was guiltless as the panther or the eagle. We had no economic or religious prejudices concerning him. His sign language, his songs, his dances were of absorbing interest to us both; and while Ernest was picturing certain phases of savage life, I was meditating a novel [*The Captain of the Gray-Horse Troop*] which would present life on a Cheyenne reservation and some of its problems. We spent many hours inspiring each other in such designs.

The amoral stance which Garland claimed he and Seton took regarding the American Indian is deterministic. It is the same determinism Garland had earlier reflected in his criticism of those who would apply the "measures of Saxon virtues" to the Indians or reject their dancing as immoral. His philosophical position is understandable in view of the scientific determinism which affected, to a large extent, the intellectual mode of the day. Garland never gave up the view that the condition of the American Indian, as he had observed him near the turn of the century, resulted from the destruction of his environment to which the Indian, as an organism, was adapted. He found this more true of the tribes that had depended on the buffalo than of those in the Southwest, where the harshness of the environment had longer deterred the white man and therefore delayed the changes.

Although he never gave up this view, Garland was steadily working away from it. While in 1900 he relegated the Indian to the level of the panther or eagle, two years later he was writing of the "human side" of the Indian and of his rights as a human being, rights which he was painfully aware of as being woefully neglected. The Indian was a human being to whom the white man was obligated to make his assimilation into Anglo-dominated culture as painless as possible.

Oklahoma in 1900: Stories From Stouch and Seger

Significant in the further shaping of Garland's attitude toward the Indian was a trip he took with Zulime to Oklahoma in April, 1900. George W. H. Stouch, now a major and agent to the Southern Cheyenne and Arapaho Indians, invited the Garlands to visit him and his wife for a tour of the reservation. Stouch knew of Garland's interest in Indians and had suggested several topics to him at Lame Deer in 1897. The writer was eager to go, for he had already begun preliminary work on *The Captain of the Gray-Horse Troop* and thought Stouch might offer some suggestions. He had also begun to think about a volume of stories, tentatively titled "Our Red Neighbors," which were "to present the Indian as a human being." For these reasons, Garland considered the invitation "a most important event" in his life.

On April 23, the Garlands left Chicago for Oklahoma. After arriving at the Darlington Agency, near El Reno, and seeing Stouch, they went to a Cheyenne village nearby, where Garland was presented to some of the headmen. The author wrote of them: "Once they held themselves erect among men. No one dared to give them orders. Now they are somebody's hired men — outcasts, tramps."

That evening the writer talked with Chester Poe Cornelius, an Oneida, and their conversation proved not only interesting but historically important. Cornelius was a lawyer, and he told Garland, "Lawyers here will always be concerned largely with Indian lands, inheritance, and titles. The agency rolls do not show family relationships. Each man and woman has an individual name and there is certain to be much litigation." Garland promised to bring the matter before President Theodore Roosevelt, whom he had met while he was working on the Grant biography.

Garland also spoke to a group of youngsters at the agency school. He said of the children: "I was much impressed with them, but could not help

thinking how arbitrary this scheme of education is: to make them conform —
to make them act like white people — to cut them off from all that is deep-
seated in them, is the purpose of their teachers. They sing our monotonous,
worn-out hymns and they wear shoddy, agency clothing. In the end they will
be merely imitations of poor whites." Garland later used these impressions in
his story "Spartan Mother." Several of his other tales of the Southern Cheyenne and Arapaho also turn about the matter of education.

It appears, from Garland's notes, that between the time he arrived at the
agency and the tour of the reservation, Garland got ideas for a number of
stories from Stouch. One titled "White Calf and the Wheel-barrow," a story
of the Blackfoot in 1879, became "The White Weasel; A True Indian Story,"
published in *The Dearborn Independent* in December, 1926. In it White Weasel,
a chief, does nothing but walk about the agency grounds, dressed in his fanciest
buckskin costumes. He is thought lazy by the agency staff and is not well liked.
There is some building going on, and the contractor has trouble hiring laborers
to dig a cellar. He asks the Indians to work for a dollar a day. The next day,
the women dig while the men lie around, sleep, and tell stories. The whites
curse the men, especially White Weasel who walks about in his usual way.

After three days, White Weasel goes to the contractor for the money the
women have earned, saying that they are hungry and need their strength to
work. The contractor is outraged but pays him anyway. That night he is
awakened to find White Weasel and the other men digging. The next day,
once more the women work and the men lie around. The contractor realizes,
then, that the men cannot afford to be seen doing "women's work." He begins
to understand and admire White Weasel, who accepts the responsibility of
feeding his people but remains proud and, in many ways, adheres to the old
ways.

"The Story of Howling Wolf," which Stouch had suggested in 1897, was
evidently retold to Garland, and it began to take shape under his pen. Another
titled "Story of Red Bird" became "The Faith of His Fathers," published in
Harper's Weekly in May, 1903. It is the story of Moeehas, a progressive Indian
policeman, whose beautiful little daughter, Washa, becomes ill and dies. When
she is near death, the Catholic missionary comes and asks to baptize the child
so that, upon death, she will "fly straight to the heavenly place." Moeehas
does not believe in "that magic," yet he consents at his wife's request as the
child sinks. The priest then tells them that they must not hide the body in the
rocks but must bury her white man fashion. After the child is buried, the priest
tells them that they must not destroy the child's things but give them away.
This latter act they do not perform but, instead, burn the things. Then with
doubts about their former acts, Moeehas digs up the coffin and finds that the
child has not gone to heaven as the priest had promised. Bitter, Moeehas goes
to the agent, denounces the white man, and vows to walk in the ways of his
fathers.

Other Indian stories, evidently suggested by Stouch, which Garland
sketched in his notebook, include "Story of the Cord-wood," "Little Man —
Keeper of the Arrow," "The Dance Houses," "The Beer-bottle Necklace,"
"Mr. Jetty from Texas," "The Drunken Driver," and "Famine of Black-feet."

Garland also sketched two episodes in which the character Mose Lee, first conceived three years before, appears as a savior to the natives. In one sketch, he is already known as a friend to the Indian and is called "Blazing Hand" by them. He comes to the Northern Cheyenne to help them avoid an impending war.

He also appears in a story of undetermined origin, "The People of the Buffalo," which appeared in December, 1900, in *McClure's*. In the story, Mose finds a young Oglala child who has been lost in a snow storm and returns him to his mother. The Indians are overwhelmed by this kind act. They hold a dance for the young cowboy, feed him, give him presents, and offer him a wife. The latter he rejects, but tells the band that he will always have a warm heart toward them. With a new attitude toward the Indians and a joyous heart, he steals away the next morning and continues his journey before the camp is awake. The story was reworked and published in *The Book of the American Indian* as "The Storm-Child." In the revised version, the story is set in a Teton camp with Waumdisapa as chief. Garland gives more treatment to the Indians' attempts to get the cowboy to remain among them and has the child's mother develop a fondness for him. The end is nevertheless the same — a considerable improvement in Indian-white relations.

On May 1, Major Stouch and his guests began their tour of the reservation. The major event of the excursion was their visit to Seger's Colony, where Garland first met John Seger, a man who proved a valuable source of information on the Cheyenne and Arapaho and who had a lasting influence on Garland's career.

In March, 1886, John Homer Seger (1846–1928) had taken 152 Southern Cheyenne and Arapaho Indians to this point, which was the former headquarters of the Washita Cattle Company, some fifty miles from Darlington Agency, and founded Seger's Colony — a subagency, manual boarding school, and 1,200 acre farm. Seger was superintendent of the school, carpenter, brickmaker, mason, farmer, and subagent. He had joined the Indians' games, listened to their stories, and faced both the hard and prosperous times with them. He considered the natives not as "treacherous fiends" or "wily devils," but as " 'folks' — men and women of the Stone Age."

On the day of Garland's arrival at Colony, Seger told him numerous amusing anecdotes and stories about the Indians, their customs, and life. Garland asked if Seger had ever written the stories down. He had not. The subagent was, in fact, poorly educated and almost illiterate; for that reason the Indian Department had considered dropping him from service. But he was invaluable in his position at Colony and was thus retained.

Garland took notes for four stories. "Carrying the Mail" was the germ for "The Blood Lust," which first appeared in *The Book of the American Indian*. In the story, Seger selects Little Robe, a Cheyenne, to accompany him on the mail route between Fort Reno and Camp Supply. At one spot along the way, Little Robe remembers that he and his family once camped there. Then he tells Seger how once, as a young man, he took his wife and beautiful daughter with him when he went south to raid the Mexicans and steal horses. The Mexicans, in pursuit, mortally wounded his child. Little Robe gathered a band of warriors and again raided the village, killing all its inhabitants and burning it. "After that I slept," says Little Robe. The story is a fine study in character.

"Story of Hippy" became "Hippy, the Dare-Devil," published in *McClure's* in September, 1902. It is the story of Beaver-tail, an Arapaho, called Hippy by the whites because of a wound which caused him to limp. A warrior of good repute, he nevertheless is derided as a weakling by the Cheyenne, who regard the Arapaho as inferiors. In an altercation with the agency school teacher, Hippy vows to kill him, but over a period of time they become fast friends. The Cheyenne deride the warrior even more, and in his anger, he vows to make the agent give them good beef instead of the bad meat they have received. He forces the agent at gunpoint to requisition the best beef and goes back to camp a hero.

Hippy is later captured and sent to prison at Fort Smith, where he reinjures his hip and is sent home to die. On his deathbed, he asks his sons to take the white man's way. "The white man's road is the only safe one. The Indian's trail here is short. . . . Be at peace. Do not fight, as I have done."

An obvious weakness in the story is that the reader is at first more interested in Sam Williams, the teacher, than he is in Hippy. The reason for that is that Garland himself was more interested in Seger than he was in the limping Indian. Williams is modeled after Seger, who told the story about himself. Like Seger, Williams is dauntless, poorly educated, fluent in the native languages, and well liked by the Indians. Hippy calls him "Mi-O-Kani," a name by which Seger was known to the Cheyenne and Arapaho.

The other stories Seger told were of "Yellow Horse" and "Laughing Man." Garland did nothing with the latter, but he worked the notes for "Yellow Horse" into a completed story called "Leaders in the Trail," which was never published. It is a story of Yellow Horse, who is so determined to take up the white man's way and farm that he refuses to strike his tent and go on the hunt because he has a setting-hen he does not want to disturb. At his death, he has his farming tools placed nearby so he can see them and puts his children in the care of the agency farmer.

On the day following their arrival at Colony, Garland attended a council, which he described as "a fine scene." To Garland, the Arapaho were "distinctly less noble in bearing" than the Cheyenne, and they remained in the background of the council. Here he learned that the Cheyenne felt the Arapaho inferior to them. It was around that concept that Garland built the character motivation in "Hippy, the Dare-Devil."

Before the party left Colony, Garland recorded sketches of two more stories told by Seger, "Whiteman's Court" and "Lizard." Garland developed the former into the unpublished humorous story of Lizard, a Kiowa, and his wife, who constantly fight and ask Seger to settle the matter. They finally go to court, enjoy the drama of the proceedings, and return home reconciled because the white man's court has been quite enough for them.

When the Stouches and Garlands left Colony, they made plans to return so Garland could see Seger again. They visited the subagent's home in Arapaho

Sympathetic Indian subagent John H. Seger, although almost illiterate himself, supplied Garland with raw material for a substantial amount of his Indian fiction from 1900 to 1905.

Oklahoma Historical Society

and went on to the Red Moon subagency, where Garland met White Shield. His impressions of Red Moon and a moving speech by White Shield, recorded in his notes, became a part of an unpublished essay, "The Other Side of the Redman," which he wrote to show the human aspect of the Indian.

Twenty years later, Garland wrote that something White Shield had said during this meeting had given him the title for a story and the theme for a volume of short stories. White Shield's statement — "I find it hard to make a home among the white men" — caused Garland to grasp "the reverse side of the problem." He wrote, "I took for the title of my story these words: *White Eagle, the Red Pioneer,* and presented the point of view of a nomad who turns his back on the wilderness which he loves, and sets himself the task of leading his band in settlement among the plowmen." The story of White Eagle consists of fifty-six typed legal sheets.

In the story, White Eagle, a Cheyenne, and various members of his camp are persuaded by Williams to carry the mail between two forts. They do it well and prosper until the mail route folds, and White Eagle is left to fend for himself. Texas cattlemen begin to drive herds through his area, feeding them on his grass. White Eagle and his men help them ford streams and take cattle as pay. He builds a sizeable herd of his own, but as the country opens up, the passing drivers rustle his cattle. In one instance, this is prevented by Blazing Hand (Mose).

The new agent cuts off White Eagle's rations in order to break his power as a chief. The leader becomes very poor and, without the protection of the agency, afraid to venture far from his camp because of the white ranchers nearby. Another blow to this man who had attempted to take "the white man's road" comes when his son is shot from ambush and killed.

Then Major Curtis, or "Crooked Wrist," is made agent. He comes to White Eagle, promising that justice will be done. He becomes the chief's friend and convinces him to protect his land by settling down, renting his land to the whites, and building a house, but he warns him not to be like the poor white farmers. White Eagle builds a house, but he and his wife find it hard to leave the teepee. Then Mose gives him news of the man who killed his son, and White Eagle sets out to kill the murderer. But the cowboy convinces him that blood revenge is not the white man's way, and after long deliberation White Eagle returns home. He has taken the white man's road.

White Eagle is modeled after White Shield and speaks many of the lines ascribed to White Shield in Garland's notes. Curtis, of course, is Stouch, right down to his crooked arm, and Williams is Seger. The story was never published. Garland shortened it and revised it as "Hotan — the Red Pioneer," changing White Eagle's name to Hotan and Williams' to Seger. The revision appeared as "Houtan, le Courrier Rouge" in *Revue Politique et Littéraire* in December, 1937.

On May 9, the party returned to Colony, where Seger and Garland discussed the plight of the Indian well into the night. The writer took notes for two more stories, "Dark Ways" and "Creeping Bear," and compiled a page of notes on sign language. He noted Seger's importance to him: "He is a very valuable man to know. He is able to give me the humorous and human side of the Cheyenne life. He *knows* these people. He has lived with them for thirty years. He uses the sign language with astonishing readiness and precision and is able to enter the actual moods of both Cheyennes and Arapahos."

On May 10, the Stouches and the Garlands went on to Bridgeport, an Arapaho camp, and then to Darlington the following day. Garland spent most of the evening there talking with Robert Burns, a young educated Cheyenne and clerk at the agency. Although Burns was able, interesting, and well educated, his "red psychology came out in his talk." The clerk admitted he could not rid himself of a belief in certain superstitions of his tribe: "After all, I am Cheyenne. One of the beliefs of our medicine men is that a magic arrow or a magic bullet can be sent by force of the will to pierce the heart of an enemy; and in spite of my education I have a kind of half belief in it."

After his evening with Burns, Garland was "fully resolved" to do his book of Indian stories. He may have had Burns in mind when he made notes for "The Carlisle Indian," and this Cheyenne was most likely the model for Iapi, the narrator of "The Silent Eaters," which Garland wrote a few months later. However, the volume of short stories which the writer planned so zealously at this time in 1900 did not become a fact until the publication of *The Book of the American Indian* in 1923.

After their tour of the Southern Cheyenne-Arapaho Reservation, the Garlands briefly visited the Wichita at Anadarko and the Comanche at Fort Sill, where Garland met Quana Parker, the famous Comanche chief. He made notes for a story, "Blowing Out the Gas," in which Quana was a character. They had dinner on the last night of their trip with Father Isadore Ricklin of the Catholic mission near Chickasha, the memories of which event Garland cherished.

Years later, the writer assessed the trip to Oklahoma as one of the most valuable of his career. He wrote, "My mind was filled with new characters and new concepts of the red people. Major Stouch, John Seger, White Shield, White Eagle, Quannah Parker, Robert Burns, Father Isadore, and his sisters — all suggested themes for my book of stories in which red men were to be treated as neighbors." In *A Daughter of the Middle Border* Garland wrote:

This trip to Indian Territory turned out to be a very important event in my life. First of all it enabled me to complete the writing of *The Captain of the Gray-Horse Troop* and started me on a long series of short stories depicting the life of the red man. It gave me an enormous amount of valuable material and confirmed me in my conviction that the Indian needed an interpreter. . . ."

Sitting Bull: An Epic Theme

However, Garland had to wait to use the material he had collected, for in July he and his wife journeyed to the Standing Rock Reservation. There the author resumed his research on Sitting Bull, about whom he had decided to write a story. Louis Primeau, Garland's interpreter, was a half-blood trader from Rock Creek. He told his friends among the Sioux that Garland was a friend and had come to write a story about Sitting Bull from the Indian's point of view. Garland said Primeau "not only comprehended my purpose in a literary sense, but he gave up his day to the task of introducing me to his people, and of interpreting me to them, as well as conveying their thoughts to me."

Primeau helped Garland to gain the confidence of a local trader named John M. Carignan, who knew Sitting Bull well and whom Garland claimed was of great value to him in writing "The Silent Eaters." Carignan talked about Sitting Bull's character, the ghost dance, the chief's death, and the reasons for the "outbreak" of 1890. Garland's notes of the interview cover over twenty pages.

Primeau had also known Sitting Bull, especially during the last years, and therefore proved a valuable source of information regarding the chief's involvement in the ghost dance movement and other matters. Garland's notes from his talks with Primeau are extensive, covering about twenty pages.

As before, the writer delved into the agency records for information concerning the famous chief and recorded what he found. From Slohan, or Crawler, the historian of the band, Garland learned the history of Sitting Bull before the wars of the 1870s. He also talked of the Custer fight, confirming what Two Moon had told him in 1897. Garland conducted three interviews with Slohan, and in the pages of his extensive notes from these sessions can be found a great part of the raw material from which "The Silent Eaters" was constructed.

Garland also interviewed others, including Lone Man, Looking Stag, Crazy Bull, One Bull (Sitting Bull's nephew), and Hawk Man. From Looking Stag and Crazy Bull, as well as from Primeau, Garland learned about a secret society called "the Silent Eaters," a group of Sitting Bull's most trusted friends, who acted as his bodyguard during his most active years as chief. They took their name from the fact that they did not sing at feasts and dances but smoked and talked quietly — "meditating on many things." The name gave Garland the title of the lengthy manuscript which was not published until it appeared in *The Book of the American Indian*.

"The Silent Eaters" is the story of the life of Sitting Bull as told by Iapi, the son of Shato, who was one of the Silent Eaters. He tells of Sitting Bull's rise to power at age twenty-two, his refusal to treat with the whites, and his decision to move his people to the west to avoid conflicts with the settlers. According to Iapi, Sitting Bull, who had been joined by the Cheyenne, was surprised by Custer. Although the Indians were disorganized and confused, they won. Iapi tells of Sitting Bull's retreat to and suffering in Canada, the capture of his daughter which forced his surrender, and his imprisonment at Fort Randall.

On the reservation, the chief tries to farm, but fails; he continues to oppose all attempts by the government to make new treaties. His people become very poor, and at the depth of their despair, the ghost dance offers them hope. A Brulé named Kicking Bear brings the news of the Messiah to Sitting Bull and teaches his people the dance. Although the chief does not believe in the new religion, he knows that it is the last resort of his people. If it is not true, his people are never to regain the old life and are, in his thinking, lost. Thus, when the agent orders him to stop the dances, he refuses. The agent sends the Indian police, composed of Sitting Bull's rivals, to arrest him. When the Silent Eaters come to his rescue, Sitting Bull is killed in the fighting.

This lively novelette of fourteen chapters appears to be in a number of ways Garland's most successful piece of fiction dealing with the American Indian, combining history with the best of the writer's literary talents. Iapi, the narrator, is a Sioux who had lived the old life and then become educated in the Anglo's ways. He at once sees the futility of Sitting Bull's resistance to the white man, yet sympathizes with him deeply, both racially and culturally.

The result is a tension which keeps the reader's attention much as the sense of dramatic irony holds one in Greek tragedy. Since the story is a first-person narrative, the perspective through which the story is presented is a limited, and therefore biased, one. It is a picture of Sitting Bull as a sympathetic Sioux saw him. In some ways it is an attempt to vindicate him.

The story is ultimately as much that of the narrator as it is of Sitting Bull. Iapi, too, can almost believe in the ghost dance because of the memories he has of his early youth in the wild. Yet the indelible stamp of the white man is on him. He knows too much to be able to believe; he likes the comforts of the white world. His position is therefore anomalous. He can never be white, no matter how well he is educated, and because of his association with the Anglos, the Indians distrust him. Yet Iapi is a Sioux who loves his chief. His ultimate evaluation of Sitting Bull is essentially that which Garland, himself, at one time expressed as his own opinion of the chief. If the story has a theme, it is in this statement:

He epitomized the epic, tragic story of my kind. His life spanned the gulf between the days of our freedom and the death of every custom native to us. He saw the invader come and he watched the buffalo disappear. Within the half century of his conscious life he witnessed greater changes and comprehended more of my tribe's tragic history than any other red man.

"The Silent Eaters" lacks the excesses of style which mark much of Garland's other work. The sentences are bare and simple, making the reading go quickly. Garland also does an excellent job of approximating the Indian rhetoric, of which generous examples can be found in his notes. Instead of the strained metaphors and similes which this writer so often produced, one finds here only those drawn from natural phenomena, which the Sioux knew well. Stylistically, as well as formally, there is a maintenance of control, which is rare in Garland's writings on the American Indian.

The author himself later evaluated the work he had done in "The Silent Eaters." The old warriors he had interviewed in 1897 had given him a clear sense of his purpose in the work: "No people is wrong unto itself. Every race, being a product of environment, bases its moral laws on its need of survival. Nature cares nothing for the individual. Whether a man scalps his enemies or eats them is all one to nature, provided such action insures the continuance of his kind." The writer questioned why we should bring into a Sioux's interpretation of life "the notions of an utterly alien and infinitely older state of organized society." He asked, "Would not an educated Sioux — if free to open his heart — make a special pleading for his chief, the Sitting Bull?"

The Garlands went from Fort Yates to Yellowstone and then to the Blackfoot Reservation. There Garland interviewed a trader, whom he identified as H. Kennerly, regarding a visit by Sitting Bull sometime before the chief's surrender. Garland rendered Kennerly's story in "The Sitting Bull's Visit," which was never published. The trader recalled how in the late 1870s six Sioux came to his trading house in Montana. Unknown to Kennerly, one was Sitting Bull himself, who then had a large reward posted for his capture. Some of the half-bloods and whites of the area tried to capture the chief, but the trader opposed them, saying that the Indian was his guest. After Sitting Bull escaped on a pony Kennerly gave him, the people found that the chief had left a large band of warriors camped just out of sight of the settlement while he came in to trade.

Sitting Bull is portrayed in the piece as a sensitive, honorable man. The notes for this narrative and other Sioux and Blackfoot matters related by Kennerly occupy over seventy pages of the writer's notebook. Garland also made extensive notes on Sitting Bull based on an interview with Philip Alvarez.

With a Blackfoot named Four Horns as a guide, the Garlands spent two weeks in the mountains. Garland found this Indian quite interesting and years later wrote a brief, unpublished sketch in praise of his character. In "Four Horns: Piegan," Garland says, "I afterward put this man into some of the scenes of 'The Captain of the Gray-Horse Troop.' " Here the writer refers to his use of Four Horns as the model for Two Horns, who dominated Captain Curtis's camps in the novel, just as Four Horns dominated those of the Garlands.

Before Garland left the West, he made plans for the use of the material he had gathered during his spring and summer travels among the Indians: "First I must put together a volume of short stories to be called *The Red Pioneer;* then I shall complete a prose poem of Sitting Bull to be called *The Silent Eaters,* and third, and most important of all, I must do a novel of reservation life, with an army officer as agent."

Family affairs interfered somewhat with Garland's work, but he was able to do preliminary work on "The Silent Eaters," which he said "took shape as a brief prose epic of the Sioux, a special pleading from the standpoint of a young educated red man, to whom Sitting Bull was a kind of Themistocles. Though based on accurate information, I intended it to be not so much a history as an interpretation." Garland initially felt inadequate for the task. He said in *A Daughter of the Middle Border* that he came to a conclusion after his investigations among the Sioux: "There was a big theme here, but I had small faith in my ability to handle it. It required an epic poet, rather than a realistic novelist."

A Time For Writing: Short Stories and A Novel

The Garlands returned to New York in October, 1900, with the author intent on writing his collection of short stories. To him, he said, the Indian was not "a subject of religious controversy"; Garland had "only an ethnological interest in his songs and supplications" and was "concerned with him solely as a human being, more or less in harmony with his environment like the panther or the eagle." Garland wanted to set down the Indian's point of view, just as other writers were attempting to do for European immigrants. He saw the Cheyenne village as he would see any other collection of people, having both good and bad. He later wrote, "My stories take the cruelty and dirt and sloth of camp life for granted — such facts have been sufficiently dwelt upon. I have drawn the tender and humorous side of their lives as well as the patiently heroic side." These facets of Indian life he tried to exemplify in his stories of character types — Rising Wolf the mystic, Hippy the dare-devil, White Eagle the pioneer, White Weasel the dandy.

In the winter, he began writing *The Captain of the Gray-Horse Troop.* By the end of March, 1901, he had finished "The Silent Eaters" and sent it to *Century Magazine,* only to have it rejected. He had also conceived an ending for his novel, but he decided in May that he needed further study of the Cheyennes. Thus he returned to Oklahoma early that month. He spent two weeks with Seger, listening to his stories and taking notes. His notebook contains jottings on no fewer than fifty-two anecdotes or stories! Of these Garland worked seven into stories which he published.

Two anecdotes, "The Rooster" and "Whiteman's Conceit" became "Two Stories of Oklahoma," published in *Century* in June, 1904. The work contains humor, which is rare in Garland's writings on the American Indian. Perhaps this light touch can be attributed to the fact that the humor was ultimately Seger's. The first story, "Nuko's Revenge," is about an Arapaho who leaves his pet rooster with the agency farmer while he goes on a buffalo hunt, only to find, when he returns, that his rooster has been killed by a turkey cock. Nuko, in revenge, kills the turkey and carries him off to eat, despite the farmer's protests that the bird belongs to the "Great White Father" in Washington.

The second tale, "A Red Man's View of Evolution," is narrated by the agency farmer. An ancient Kiowa is asked why he does not light his pipe with a match instead of a flint and steel. The old man replies that in spite of fancy inventions like matches, the white man is not very clever. In fact, he is foolish. He wears hair on his face and is not a man but a hair-covered animal. However, the hair is wearing away in spots, and the old man believes that the whites will be men by and by.

Seger's tales "Big Nose" and "A Decree of Council" were developed into a story with the latter as the title. "A Decree of Council" first appeared in *The Book of the American Indian* in 1923. It is the story of Big Nose, a Cheyenne, who one night gambles away his money, blankets, teepee, wives, and even his clothes. He walks naked through the camp asking people to take pity on him. Finally the headmen in council decide that Big Nose should be given a teepee and the necessities of life and that one wife — old and shrewish — should be returned to discipline him.

Big Nose changes his ways and becomes "progressive," farming and carrying freight for the agency. One day he complains to Seger that he wishes to take a new wife and get rid of the old one, who will not stay home and keep house. Seger goes to White Shield on Big Nose's part, but when White Shield tells Seger the facts of the case, the subagent knows there is no appeal from the decree of council. Garland uses the story as an editorial springboard to discuss the social nature of the Indians:

It is this feeling on their part which makes it so difficult for the Government to carry out its theories of allotment. It is difficult to uproot a habit of life which has been thousands of years forming. It is next to impossible to get one of these people to leave the village group and go into his lonely little cabin a mile or two from a neighbor. And the need of amusement is intensified by the sad changes in the life of these people.

"Lone Wolf's Camp" and "Lone Wolf's Old Guard" became "Lone Wolf's Old Guard," published in *Harper's Weekly* in May, 1903. It is the story of Lone Wolf, a Kiowa, whose camp is on the line between the Cheyenne and Kiowa lands. The Cheyenne lease their land to a cattle company, and when the whites come to run the fence line, Lone Wolf tells them he will fight to prevent their taking his camp, which the line would split. The crew go to Darlington, where the cattlemen persuade John Seger to run the line. Lone Wolf holds council. He knows his predicament. To fight is certain death; the Indians could kill the crew, but then the army would come.

At last the old men of the camp decide to go to battle and do one more heroic deed before they die. That way, retribution will not be visited on the younger Kiowa. In war paint and led by Lone Wolf, they confront Seger and his crew. In a dramatic scene, Seger convinces them that the line has been authorized in Washington. Lone Wolf finally agrees not to fight and says he will accept the line if it is run by the army. This will assure him that the line is not a trick of the whites to steal Indian land. "Lone Wolf's Old Guard" reappeared in *The Book of the American Indian*.

"Big Horse" became "The River's Warning," published in *Frank Leslie's* in January, 1902. The story is told by Big Elk, a Cheyenne, who as a young man was taught to hate the white man, though he had never been close to one and had never seen one's house. After the first agent had come to Darlington, Big Elk, as leader of a band of youths, suggested that they raid the agency and steal the horses and thereby become heroes among the Cheyenne. Big Elk scouts ahead and finds that whites and Indians work peaceably together about the agency and that the whites are kind to him. He returns to his men determined not to perpetrate the raid, but they revile him. He goes back to the agency to make sure he has not been tricked, but the Indians he meets tell him the agent is kind. Again the leader returns to his men, determined not to raid, and again they mock him.

Angered, Big Elk at last agrees to the raid on the following morning, but on arising the Indians find that the Canadian River between them and the agency is too high to cross, though the sky is cloudless. They wait two more days, but each day the river is higher. They give up the raid, certain that the Great Spirit has spoken. Garland uses the story to make editorial statements about the social nature of the Indians and their fascination by the "wonders" worked by the whites. The story reappeared in *The Book of the American Indian*.

"Curley's Scars" was worked into "Red Plowman," which appeared in *Craftsman* in November, 1907. It is a single scene. Osca is plowing — unused to it and doing it badly — but determined. "It was as if a man of the stone age had met and taken lessons of the advance guard of the age of steam," says Garland. A party of young Arapahos ride up and chide the plowman as a great chief reduced to a squaw. Osca answers that their fathers and his enemies do not call him a squaw. He follows the white man's way, but he does not beg from him with one hand and strike him with the other. Osca tears open his shirt and shows them his battle scars. He has fought "the wonder-workers"; now he has turned from war. Ashamed, the youths leave.

Finally, "The Love of Matches" became "Nistina," which appeared in *Harper's Weekly* in April, 1903. Nistina's beloved Hawk is sent off to prison in Florida because he organized a raid in retaliation to abuse he had suffered from some cattlemen. Nistina laments her loss, and as time passes and she hears no word from Hawk, she becomes depressed. Without confiding in her father or mother, she decides that she must learn to read and write English in order to inquire after Hawk.

When a young man returns from prison and tells her that Hawk will write her in the white man's language, Nistina becomes more determined and soon sends him a letter. She receives no answer and writes again. In the third year she receives a letter in poor English from Hawk along with a photograph of him dressed in white man's clothes. Nistina is happy, and when she tells the story to her father, he says, "It is good. . . . Surely the white-people are wonder-working beings." "Nistina" reappeared in *The Book of the American Indian* in 1923. The name "Nistina" does not appear in Garland's notes on the story, but toward the end of his notebook is a list of Indian names in which it does appear.

Another name on the list is Tah-You, the name of the central character in "The New Medicine House," which appeared in *Harper's Weekly* in December, 1902. The story, of uncertain origin, may have been suggested by Stouch rather than by Seger, for its setting is the Northern Cheyenne Reservation, and it deals with a new hospital which has just been built there. The Indians are reluctant to use the clinic, and the situation is complicated by a zealous nurse and a preacher.

When a man dies in the hospital, the Indians will have nothing to do with it. A youth named Robert falls ill, and his grandfather Tah-You, a medicine man, wants to see the young man and treat him. The agent refuses but tells the old man that he may take the boy home if he is no better on the following day. This he does, and when the agent visits the camp he finds the youth nearly recovered. He knows that the security of home has helped, but old Tah-You insists that it was his good medicine. The story reappeared in *The Book of the American Indian* in 1923.

Another story of certain origin but one for which there seem to be no notes is "The Spartan Mother," which Garland said was based on "Seger's experience as a teacher in Darlington" and which he considered one of the "most significant" of his Indian stories. It appeared in *Ladies' Home Journal* in February, 1905. The story is, in reality, about Seger. Out of love for the Indian children, Seger recruits students. Many parents resist. Among them are Tomacham and his wife Wahiah, who finally bring their son Atokan, a proud youth, to the school but ask that his hair not be cut and that he be allowed to dress in the old way. Seger refuses, and after a heart-rending decision, they send Atokan anyway.

Seger is not able to break the boy's spirit, and Atokan leads the others in refusing to return when the bell rings after noon. Seger sends word that he will whip the children who disobey. This causes alarm because the Indians traditionally do not whip their children, and they are angered by the threat of a white man to do so. The old people come to school to watch. Atokan disobeys, and Seger whips him several times until the boy's spirit is finally broken and he cries. The superintendent then asks Tomacham why the Indian sends his children to school if not to learn and how they are to learn if they are not in school. The chief sees Seger's logic and tearfully retires, realizing their final subjection to the white man — they had given him their children.

As Garland sometimes did, he wrongly named the piece. Wahiah, the spartan mother, is a silent figure in the background. She is torn between the love and pride for her son and the desire for him to survive. She tearfully gives her boy over to Seger's hands. Though Garland evidently wants the reader to sympathize with the motives of Seger, the methods he has the superintendent use are less than flattering. The story reappeared in *The Book of the American Indian* as "Wahiah — A Spartan Mother."

Besides the new stories, Seger told again the story of Little Robe, which Garland would render in "The Blood Lust" in *The Book of the American Indian,* and gave the writer more instruction in sign language. In terms of literary production, Garland's trip in 1901 was one of his most important. By this time, he noted later, his mind had completely turned away from the scenes of his youth to "the red people of the plains and the men and women of the High Country," and he considered *Main-Travelled Roads* "a picture painted."

During his trip to Oklahoma, Garland had found time to work on the Curtis-Lawson dialogue for *The Captain of the Gray-Horse Troop* and to interview Stouch concerning his attitude toward the Indians and the civil service system as it applied to Indian agents. He worked on the novel in June, and then, with Mrs. Garland, traveled in Colorado, New Mexico, and Arizona during July, August, and September. The only Indian matter in his notes from this trip is a brief entry on Laguna, where the Garlands went to see the Corn Dance.

Garland's major project during the fall and winter of 1901 was completing his novel, which began appearing serially in *The Saturday Evening Post* in December. He then faced the problem of getting it ready for publication in book form. Harper and Brothers brought out the volume in March, 1902.

Theodore Roosevelt praised it; but, according to Garland, to George Bird Grinnell, a frequent traveler to the Blackfoot Reservation, it was "a fictional study of no great importance." Garland valued Grinnell's opinion and had sought his criticism in writing the novel. Generally, Grinnell praised Garland's Indian stories, "not for their truth, but for their sympathetic view" and applauded Garland's attitude that a village of Sioux or Cheyenne was "like a village of white men — a mixture of good and evil with its hoodlums, poets, and philosophers."

Over the years Garland's novel has failed to pass the critical tests for good literary art. Roy W. Meyer deals well with the novel as a piece of fiction and aptly points out its problems: the weak love plot, the strained dialogue, and the unbelievable swiftness of the Indians' conversion to agriculturalists. Garland tried to justify and make apology for the love plot: "After all, it is intended to entertain rather than instruct." And too, an artist in the midst of an outbreak was not odd, for artists often toured the reservations. At any rate, he says that his main concern in the novel was "with the outlook and action of the Cheyennes," the last stand of these "people of the polished Stone Age confronting an age of electricity and the machine gun."

The conversion of the Indians perhaps was symbolic of what Garland hoped would happen to the natives in the process of assimilation, since it was unavoidable. Nevertheless, Meyer's criticism of it as an artistic device stands. The only other bit of commentary that might be to the point here is that the characters of the novel are types like those in Garland's short stories. One finds the Indian lover, the Indian hater, the ethnologist, the politician, and so on. Characters and their motivations seem too thinly drawn here, as they are in his shorter works. The author was often more interested in the event than in the character; therein lay his artistic sacrifice.

Meyer clearly develops the thesis that Garland presented through Curtis the same philosophy he presented the following April in his article "The Red Man's Present Needs." But, says Meyer, it was not nearly as effective in the novel because of Garland's failure to execute well the fictional mode of expression.

At the time of its appearance, the novel was generally well received. Army officials were pleased with the sympathetic treatment of the army. Reviewers "accepted the novel as a truthful presentation of life on an Indian reservation in the nineties." In its serial form, the book had caused a sensation in the West, particularly at the Standing Rock Reservation. To the Indians and the people at the agency there, Garland's novel was "a reality," for the commissioner of Indian affairs had recently proposed the leasing of Sioux lands to the cattlemen, the Indians' old enemies. The Sioux chiefs were opposed to the leasing and prepared to send a delegation, accompanied by Louis Primeau, to Washington. J. M. Carignan, whom Garland had met at Standing Rock in 1900, asked Garland to meet the delegation in Washington to help in putting their problem before the public.

Some reformers had great hopes for *The Captain of the Gray-Horse Troop* as a reform novel. B. O. Flower of *The Arena* wrote:

I think that in very many respects this is your best work. It combines the excellencies of your more recent long books with the strong altruistic and moral motive which was so marked a feature of your earlier novels. . . . We have so many writers now who are writing merely for art's sake, and so few who seem to have a broad grasp of the fundamentals of justice, that I have regretted to see so many of your recent works lacking in the strong moral motive that characterized "Jason Edwards," "A Member of the Third House," "A Spoil of Office," and most of your earlier short stories.

The novel was Garland's greatest literary success up to that time in terms of the number of copies sold, but, at that, it was not as successful as the writer had expected. He felt that the publishers had failed to give the novel the publicity it deserved.

Renaming the Indians: An Unfortunate Project

One significant result of *The Captain of the Gray-Horse Troop* was that Roosevelt became convinced that Garland knew the conditions on the western reservations. Shortly after the first of April, 1902, the author was called to the White House to discuss "the Indian problem" with the president. Also present at the meeting was Clinton Hart Merriam, head of the Division of Ornithology and Mammalogy of the U.S. Department of Agriculture. During the conference Garland argued that the Indian must have time to pass from his age to the age of electricity:

It is a mistake to imagine that a single generation or even three can bridge the chasm. They are gregarious. To make solitary homesteaders of them is to destroy them. Their land should be allotted in such wise that they can live as the French peasants do, in villages, and farm their outlying lands. Others of them, like the Navajo, are natural herders and should be allowed to continue as such. They must have time of adjustment.

Then Garland introduced the idea of renaming the Indians, a project which first had been suggested to him in 1900 by the Oneida Chester Poe Cornelius at Darlington.[4] Actually, the entire matter of Indian names stemmed from the problems surrounding allotment, which resulted from the execution of the General Allotment Act of 1887. This congressional act was looked upon as a possible solution to the "Indian problem" that had existed for the better part of the nineteenth century. It gave the president of the United States discretionary powers to force the Indians on certain reservations to take allotments of land in severalty. Allotment was in reality thrust upon the Indians as a means of assimilating them into the Anglo-dominated culture.

As the government proceeded with allotment by taking tribal censuses and assigning parcels of land to each Indian, officials noticed that the nature of native names made their work difficult. Reformers such as Garland felt renaming necessary because the names of Indians in many tribes were not compatible with the Anglo custom of giving children the surname of their fathers. Since the laws governing inheritance were based on this custom, there was the possibility of confusion, litigation, and fraud in the matter of an Indian's inheritance of land unless some reform in naming practices occurred.

Since his visit to the Southern Ute reservation in 1895, Garland had been concerned with those names which were "bungling translations made by ignorant interpreters or by contemptuous whites" and those which were arbitrarily given by teachers and missionaries. Some of the finest and most dignified chieftains he knew had been burdened with names like Tail Feathers Coming, or Scabby Horse. He suggested that each family group be asked to choose a surname of its own — the same as if they were Russians, Italians, or any other

---

[4] A complete account of Garland's renaming efforts appears in Daniel F. Littlefield, Jr., and Lonnie E. Underhill, "Renaming the American Indian: 1890–1913," pp. 33–45.

foreign people — so that each member of the family would have a distinct name. He stressed the legal reasons that their relationships be shown, for many of the Indians already owned valuable lands and other property. In this discussion Merriam supported Garland.

Roosevelt pledged his full support in the matter of Indian renaming. Garland then received the support of the secretary of the interior, Ethan A. Hitchcock, and of William A. Jones, commissioner of Indian affairs. The worst feature of the situation, the writer told Jones, was that lands already had been allotted to many Indians and that the new land-owners appeared on the rolls with "silly or disgusting translations" of their proper names. Garland stressed that "it should be possible, however, to apply the white man's system to those tribes whose lands are still held in common." Jones asked Garland to compose a circular which could be used as a guide to naming by agents, teachers, and interpreters. Since the plan had caught the attention of so many, Jones asked the author to supervise the work which lay ahead.

Garland set about gathering a staff to assist him in effecting his plan. He selected George Bird Grinnell, Clinton Hart Merriam, W. J. McGee of the Bureau of Ethnology, and Dr. Charles A. Eastman, a three-quarter blood Sioux and government physician at Crow Creek, South Dakota. Other persons who advised or assisted Garland in the renaming project included Charles F. Lummis, Robert Burns, and Seger.

The circular which Garland wrote was issued from Jones' office in December, 1902. It "amplified and reissued" a circular that had been put out from the commissioner's office in 1890. It called for (1) the establishment of the father's name, shortened if necessary, as the family name; (2) retention of the root word in abbreviated names and avoidance of the creation of words of evil significance in the process of abbreviation; (3) retention of long Indian names in translation; (4) elimination of foolish, cumbersome, or uncouth translations; (5) elimination of nicknames; (6) the spelling of each name as one word; (7) preference over English names of any acceptable Indian names given by parents to children; (8) retention of names by which Indians were already well known, after which name the family name was to be placed; (9) consultation with parents in naming children; (10) annotation of existing allotment rolls to show both the old and the modified name; (11) consistency in spelling, for which suggestions were given.

In April, 1903, work began in earnest on the Southern Cheyenne and Arapaho rolls, Robert Burns doing the work at Garland's request. A month later, the effort had progressed far enough that sample sheets were sent to Commissioner Jones for Garland's approval. The writer found the names generally improved, but he wanted the Indians' wishes concerning their names more clearly represented. Translations of Indian names and school names, which the Cheyenne did not recognize at all, were common on the lists. In a letter to Jones, Garland wrote:

I should like to know whether there are insuperable objections or whether the ones working on the rolls are not revising from the white man's point of view with a feeling that the names ought to be as nearly Anglo as possible. My notion is to treat them as we would Polish or Russian names — *retain as much of the Cheyenne as we can easily pronounce* and above all secure the pleased co-operation of the red people themselves.

The project of renaming the Oklahoma Indians did not go very far, for interest in it soon dwindled on the part of officials in the field. However, Eastman was successful in assigning family names to most of the Sioux in the Dakotas. Although Garland worked at the project for over a decade, at the end of that period many of the problems which the writer had sought to solve still existed. A letter to Garland from the secretary of the interior in 1913 indicates why the plan failed:

The plan has, as you say, never been fully carried out, but the difficulties in the way should be borne in mind. Under the instructions of the circular to which you allude, this work has so far been left chiefly to the Superintendents of various schools, and it appears probable that, in the press of other duties, this matter has been somewhat overlooked. Your offer of cooperation is appreciated and any suggestions from you will be considered.

Unintentionally, Garland actually may have done some harm to the Indian. His attempts to rename them were made in a spirit of humanitarianism to protect the Indian's remaining land and to make his assimilation easier. Those attempts, unfortunately, struck at times at the Indian's very identity — his name. Unfortunately, too, the project absorbed much of Garland's energy. About the time the effort got under way, Garland's rate of production of writings on the Indian was at its highest. Twenty-four months later, it was at its lowest in several years.

Mature Reformer: Hamlin Garland, 1902–1903

At the time of his meeting with Roosevelt in April of 1902, Garland was more deeply involved in Indian reform than at any other time in his career. That month, in fact, there appeared an article which reflects his most mature thinking on the American Indian. It was "The Red Man's Present Needs," published in *North American Review*. By this time, Garland had traveled among the Indians for almost a decade. The changes he had seen them undergo were vast, and his writing reflects the sober and mature thought which the writer had put into the subject.

Garland realized that the "unofficial inspection" he had made of so many reservations "for fictional purposes" had, over a period of years, given him "a clearer understanding of the present conditions of the nation's wards." Thus he writes with authority, aimed at reform in government policy, on such subjects as the diversity of peoples under the name "Indian," climatic conditions which affect the various reservations, political differences within the tribes, allotment as a failure in Indian policy, and the social nature of the native.

Garland then offers eight suggestions whose purpose is "to make better Indians, and to make the transition from their old life to the new as easy as may be, to lessen rather than to add to the weight of their suffering." Among the eight are the settlement of Indians in family groups, the rescue of dying arts, and the prevention of missionaries from regulating the amusements and daily lives of the natives. The language of the article is clear, the statements concise. Sentences are well balanced and restrained. Garland is in control of his subject. As a result, this is perhaps his best piece of nonfiction on the American Indian.

A related piece, apparently written at about the same time, is "The Indian Agency," which was not published. In it Garland makes the same points concerning the isolated life of the agents, the methods of appointing them, and the work of missionaries among the Indians. The first three paragraphs of that piece, with minor revisions, became the first four of "The Spartan Mother."

A few days after his historic meeting with Roosevelt in 1902, Garland went to Oklahoma "to see Major Stouch and John Seger, and to make certain observations for President Roosevelt." His primary purpose, however, was to get Seger to record his experiences among the Indians. Seger consented to talk in the presence of a stenographer, and for ten succeeding days, an hour or so each day, Seger highlighted his most interesting experiences. Garland himself took over a score of pages of notes, presumably about incidents related by Seger when he was not with the stenographer. After ten days, Garland had obtained a chronicle, "more or less consecutive." He evaluated the notes as a "confused mass of raw material, valuable only for its historical data." He said Seger's memory was "prodigious, but he had no power of construction. He could not write and his talk was repetitious."

Garland took the original typed copy and left the carbon with Seger, intending to rework the manuscript and if possible find a publisher for it. However, he later said that if the tangle of material were ever acceptable to an editor, it would have to be entirely rewritten. He could not devote sufficient time, which he said would require a year, and he suggested that Seger and his son Neatha rework it.

The subagent agreed to do so and spent time on it occasionally during the next few years, but the manuscript was never put in final form. Among Garland's papers are 183 pages of drafts of Seger's story, historical in part and fictionalized in part. The manuscript was frequently mentioned in the correspondence between the two during the following years. Seger, however, blamed his busy schedule for not revising the material. That was probably the case. Like Seger, Garland, too, was too busy to devote the necessary time to the work.

It is difficult to overemphasize the importance of Seger in Garland's career. Out of their relationship, which lasted until Seger's death in 1928, came many stories, sketches, and articles dealing with the Cheyenne and Arapaho. Many of the ideas for them came directly from Seger, he suggested many others, and he greatly assisted Garland in gaining insight into the Cheyenne and Arapaho customs, condition, and character. Finally, Seger appears as a character in several chronicles which deal with the Indians of Oklahoma, which, as a body, are the greatest number of stories Garland did about the Indians of a particular locale.

In 1924 Stanley Vestal (Walter Campbell) of the University of Oklahoma edited Seger's *Early Days Among the Cheyenne and Arapahoe Indians.* In his introduction, Vestal suggests, at least in tone, some impropriety on Garland's part in using Seger's material. Garland readily admits the use of the material in his Indian stories:

None of them are true in the sense of being precisely the way they were told, for I took very few notes. They are rather free transcripts of the incidents which chanced to follow my liking — but they reflect the spirit of the original narratives and are bound together by one underlying motive which is to show the Indian as a human being, a neighbor.

Garland also told Stouch, "I am going to tell of the red man as you and Seger have known him, as a man of the polished stone age trying to adapt himself to steam and electricity." The writer said that he used the subagent's material with his consent: "As compensation for the suggestions he gave me, I bought a farm and helped him make a home upon it after the department had dropped him from its rolls."

During 1902 and 1903 Garland saw published more of his writings on the American Indian than at any other time: five short pieces and a novel in 1902, and six short pieces in 1903. Among these latter was an article titled "The Redman as Material," published in *Booklovers' Magazine* in August. Garland says that the Indian has always been "material" for New World writers, who are responsible for many misconceptions about the savagery and treachery of the native. Writers have consistently failed to show his "human side" — his family life, his concept of life and duty. With "supposed altruistic intentions," such writers have "helped to make the English-speaking peoples the most ruthless conquerors the world has ever seen, ruthless in the sense that they displace and destroy with large-hearted, joyous self-sufficiency, blotting out all manners, customs, religions, and governments which happen to differ from their own."

Garland's interest here in the human side of the Indian reflects an idea he had long entertained. He left some unpublished pieces whose titles and content suggest that they were aimed at destroying the popular, stereotyped images of the American Indians created to a large extent by American writers. They are summary pieces, gleaned from his years of travel among native Americans.

"The Other Side of the Redman" begins with criticism of writers who have failed to take into account the human side of the Indian. To show the "other" side of the native, Garland recounts episodes of his visit to see Seger in 1905 and anecdotes of Looking Stag at Standing Rock in 1900 and of the Red Moon subagency and White Shield in 1900. "The Gentle Side of the Red Man" was an attempt to show that the Indian was not always the "stolid and very serious" person he was thought to be. Incidences witnessed during Garland's visit to the Utes in 1896, Hubbell's trading post in 1899, and the Standing Rock and Blackfoot Reservations in 1900 make up the body of this work. Internal evidence indicates that these essays were produced about 1905.

Decline in the Indian Writings: New Directions

After 1903 Garland's writing on the American Indian drastically decreased. He published only one piece in 1904 and 1905, none in 1906, one in 1907, and no more until the publication of *The Book of the American Indian* in 1923.

Family obligations had something to do with the decline. Because he was married and wanted to establish a home, he had taken less than he wanted for the serial rights to *The Captain of the Gray-Horse Troop.* The birth of his first daughter increased his desire to settle down. He said that after the publication of *Hesper* in 1903, "I counted my days of controversial writing at an end. As a householder I was in league with the capitalistic forces of society. Like the Irish reformer in the old story I found myself changed."

By 1910, Garland was reluctant to travel because of his family, and by 1913 he felt his fictional powers waning: "I no longer feel it my duty to enlighten the world, I am content to feed and house my wife and daughters." In retrospect he wrote, "Marriage, paternity, householding, during these years unquestionably put the brakes on my work as a writer, but I had no desire to return to bachelorhood."

But Garland had in his possession huge amounts of material on the American Indian, which he could have used. Thus, there were other, and more central, reasons for the decline of his writing on that subject. In June, 1904, Garland began a novel based on his twenty years of psychic experiences. Called *The Tyranny of the Dark,* the novel marked a turning away from the subject he had found so vital after his trip to the West in 1901. Several of his friends warned him against changing directions in his writing, but he asked himself, "Why should I confine myself to writing stories of the plains?" He ignored their warnings in 1905, but in 1930 he recognized that he had made a mistake in "exploring the dark chambers of religious controversy."

Garland had also become very interested in forestry. He had had a casual interest in it since his visit to the White River Plateau in the early 1890s. Then he had met in 1902 with Roosevelt and Gifford Pinchot concerning the conservation of the nation's forests; to Garland that meeting was signal in his growing interest in forestry and the mountain West. By 1907, forestry was his chief interest, which culminated in *Cavanagh, Forest Ranger* in 1910 and subsequent works. His notebooks from 1902 through 1913 contain page after page of notes on forestry matters.

There was also in the writer a growing sense that the "wildness" of the West was fading. After the publication of *The Captain of the Gray-Horse Troop,* Roosevelt pointed out that Garland had changed his attitude toward the pioneers whom he had idealized in his earlier Midwestern stories. Garland had shown in his novel "that these advance men of our civilization were a grim lot." Said Roosevelt, "Now when you have become the advocate of the Sioux, your eyes are opened to the greed of the white cattleman to whom the Indian is a cumberer of the earth and should be destroyed. Your pioneers in similar case would be similarly minded."

More and more in his travels, Garland became convinced that the West was peopled by shiftless, dirty whites. In 1907 he made notes for a speech called "The Lawless West." As a novelist, he hated the passing of cattlemen, cowboys, sheep-herders, and boomers, but as a citizen he did not. In 1913 he wrote of the squalid western towns: "I fear I have gone beyond being interested in these conditions — they are neither one thing or the other, towns in transformation, transition." His disgust with such towns reached its height in that year:

The people have changed for the worse — or I have come to them in a less idealistic mood. The settlements are no longer picturesque — they are pitifully squalid. The present phase of development is cheap, flimsy, and ugly. At fifty-three a man does not so easily overlook tin cans, flies, and dirty hotel rooms. This is my last expedition to this part of the West; nothing seems worth while but my wife and daughters.

Since his trip to the West in 1897, it had been Garland's contention that it was the dirty, shiftless whites that Indian agents and missionaries had used as models for the Indian. Perhaps that explains, in part, the writer's declining interest in the Indian. Although he continued to travel in Oklahoma, his interests there were mainly in his real-estate investments. He also visited the Wind River Reservation in Wyoming in 1908, the Crow Reservation in 1909, and the Flathead Reservation in 1913, but his primary interest during these trips was the forest lands on the reservations. In all of these travels, his notes on the Indian are scant and do not reflect the vital interest they did up to 1902.

However, Garland did not give up completely his writing on the American Indian during the period 1904 through 1923. He continued revising "The Silent Eaters" because he felt the story was a potentially good one. After its rejection by the publishers, Garland had considered rewriting it as a play and went so far as to sketch out five acts for the drama called "My Chieftain — Sitting Bull." In June, 1907, he completed a revision of the manuscript, failing to make it what he had hoped, "a short prose epic of the Sioux race, ending with the Ghost Dance which is its final tragedy." Garland revised the material again in 1912. He thought it was one of his best pieces of writing. "It had no popular appeal, however," he wrote. Though finally published in *The Book of the American Indian,* it never received the wide reading the writer felt it deserved.

Garland also did a few new pieces of writing and drafted plans for others. During his trip to Oklahoma in 1905, he had observed and taken notes on part of the proceedings of the last national council of the Creek Nation before the tribal government was dissolved in 1906. Garland sensed in the voices of the Indian legislators "the sadness of a vanishing race whose history was fading into myth." He gives a graphic account of his observations in an unpublished essay, "The Final Council of the Creek Nation." He interviewed Pleasant Porter, chief of the Creeks, who conveyed to him "the attitude of the chief who, while not content to see his people's traditions disappear, is, after all, resigned to the inevitable laws of civilized society."

Perhaps Porter's attitude offers a clue to the most significant cause of Garland's declining interest in the Indian — the decline of the Indian himself as Garland had observed and known him in his early travels to the reservations. Instead of giving up the subject, the subject faded out. Government policy had won. The old Indians were dying, and the new generation were like Iapi of "The Silent Eaters" — caught between two worlds, despairing of one and unable to find a place in the other.

Among the records of the Sac, Fox, and Kickapoo Indians at the Oklahoma Historical Society is a government report from the early part of the twentieth century. It makes clear the intent of the policy of allotment — the rapid transformation of the Indians into red members of the Anglo-American society. It says, in part:

Upon final allotment of their lands, most of our Indians have accepted the situation gracefully, and are "catching" the habits and ways of their white neighbors. This status of the Indian problem of the United States is nearing the desired end toward which our Government has been working for many years and in bringing about which we have spent millions of dollars.

As a result of allotment, in other words, the Indians had been thrown suddenly into the midst of a people whose habits they had to "catch" in order to survive; it was a situation they had to make the best of. Thus, assimilation into the Anglo-dominated culture on white terms was the "desired end" of many years of Indian policy. If Garland's contention was right — if the habits the Indians had "caught" were those of poor whites — how drab the natives must have become to him!

In 1909, Garland made notes for a story called "The Seminole Strain." It was to be the story of a young white man who falls in love with a Seminole girl. She suddenly disappears when one of her Seminole friends has a black baby. Knowing that many Seminoles have a "negro strain" in them, she flees for fear that she will bear her lover a black child. From his notes, it appears that Garland intended a happy ending for the story. Perhaps the subject was too controversial for him to finish at the time. He left parts of five drafts, consisting of 240 leaves.

During his visit to the Flathead country in 1913, Garland drafted a poem titled "The Dance" and made notes for a story to be called "The New Agent." He also made notes and sketched a story about Charlot, which became the story of "Chief Charlevoy," later included in "The Human Side of the Redman," which Arvidson indicates was published in *Current Literature* in 1927. This article consists of three parts. "The Red Man's Gift" is a recounting of a story Seger told Garland about Hakano, a Cheyenne, in 1901. "Redman's Magic" recounts, for the most part, the stories of Jicarilla magic told to the writer in 1896 by John Gaylord. The third part, "Chief Charlevoy," is about the chief who, on the verge of death, reflects how the Flatheads once thought their reservation a prison. But it was really a haven when compared to the moral and social decay of these people following allotment. Divested of the old beliefs and unable to accept the Christian, Charlevoy dies without spiritual comfort.

After 1904, Garland also continued to attempt dramatic works, both plays and photoplays, using the American Indian as subject matter. In 1906, he worked on a play called "The Storm Child," an adaptation of his story of the same name. The writer left eight pages of dialogue from the first scene, in which he adds to his original story by having Hokah, the Chief, give background information about Blazing Hand (Mose). Among Garland's papers is also an undated libretto for an operetta, "Wamdesapa," based on his story "The Remorse of Waumdisapa." This piece is complete and follows closely the story line of the prose narrative. Mattowan is given the name Iapa, but his character remains the same. The dialogue, of course, is presented in verse form; nevertheless, Garland ably maintains the dramatic scene around the council fire.

The writer's most ambitious activity in this direction, however, came in 1916, when he was approached by representatives of the Vitagraph Company of America in Brooklyn about putting some of his stories on film. After talking to the president and the head of the scenario department, Garland signed a contract which gave the company the right to produce four of his stories each year for five years. The crew went to work on *Hesper*.

In April, the president of the company called Garland to discuss the filming of *The Captain of the Gray-Horse Troop*. He got the company to agree to introduce the film with scenes of the Cheyenne before the white man came. Garland adapted his novel in a scenario for a silent film called "The Red Pioneer." The film was to have two parts. The first was to be an introduction consisting of seven scenes showing a group of Indians before the white men came, the coming of the whites, their trading with the Indians and introducing them to whiskey, the Indians deciding to go to war against the whites, their captivity, their being robbed by a bad agent, and their plea to the president, who promises to send them a new agent, an army officer. The second part of the film was to be an adaptation of *The Captain of the Gray-Horse Troop*. Garland drafted the dialogue for the first scene, which depicted George and Jennie Curtis's stay at the Streeter ranch on their way to the agency.

Garland had high hopes of filming the reservation scenes on the Tongue River Reservation, with Northern Cheyennes acting out the scenes. He sought the aid of his old friend George Bird Grinnell in getting permission from the Indian officials, but he got nowhere. By winter, it became apparent that the Vitagraph Company would not make the film in Montana but rather in California. William Wolbert of the film company sought the assistance of Charles F. Lummis, a well-known authority on several of the Southwestern tribes, in the matter of sign language. Lummis advised him, in spite of his previous bad experiences with movie companies, but he told Garland that he expected the company would "make a travesty" of the sign language. In the end, Vitagraph lost interest in the project. That was perhaps well, for *Hesper* was filmed, and Garland was most disappointed in the results. He was released from his contract in 1920.

Garland's last major work on the American Indian came in 1923 with the publication, by Harper and Brothers, of *The Book of the American Indian*. It included fifteen stories: "Wahiah — A Spartan Mother," "Nistina," "The Iron Khiva," "The New Medicine House," "Rising Wolf — Ghost Dancer," "The River's Warning," "Lone Wolf's Old Guard," "Big Moggasen," "The Storm-Child," "The Blood Lust," "The Remorse of Waumdisapa," "A Decree of Council," "Drifting Crane," "The Story of Howling Wolf," and "The Silent Eaters." This was the first publication of "The Silent Eaters," "A Decree of Council," "The Remorse of Waumdisapa," and "The Blood Lust." The other items appeared in slightly revised form from their former publication.

This was the work that Garland had for over twenty years planned to call "The Red Pioneer." All of the stories were faithful to his impressions of the Indians he had studied and were written without "the settler's bias." He wrote:

I took the red man as I found him. To me he was a product of his environment, like the eagle or the mountain lion. To call him a fiend, a devil, was unscientific. The question of his origin, the basis of his customs should not be clouded by social or religious prejudice, nor confused by the hate of those who desired the lands he occupied. In short the red people were to me human beings who had come up along another line of civilization from ours. Although in some ways our inferiors, they possessed certain singularly noble habits.

Harper and Brothers had wanted to publish the volume as a large book, illustrated by Frederick Remington. Garland had doubted that the people would buy it, and he disliked Remington's illustrations, which he called "conventional" and "prosaic." Perhaps he was doubting because of what various editors had told him earlier: "Stories about Indians are no longer in demand." Although *The Book of the American Indian* did better than Garland expected, it was not widely read. Most of the stories had been published more than twenty years before. Most of the Indians about whom Garland wrote were citizens of the United States by 1923, and the wild life and reservation scenes depicted in the works were one or two generations past.

Garland still had his extensive notes and diaries. From his "careful study of real people and real conditions" had come his historical fiction. "My stories might have been better stories, that I will admit," he said, "but they are never falsifications of life and character. They are based on studies in the field. . . ." He said of his notes in 1930:

In them are intellectual snapshots of half-breed interpreters, grave red chieftains, grim old cattlemen, and the lovely daughters of bent and querulous mothers in lonely ranch houses. They picture of miners, prospectors, Navajo teamsters, stage drivers, and scores of other forms and faces of interest to me at the time, some of which are to be found in my stories, but many are still waiting use, preserved as if in amber. . . . I cannot quite bring my hand to destroy these records — it would be like destroying some part of myself, and yet I doubt if they will ever find their way into print.

From these notes he constructed the narratives of his travels among the Indians for his subsequent autobiographical volumes, especially *Roadside Meetings* (1930) and *Companions on the Trail* (1931). At times in these accounts Garland almost recaptures his enthusiasm for the subject. But for the most part, *The Book of the American Indian* marked the end of Hamlin Garland's thirty years of research and writing on the American Indian.

PART II
The Essays

Background

The Southern Ute Reservation, which Garland visited in 1895, was the home of the Moache and Capote bands, part of a large group of people who once occupied the area that is now central and western Colorado, eastern Utah, and northwestern New Mexico. A treaty in 1868 established in western Colorado a reservation for these bands, along with the Uinta, Wiminuche, Tabequache, Grand River, Yampa, and other bands of Utes.

In 1878 the Moache, Capote, and Wiminuche gave up their right to the lands of the confederated Utes in return for a reservation on the San Juan River in southern Colorado. These bands became known as the Southern Utes. In 1880 they agreed to settle on the La Plata River, where they remained. Their reservation, in the southwestern corner of Colorado, was approximately 110 miles east and west and 15 miles north and south, embraced about 1,710 square miles, and contained over a million acres. It was traversed, generally north to south, by seven rivers: Animas, La Plata, Mancos, Pine, Piedra, San Juan, and Florida. It was an arid land, yet fertile and productive if irrigated.[1]

Early in 1895 Congress passed an act providing for the allotment of land in severalty to those who wanted it and the removal of those not taking allotments to the western forty miles of the reservation and to portions of New Mexico. Generally, the Moaches and Capotes supported the idea of allotment and the Wiminuche opposed it. The result was two reservations, the Southern Ute, with its agency at Ignacio, and the Ute Mountain, with its agency at Navajo Springs.

By the time Garland arrived in the summer of 1895, most of the nearly 400 allotments had been given. At that period, sixty percent of the Southern Utes gained their subsistence from hunting, fishing, and root gathering, twenty percent from what the government called "labor in civilized pursuits," and twenty percent from issue of government rations. Those engaged in farming cultivated 296 acres. Fifty-three dressed wholly in citizens' dress, and 127 dressed that way in part, gaining the appellation of "blanket Indians." The Utes were generally opposed to education and maintained many of their traditional customs regarding birth, burial of the dead, and religion. Only nine could read, and thirty-one could speak English. At this time there were 269 Moache, 193 Capote, and 680 Wiminuche Utes.[2]

Garland's impressions of the Utes were carefully recorded. His general observations and descriptions of the condition of these Indians are accurate and can, for the most part, be substantiated by historical evidence. Hence, although "Among the Southern Utes" appears to be one of Garland's weaker pieces of writing on the Indian, it is an interesting contemporary account of the social life, customs, amusements, and demeanor of that group of people in 1895.

---

[1] Frederick Webb Hodge, ed., *Handbook of American Indians North of Mexico*, Pt. 2, pp. 846–876.

[2] *Ind. Commiss. Annual Report, 1895*, pp. 138–140, 444.

1. Among the Southern Utes[3]

The Agency sits amid sparse cottonwoods on an arid plain spotted with sage bush and juniper, and flooded with excess of sunshine. The Pinos river, shallow and swift, roars in high key past the rambling buildings.[4] The river valley is not wide nor deep. The whole reservation is most barren of useful vegetation, smitten by the sun in summer as if by falling fire, and by the winds that sting and benumb in winter. It is an oblong tract running along the southern boundary of Colorado. It impressed me as a bare and lonesome land, with noble horizon lines.

Doubtless it was made the home of the Utes because it was supposed at the time to be unhabitable by any other human being.

The agency wagon at the little brown station loaded the painter[5] and myself into its capacious bed, and rolled up the dry, smooth road. It was 9 o'clock of an August morning.

A powerful young Ute, in cowboy dress, strapped the mail up on his horse and set off behind us. He had large, black eyes and a lithe figure. He rode magnificently, and was manifestly proud of his office.

Half way up the road he was joined by another youth, who wore a blue sack suit and a broad, black hat, bound with a ribbon and pricked off with an eagle feather. He had beautiful blue, yellow and white moccasins, and a most gorgeous plum-purple neckerchief. His eyes were surrounded by radiating lines of red, white and green, which showed on his clean, shining face as markedly as his white teeth. He smiled with excess of delight at himself, and his arms flapped up and down like the wings of a heavily laden crow.

---

[3] Item 434, Hamlin Garland Collection, University of Southern California Library, Los Angeles; published by permission of the University of Southern California Library and Constance Garland Doyle and Isabel Garland Lord.

[4] The agency at Ignacio was located one and three-quarters miles from the Denver and Rio Grande Railroad and twenty-four miles southeast of Durango on the Pine River.

[5] The painter was Charles Francis Browne, an artist, lecturer, and critic, whom Garland met in Chicago during the early 1890s. (*The National Cyclopaedia of American Biography,* 16: 40–41.)

A little further we came upon a ranch, half cabin, half wickiup (Indian tent).[6] At the irrigation ditch,[7] which was filled with clear, cool mountain water, an Indian woman was washing the head of a babe. The babe came up out of the shower of water plump and shining as a muskrat, and as brown. Behind us the young Utes chattered with jovial cries.

We turned up at the agency buildings, which are of hewn logs, painted a dull red.[8] Indians were standing about the store. A middle-aged man in a white man's suit of denims was grinding a sickle. His wife was merrily turning the grindstone. A plump little papoose stood by intently watching the operation.

The white people consisted of the agent, Col. Day, his son and his son's young wife, the doctor, the cook and the trader.[9] The buildings were all alike, long low, log or frame structures. The offices were quite interesting within, by reason of the large fireplaces and a marked appearance of age. Several Indians were waiting about, dressed strangely like Orientals. Some of them wore a white blanket, which they held to their faces like Nubians. One or two of the girls, looking like Japanese pictures, peeped shyly at us from the house corners. A number of wolfish-looking dogs were prowling about.

As I stood looking around me at the strange figures coming and going, I heard a wild, sweet fluting, and a boy, robed like an Egyptian, with head covered by a white robe, rode by piping intently. The strain was as wild, as sweet and as lonely as the melody the fisherman pipes in *Tristan and Isolde,* and brought that scene instantly to my mind. It was mournful, and somehow seemed inwrought with silence and vast space. It was undoubtedly an Indian love song, declined to a flute phase. I marveled that in this far land an untrained Ute boy should sound a strain which might go into Wagner's great opera. It began with a high note, and fell in long drawn mournful cadences to a tone which was like the moan of the November wind. The Ute lover no longer sings to his sweetheart, but, no doubt, this fluted strain has been used for ages to express the lover's longing and despair.

The fluter was a lad with large, dark eyes and beautifully arched eyebrows. His white robe came over his head and draped his whole upper person.

---

[6] A wickiup is not a tent in the usual sense. The term ordinarily refers to a dome-shaped shelter covered with brush. (Hodge, ed., *Handbook of American Indians North of Mexico,* Pt. 2, p. 950.)

[7] The irrigation system was not extensive in 1895, and the Utes were faced with problems of water rights under Colorado law. In 1895, only 269 acres were cultivated by the Utes. During that season, they raised 1,980 bushels of wheat, 4,800 bushels of oats and barley, 400 bushels of corn, and 300 tons of hay. (*Ind. Commiss. Annual Report, 1895,* pp. 582–583.)

[8] Pending a decision on allotting land to the Utes, a general disregard had been shown the agency buildings. Agent David Day wrote: "The buildings of this agency are conceded by inspectors to be the most worthless in the service, and will no doubt continue to monopolize distinction in this direction until the element of doubt respecting the future home of the Utes shall be removed." (*Ind. Commiss. Annual Report, 1894,* p. 127.)

[9] The agency personnel who can be identified include Colonel David F. Day, the agent; Stanley Day, his son; Dr. Frank C. Blackly, the resident physician; and George H. Kraus, the trader.

To see him was like seeing something Oriental and something far into the sorrowful past.[10]

Down around the store I found a group of Indian children, playing with sticks and stones and chattering like white children, only with softer voices. Some of them were very bright and attractive, lithe little creatures of nine or ten, draped with shawls like old women. They were not at all afraid of me though they studied me carefully.

At the door, there were Indians playing checkers — and playing a good game — which made the store seem like a country store. One old fellow whistled and trotted his foot quite in the manner of a crossroads champion. One very gaily attired young fellow stood looking on. He wore wide, vividly yellow trousers with red folds at the side, a belt of silver bosses, a black waist with a pink undershirt, and over all the blanket which he handled with a grace of a prince.

Others came and went on strong, swift little horses. On arriving they tied their ponies to a long pole before the store, quite as people do in the little timber towns in the south. They all greeted each other with smiles. Their faces were generally broad and kindly. Mainly, they wore a mixture of American and Ute dress, that is, American boots and trousers with a cowboy hat and a white blanket. They sat in groups under the trees and smoked and talked, breaking into laughter occasionally.

They seemed to enjoy coming to the store (bare and unattractive as it seemed to me), precisely as settlers in Dakota make a visit to the village, apparently to gossip and be amused. The young men scuffle good-naturedly under the trees, the women visit, the more active men consult with the blacksmith or farmer, others grind sickles or study the action of mowing machines, the women trade.

The trader speaks Ute fluently, and the Indians, both young and old, seemed to enjoy a talk with him. The little ones swarmed about him fearlessly, and the women answered his jocular greetings in kind. It takes patience to be an Indian trader. The Indian is so poor; his methods are so slow and rambling, his speech so meagre;[11] an impatient trader soon wears out and becomes crusty and unjust to them, though he began with the best intentions in the world.[12]

The Utes, the trader told me, have Spanish as well as Indian names — Aglar (the eagle), Antonio, etc. They have also American names, at least on the rolls of the Government. One very dignified and splendid young dandy

---

[10] This experience was later used by Garland in a poem titled "The Ute Lover," which appeared in *Century* in June, 1899.

[11] This, of course, is a white man's judgment. Although Garland was sympathetic toward the Utes, clearly he had not yet learned to judge them on their own terms.

[12] Garland later wrote in his notes that "few white men were able to speak the Ute language except those who use the language as a means to get money." ("Colorado, Ouray, 1896," p. 118.) In "The Red Man's Present Needs" (1902), reprinted in this book, he strongly condemned the reservations that had only a single trader, which allowed for an intolerable monopoly.

suffered under the name of "Biscuits." "Mr. Biscuits" he was satirically called by the agency clerks. He was not at all contemptible, however; he was very dignified and dressed with rare skill and taste.[13]

Like all people suddenly forced out of their own environment and exposed to totally new conditions, the Utes are a mixture of apparently impossible characteristics. They love their children and are very kind to them, yet they do not allow a deformed child to live. Immediately after birth it is wrapped in a thin cloth and laid outside the wicki-up. They do not allow twins to grow, because they feel the mother cannot suitably take care of two babies. The weaker of the twins is exposed to die at once after birth. From their point of view these things were justifiable.[14]

They are neighborly and full of good cheer. "They did not lie nor steal nor debase their women," said the trader. "They are good people. If you take into account their conditions and surroundings, they are doing as well as anybody could. I trust them here as quickly as I'd trust anybody. In fact, I doubt whether among the same number of white people I could trust so largely and lose so little."

He showed me his books, whereon were the names of his customers standing opposite large credits. The names as he read them to me seemed a curious mixture of Spanish, American, and Ute, but he knew them all. There are about 2,000 Utes altogether, but less than 1,000 live at this agency. In a long talk with Mr. Kraus I came upon many of the hidden traits of the Utes, for they have come to trust him and have admitted to him much of their inner life. What he told me ran closely parallel to the perceptions of Kemeys and other of his artist friends who have been among these desert peoples.[15]

It requires a peculiar mind to understand the Indian. First, his inherited habits of thought must be understood and, second, the power, the almost infrangible power of his environment. He must be considered as a man born of a certain race, and situated in a certain environment — he must be considered relatively in all questions of morality. It is absurd to apply to him the measures of Saxon virtues. From his point of view it is well that the deformed babe should die at birth. It is the power of the environment which makes them seem paradoxes. They foster childhood, caress and shield the babe, but find old age in the way. They are indolent in some things, but capable of the most prolonged and painful exertion in other ways. Their thought is a mixture of the

---

[13] In Garland's papers are to be found several pages from the ration books for the Southern Ute Agency, which illustrate Ute Indian and European-American names, such as individual #271, Co-cep-e-wi-run (Jane Miller). (United States Department of the Interior, "Rosters and Lists of Indian Names.")

[14] According to Kraus, a baby with blue or gray eyes was also allowed to die of exposure following its birth. (Garland, "Colorado, Ouray, 1896," pp. 120, 156.)

[15] Edward Kemeys (1843–1907), a self-taught sculptor, became interested in the Indian and wild animals around 1870. He spent a great deal of time studying his subjects in the West. In 1892 he moved to Chicago, where he became acquainted with Lorado Taft. When Garland moved to Chicago in 1893, he met Kemeys and had many talks with him on the topic of art, sculpture, literature, and the American Indian. Kemeys is perhaps best remembered for "Bison and Wolves," "Still Hunt" in Central Park, New York, "Wolves" in Fairmount Park, Philadelphia, and the gigantic head of a bison for the Omaha bridge of the Pacific Railroad. (*The National Cyclopaedia of American Biography,* 8:279.)

lofty and the childish.[16] They believe stones grow, that a medicine man can heal the sick, that taking a man's picture may take away his life, and yet they reason their way to various fundamental conceptions with the directness of modern science. Many of them have reached the idea of "one God in the centre of the sky."

Nothing is unexpected with them. They are fatalists in many ways. If a man were to return suddenly after years of absence they would treat him as if he had but just been across the Mesa on a hunting trip. There is no word of welcome,[17] no word of thanks in their language, but that does not mean they are cold-hearted or ungrateful. Such things are taken for granted. Those who have are expected to share with those who have not, and so even the children carefully apportioned my gifts of candy. This is their training. They enter your house without knocking, simply because that is the custom, to lift the tent flap and walk in. Their only caress is shaking of hands, and in their letters they say by way of greeting, "I shake your hand." I. heard Charlie[18] dictating a letter, and it sounded very kindly indeed to hear him begin by saying: "I shake your hand."

In thought they are fatalists, and many of them, especially the older ones, are agnostics, and the idea of the Trinity and of the redemption they wag their heads at. They have wise talks around the winter fires — slow, quiet, long dialogues wherein all things they know are sifted. They are fatalists because the Creator knows what He is doing, they say, and they do not question only to discover His purpose.[19]

Their idea of heaven, as the trader related it to me, has its ingenuities, even humors. They believe, as do all other tribes, that they are "the chosen people," the people here first, and that they are to have the best of this world and of the world to come. Heaven with them is in three great strata. In the highest is the Ute spirit land, and all the Utes have wings. In the second are the buffalo and all the game and beautiful forests and meadows. In the lowest strata are the white men.

---

[16] Garland has asked that the Indian be judged relatively, but the writer himself here offers Anglo-American assessments.

[17] Garland belies this statement later in this essay, when he cites the word *"mike-eh"* as the Ute word for "howdy." Sapir gives the word maik·i as "hello." (Edward Sapir, *Southern Paiute, A Shoshonean Language,* p. 564.) It is true that in Numic-speaking cultures, thankfulness is not normally verbally expressed. Perhaps this attitude was best described by Washakie, chief of the Wyoming Shoshones: "Do a kindness to a Frenchman, he feels it in his heart and his tongue speaks; do a kindness to an Indian, he feels it in his heart. The heart has no tongue." (U. C. Irenholm, *The Shoshonis, Sentinels of the Rockies,* p. 254.)

[18] This was Chief Charlie, Buckskin Charlie, or Charles Buck (1840–1936), whom Garland describes later in this essay. He was first chief of the Moaches in 1870. In 1895, he farmed sixty acres of land, which act served as inspiration for others to follow. He built rude, but substantial, buildings for himself and his livestock. His wife took up habits of the white women. In 1896, he invited Garland to visit his farm. (Garland, "Colorado, Ouray, 1896," p. 125.)

[19] The Utes received Christian training from the Reverend and Mrs. A. J. Rodrigues, Presbyterians, who gave them Protestant views. The Mexicans on the borders of the reservation were Catholic. In 1895, Agent Day said that the Utes were undecided as to preference for Protestantism or Catholicism. (*Ind. Commiss. Annual Report, 1895,* p. 140.)

The Indians have wings, and when they wish to hunt they drop down to the second world to chase the buffalo. If they feel like taking a turn at the white man they drop to the third and lowest world. The white man cannot rise higher or fall lower, and so they are forever at the will of the Indians. This arrangement of their enemies is less barbarous than Dante's and much simpler in design.[20] I am free to say there are plenty of white men who ought to occupy that lower world.

They do not fear to die, but speak of death calmly. They are like the spiritualists in believing that death is a mere transition moment between a hard wearisome world and a higher, freer life.[21] Doubtless they have the shrinking from death which all healthy organisms show, but so far as their thought is concerned death is not a gloomy end.

Their burial customs, however, are mysterious and sombre. The dead man's face is covered at once, and at the end he is carried out in the dark and buried secretly among the rocks. Even so great a chief as Ouray was thus buried, and to this day, it is said, no one knows where he lies.[22] Perhaps some boulder was pried out of its bed and the great orator and warrior placed there and the boulder rolled back into place. Such is their custom — much like the Hopi people, who drop their dead into the crevices of the cliffs and never look at the place again.

Upon the death of a man his personal property is considered valueless, and is burned up: blankets, saddles, even his tent and wagons. Two or three years ago a thousand dollars' worth of property was burned upon the death of a prominent Ute, but this custom is not binding, and the younger Indians do not countenance it. Doubtless the custom arose originally from the feeling that the clothing of the dead might be infected with disease.[23]

Col. Day and his assistants are trying to induce the Indians to bury their dead in a cemetery, in American fashion. I doubt the wisdom of that, but their motive is good. They have already had several burials in a little lot on the Mesa.

Not long ago Peter, one of the most intelligent Indians of the reservation, on his deathbed asked to be buried in white man's way in his uniform as a

---

[20] In his *Divina Commedia* (1300–1311), Dante Alighieri consigned people to one of nine circles in Hell, according to the magnitude of their sins in life.

[21] Garland was more than casually interested in spiritualism and its premise that the spirits of the dead can communicate with the living. This was the subject of several articles he published in *Psychical Review* in 1892 and 1893, as well as his novel *The Tyranny of the Dark* (1906).

[22] Ouray (1833–1880), a noted leader of the Utes, was considered their head chief at the time of the outbreak of 1879, when the agent and other whites were killed. Ouray commanded the Utes to cease hostilities, but army interference caused them to continue. (Hodge, ed., *Handbook of American Indians North of Mexico*, Pt. 2, p. 175.) Wilson Rockwell states that the remains of Chief Ouray were collected and buried in a Catholic-Protestant cemetery near the agency at Ignacio. (*Utes: A Forgotten People*, p. 207.)

[23] The Utes who adhered to this practice burned the effects of the deceased out of fear. A good example is the death of Karrach, probably the "prominent Ute" to whom Garland refers. After he died, his relatives concealed his body and burned his clothes, wickiup, and some implements, declaring his ground bewitched. To make inroads on such superstitions, Agent Day had the ground broken and in 1894 planted it, irrigated it, and raised an excellent crop. He persuaded Karrach's family to return and take over the farming operations in the spring of 1895. (*Ind. Commiss. Annual Report, 1894*, p. 129.)

patrolman.[24] He wished also to wear a white shirt and a necktie, like the white man. All this was done for him, and it all appealed to me with great pathos some way, that desire to die proudly and at his best as a man who had tried to comprehend the white man and serve his own people. His broken speech flashes a vivid light in upon his own striving mind. He wanted to be good and right, as I believe most of these people do.

They need instruction, not in religion, but in living, in working, in daily habit. I felt this deeply as I talked with the trader and with the agent. In the war of political factions they have been neglected in the matter of schooling.[25] In the war of greed and political brigandage they will probably be sacrificed in the end. Such is the process concealed under the glib phrase "the war of races."

In their last removal the Utes were paid in some part for their lands, and their money was invested for them in bonds, so that they now have a small annuity; also they are served a ration once a week. The serving of this ration brings them together on Wednesday in holiday attire and I remained over to see them under such favorable circumstances.

There is a failure to meet the needs of the Indians on the part of the [Department of the] Interior. As for example, plows were issued to them which were far too large for their little ponies. They could not use them, and the Indian was blamed for it. They needed ten inch plows, not sixteen inch plows. Similarly, to several of the tribes huge brogans have been issued to displace the moccasin with ill-success because the Indian has worn immemorially, a well-shaped shoe with soft sole. The brogan was almost impossible to him. I saw the Utes trying to wear the absurdly large over-alls which were sent out for them to wear. It was pathetic to see them winding the shapeless bags about their slender waists. This is not the fault of the agent but of the Department. The agent is the disburser; he does not select the supplies. If neat blue suits with brass buttons and cavalry boots were issued to them they would wear them, for they admire the soldier's uniform.

The morning of ration day dawned clear and warm. About ten o'clock the Indians began to assemble; they came fording the river on horse back, the women riding astride like the men, the squaws with children behind them. They came down over the hot mesa and winding down the trail from the North. They came afoot, the women wobbling laboriously, holding parasols, the old women carrying children in their blankets on their beautifully ornamented cradleboards at their backs. Some of the wealthier and progressive families came in wagons dressed almost entirely in American dress; others wore combinations of their own and cow-boy clothing, thus showing in their dress, as in their cabins, their transitional state of mind.

---

[24] It was common practice for the government to hire Indians as policemen on the reservations. They acted under orders from the agents.

[25] Garland felt that the Utes should be compelled to attend a school on the reservation. (Garland, "Colorado, Ouray, 1896," pp. 127–128.) The Utes had practically no children attending school at that time and were almost totally indifferent about education. (*Ind. Commiss. Annual Report, 1895,* pp. 138–139.) In 1894, out of 274 school-aged children, only eight attended the Fort Lewis Indian School and three attended the Colorado Institute for the Deaf and Blind. (*Ind. Commiss. Annual Report, 1894,* p. 128.)

National Archives

The elaborate finery of the Utes at Ignacio on ration day reflects their love of social gatherings. Chief Buckskin Charlie stands in a feathered headdress fourth from the left. The Anglo seated in front of him is probably the trader George H. Kraus.

There came two flute players riding side by side playing more songs, other songs yet closely related to those I had heard the day before and all unutterably sad. Some of the young men were superb in their finery, strings of beads and belts of Navajo silver work, and with their horses draped with the soft skins of mountain lions and foxes. They came riding magnificently, in twos and threes, and by twelve o'clock they were swarming about the store and grouped under the shade of the scant cottonwoods, in irregular masses of rich color. They act very much like white people at a Fourth of July celebration. Their faces were generally pleasant and many were very attractive. The women were heavily-built with thick black hair, well brushed. They wore beaded moccasins and leggings of buckskin; some carried a shawl blanket-wise. Some were tattooed as well as painted,[26] though most of them were not. They impressed me as a simple, good-natured people.

A few of the older ones speak English, but they have been neglected as far as education goes. Buckskin Charlie, the sub-chief, speaks a little [English] and is one of the most progressive men.[27] He drove into town with a platform spring wagon, with his wife, a handsome, dignified woman, sitting beside him and his children sitting behind on the hay. He was glad to have his picture taken and asked the painter of our party to come up and paint a picture of his house. His wife impressed me deeply by reason of her dignified reticence

---

[26]See further descriptions in Garland, "Colorado, Ouray, 1896," p. 123. Tattooing was common among the Indians of the American interior. Among men, it at times designated special offices or personal achievements and at others success in war. Among women, it sometimes indicated the tribe to which they belonged, the achievements of their male kin, or their marital status. (Hodge, ed., *Handbook of American Indians North of Mexico,* Pt. 2, p. 700.)

[27]See note 18, this essay, for background on Chief Charlie.

and the smiling interest she showed in all that went on. A young girl of her family mounted on a fine pony followed the wagon, making a very pretty young horsewoman.

Charlie lives in a house and has beds and tables. He purchased a new stove that very day, which probably helped his wife to look proud and happy. He was at one time a government scout, and there are said to be two others living here who served the United States in the same way. I saw one of them, a gray old fellow who said "Mike-eh" to me as he passed, to which I answered "Wai-no." "Mike-eh" is Ute for "howdy" and "waino" is the universal pronunciation of the Spanish for *bueno* and means "good," "all right," and the like of that.

The men, even Charlie, wear long hair, and the trader told me that the last sign of the Indian which the Ute has not yet sacrificed is the long hair, which he wears braided in two heavy strands, drawn down on either side of the neck upon the breast. They only cut these short upon the death of a very near relative, and they allow it to grow again.

These people, I saw at once, are quite unlike the stoical Indian of the North.[28] They are full of laughter, joking and gossip, they show what they feel quite plainly, and their gestures are not grandiose like the Sioux, but quick, ready like the Spaniards. No doubt their contact with the Mexican on the South has given them something of this ready speech and gesture. They are unquestionably of an entirely different race, however, from the Indian of the North.[29] They are of the great Shoshonean family.[30]

They are very kind to their wives and deeply affectionate to their children. I saw men leading their little babes about by the hands, considerate as any father; I saw one stalwart old fellow pass by leading a little girl of nine or ten, one of the most beautiful creatures I have ever seen. She carried herself with the loftiest grace and was as lithe as a little tigress. Her dainty moccasined feet lifted from the ground as lightly as the paws of a kitten. She wore a gown of dark-brown and dull-red, and a turquoise-green girdle displayed her upright little body as exquisitely as the gown of a stage Juliet; she was full of natural unconscious pride and moved like a Queen's daughter. Many of the little girls

---

[28] This reflects a stereotyped view of the Indian as stoical, a view which Garland often criticized later. At this point he had not traveled among the Indians of the North.

[29] Garland was probably familiar with George Bird Grinnell, whom he had met by the time he wrote this piece and who knew much about the Pawnees, Cheyennes, and Blackfeet. Grinnell had lived with the Indians during early expeditions to the West, and in the early 1890s he was voted head chief of the Blackfeet by the entire tribe. (*The National Cyclopaedia of American Biography,* 30: 278.) For more regarding Grinnell, see Essay 10, note 4.

[30] The Shoshonean Family is a linguistic designation for the peoples who occupied southwestern Montana, almost all of Idaho, southeast Oregon, west and central Colorado, a strip of northern New Mexico, eastern New Mexico, and all of northwestern Texas. The tribes which belong to this family are numerous; among the better known are the Hopi, Ute, Shoshoni, Bannock, and Comanche. (Hodge, ed., *Handbook of American Indians North of Mexico,* Pt. 2, pp. 555–556.)

looked to be Japanese in type and their loose gowns belted in like a blanket helped in the likeness.

At one o'clock the weekly distribution of rations was to take place and going up to the store room, I found the negro interpreter and some Ute assistants getting ready the flour and wheat.[31] The doors were open at length, and the squaws came crowding in at one side, holding small sacks in their hands and carrying their ration tickets between their teeth. Some of them looked anxious and cross, but most of them laughed and joked in low voices to each other. They presented a curious sight as they were thus massed together. They were all dark-brown of skin, and their densely black hair (which was cut short) stood out thickly from their cheeks. They were almost all of the same stature. Their teeth shone in their faces and their eyes moved to and fro comically as they wiggled along toward the clerk.

As they passed the counter, each one received a scoop of flour for each member of her family and a hunk of fresh beef. A box of baking powder was slipped in to the bag of flour, and as they passed out of the door each was tendered a cake of soap. Most of them took the soap, and their cleanly appearance showed plainly their use of it. Several of them passed through two or three times, drawing rations for other families living up in their neighborhood.

Mrs. Charlie came through like the rest, an amused smile on her lips. She presented her ticket and received her meat and flour in the same wordless dignity she showed at the store. The men did not take part in this drawing of rations at all; only a few of the old men took any notice of it; the rest were down at the store or studying mowing machines or talking the equivalent of politics or grinding sickles.

There came by in the crowd a pretty girl in a white blanket. She was very young but had the most wistful eyes and sad lips. The white women looking on exclaimed at the sight of her, she seemed so beautiful among the crowd. She was jostled about but showed no anger, she only looked patient and sad. She could not have been more than sixteen or seventeen and her face was very sweet. She was a little lighter in complexion than the others, but her hair was perfectly black. Her teeth were perfectly white and her hands were dainty. She was counted the belle of the reservation by the clerk; the sculptor said, "I wouldn't want a better model for a Madonna."[32] Her name was "White-wind."

Her story we learned was as sad as her face, for she was the second living wife of a young Indian who liked his other wife better — which was incredibly bad taste on his part. He merely tolerated her. Plurality of wives is not uncom-

---

[31] Garland identified the interpreter simply as John, a black who had come west as a soldier in the 38th Infantry at Fort Wingate. He first became an interpreter at the Terra Marilla Ute Agency in 1877. (Garland, "Colorado, Ouray, 1896," p. 161.)

[32] The sculptor was Hermon Atkins MacNeil, who became interested in the American Indian during 1893. Following the 1895 trip to the West, MacNeil received the Rinehart Roman Scholarship from the Peabody Institute for his work, "The Last Act of the Moqui Snake Dance," completed at Walpi, Arizona. (*The National Cyclopaedia of American Biography,* 34: 482.)

mon among the Utes.[33] It was plain she wished to rise into something better than her present life. Crowded on all sides by the older and ruder women, she was distinctly not a part of them. She did not associate with the women the clerk told me but spent her time with the children, with the little girls. She wanted to reach the whites, but could not. She liked to be about the white women to look in their faces and feel the touch of their hands.

She could not speak English the clerk told me, and she had thus far refused to talk through an interpreter. It was a singular and sorrowful situation to be voiceless and to look out upon the white man's world across impassable chasms. Her look is with me yet; I shall think of her as a lonely soul asking help with dumb lips and beautiful eyes.

After the rations were all drawn, groups of squaws could be seen getting their meat and flour fastened to their saddles. The men in some cases assisted in this, though generally they leave all that pertains to the household to the women. I walked about listening to them. They spoke in low voices rising occasionally to a soft diminuendo, like the Oriental women with the same droning nasal quality in their speech. They are quite theatric in the sudden changes from a laughing rapid speech to this droning, almost whining nasal. Whether this comes from the Spanish or not I do not know. They seemed to use it in mock anger and protest.

Sometimes on ration day the young women play "Shinney," a game familiar in the east.[34] They play a good game, it is said, and the men look on and laugh and cheer in high glee, though they do not play themselves. Under a tree, I stood to watch a group of women seated around a blanket playing a game of cards with a "five cent ante." I did not learn the name of the game. It was probably such sights as this which cause the casual observer to think they are gambling away their annuity. As a matter of fact, the trader told me, this gambling is more in fun than anything else and it is entirely among themselves. Anything like gambling in the ordinary sense they do not do.[35] They play this game quite as they would play a game of checkers or shinney.

---

[33] Kraus later told Garland that at maturity the Ute girls were sent out to become mothers. They were welcome at all wickiups, but their objective was to get a husband and add children to the tribe. A man could select several wives if he desired. If a man wanted another's woman and she was willing to become his wife, the new husband was entitled to claim all the woman's property. (Garland, "Colorado, Ouray, 1896," p. 167.) Day reported that there was no marriage ceremony among the Utes and that immorality prevailed, rendering "loathsome diseases quite common." However, Dr. Frank C. Blackly reported less venereal disease in 1894 than "sometime back" because Day had excluded "Mexican women of known bad character from the reservation." (*Ind. Commiss. Annual Report, 1894,* pp. 127, 130.)

[34] Shinny is a game in which a ball or some other object is hit with a stick. It is somewhat like hockey, except that there are usually no player positions assigned, except for a guard at each goal.

[35] In 1894, the agent wrote of the Utes: "All are gamblers; success in winning at 'Monte' or 'coon-can' being equally divided between the sexes. The victors loan to the vanquished, and the agent has yet to hear of an encounter resulting from gambling differences. It is gambling in one sense, but when we consider the losers are at liberty to restake themselves out of their more fortunate neighbors' winnings, it differs materially from the methods utilized by the whites." (*Ind. Commiss. Annual Report, 1894,* p. 127.)

Down at the store I saw a pretty and suggestive sight. The trader, a big bluff fellow, had invited two tiny Ute babes to dine with him, and as I came along they were sitting at the table by his side, grave as Judges, intent as honey bees. One of them, a little girl, had on a rich, new calico dress with puffed sleeves, which the clerk's young wife[36] had made for her and which she was trying to be worthy of. The other little fellow was smaller yet but equally serious. He was taking his first lesson in the use of a fork and it was comical to see how diligently he followed instructions.

It was an interesting commentary on the Indians' attitude toward this trader. Evidently the mothers of these children felt perfectly easy in mind with regard to them, for they were nowhere about. He told me that when he first came to Ignacio the children were scared as rabbits. "Now you see how they feel."[37]

"How well the little fellow does it," I said.

"They are all like that," the trader replied. "They are quick to learn and they *want* to learn, and they *will* learn if they have a chance. They want to know how to live, they don't want fractions and cube root, they ought to be taught how to build a house and how to keep it clean, how to mend a sickle bar and things like that. Now the women are crazy about sewing machines. I had a sewing machine here for a while and they swarmed in to see it and try it.[38] They want to make things like the white women and they like to see the inside of a white woman's house. You must remember these Indians have no example set them, the most of them never see the inside of a white man's house, that is to say they don't know how the white man actually lives and the way a white woman takes care of her house. The traders are almost always bachelors like myself and are able to offer very little in the way of this practical instruction in housekeeping."

"What is the reason they do not farm more?" I asked; I had well defined ideas of my own on the subject but I wished to hear what the trader would say.

"Well I will tell you," he replied. "I am a trader and not a Philanthropist. It's none o' my business, of course, but if I wanted to do something for these Indians and could, I'd do about four things. First I'd put them on land where a human being could live, then I'd issue tools suited to their needs and clothing which they would wear. Then I'd scatter some good western farmers among 'em with complete outfits, and I'd have some matrons to teach them how to keep house, and finally I'd try to remember that they are not white people with red

---

[36] This was Mrs. Stanley Day.

[37] Kraus, from Durango, came to Ignacio in 1893 and traded until 1897. (Frank McNitt, *The Indian Traders,* p. 308.) Both the Ute women and children had at first distrusted Kraus. However, after he had been at Ignacio for several years and had learned their language, they came to trust him and liked him very much. (Garland, "Colorado, Ouray, 1896," p. 121.)

[38] Francis E. Leupp, speaking at the Thirteenth Lake Mohonk Indian Conference, October 10, 1895, praised Kraus and called him a "field matron" for Day in the process of transforming the Utes. Kraus had bought a sewing machine and invited the women to learn sewing. A number had taken lessons, got the idea quickly, and were soon able to make their own clothes. But Leupp had few misconceptions about Kraus who, he said, had "an eye on the main chance. He realizes that the more the women can sew, the more dresses they will want." (*Ind. Commiss. Annual Report, 1895,* p. 1003.)

skins, and I wouldn't try to make Presbyterians of 'em the first week and saints of 'em the next. You can't drive them to be civilized, you got to lead them and you don't want to jerk too hard on the rope at that."

There seems so much hard sense in this, I quote it on its merits without further comment.

That they are changing fast, my brief glimpse of the Utes convinced me. In language, dress, in house-room, everything they have or touch shows a transitional stage. A few years ago only an occasional man had taken to white clothing. There were a hundred who had dropped the blanket altogether and a hundred more who only used the blanket ceremonially.[39] So far as I could see, the officers at the agency were affording them (in so far as they could) good practical instruction. They are crippled, of course, by lack of time and means and by reason of the isolation of the agency.

The language of the Utes has become far too narrow to express their swiftly expanding life and thought, and therefore they have incorporated many Mexican words and phrases together with a few American words. Nearly one quarter of their language as they speak today is Mexican-Spanish and Western dialect. In using American words they have a curious fashion of adding a syllable like "muts," "Coffee Muts," "Peanut Muts," etc.[40]

Whether they will survive the complete breakup of their tribal manners, customs, and laws is a grave question. One man whose opinion was authoritative said to me gravely and emphatically "they are disappearing from the face of the earth," and undoubtedly they are fewer today than ever before in their known history; yet it may be that if justice is done them, if they are properly instructed, they may increase in numbers rather than diminish.

It is not my purpose to enter into controversy on this question. The art side of their life, its dramatic and pictorial aspects are nearest to me at this time.

To pass a definite opinion upon any question connected with these people requires long and severe study of their language and living. This I know. It was all superb material for the painter and sculptor, this large movement of mounted men and women in their flowing and richly-colored garments. They formed a hundred themes for great paintings as they trailed over the glowing palpitating crests of the mesas or halted beneath the solitary cottonwood trees to rest in shadow. Their life suggested the desert life of the far East.

Out of a scurry of dust a group of superb riders would burst like Bedouins, their gay colors flaming, their white blankets streaming. Behind them, slowly, with stately calm a woman would come seated astride, her papoose strapped to her back, its fringed cradle-board nodding above her head.

They were as loathe to leave as country people at the circus. Here were the white people and here was gossip and sport and friends and relatives they had not seen for weeks. They were, beside, in their best clothes, and youth

---

[39] The blanket was the gauge by which officials of the Indian Office marked the "progress" of the Indian toward "civilization." They designated as "blanket Indians" those who refused to dress like the white man.

[40] Research reveals no Numic word to correspond exactly to Garland's word "muts." It is probable that the author heard the Indians imperfectly, perhaps misunderstanding their pronunciation of the English word "nuts."

and maiden passed swift glances of admiration. To go home meant to go to the poor little wicki-ups in the distant valley. It meant putting away the gala dress and putting on the old rags. It meant return to the actualities of their severe life, and undoubtedly it meant in some cases a return to sloth and dirt.

Then, too, here was a painter painting pictures, and a group of Gypsies, whose monkey was eating peanuts from the painter's shoulders. Here also was a sculptor who pinched clay till it looked for all the world like "Mary" and little "Whitewind." And there was a man with a beard who taught them to play games and gave the children candy. No wonder they waited long after their usual time to go home.

But slowly in groups, in squads, in files, in rushing cavalcades they disappeared, and when the red sun-set grew pale the far-off mournful voice of the receding flute alone was heard above the high keyed snarl of the river.

They attracted me mightily, these people; they trailed behind them such mystery of ancestry, they were such a mixture of child and man, of mirth and gravity. I feel sure we will be good friends when they come to know and believe in me.

As I think of them seated here in the center of a vast city, I see Mary's broad smiling face as she shakes her thick black hair in smiling protest. I can see the magnificent young "Jim" leaning against the doorway. Charlie's wife smiles that curious amused smile and Charlie stands proudly beside his team. But out of it all, most lasting of it all, comes the face of little Whitewind. So sad, so wistful, so wordless that it seems to me as if the wail of the flute were the heart of her finding utterance in song.

Background on
A Day at Isleta

The Tiwa pueblo of Isleta, which Garland visited in 1895, apparently stands on the same site it occupied in the sixteenth century, when the Spanish discovered it. Early in the seventeenth century, the Franciscans established the mission of San Antonio de Isleta. Its population swelled some time around 1675, when it gave refuge to the people of neighboring Tiwa pueblos, who fled from the Apaches.

In 1680, the inhabitants of Isleta did not participate in the Pueblo Uprising but later joined the rebels. In 1681 New Mexican Governor Antonio de Otermin captured Isleta, taking over five hundred prisoners. Many of the Tiwas apparently took refuge with the Hopi. Some of Otermin's prisoners escaped, but most were settled near El Paso at Isleta del Sur. Refugee Tiwas apparently refounded Isleta early in the eighteenth century. The mission was reestablished as San Agustín.[1]

In 1895, the inhabitants of Isleta, as well as of the other pueblos, made their living essentially from raising wheat, oats, barley, and corn, along with some fruit and livestock. Education was not popular. During 1895, indeed throughout the 1890s, the Indians found their water, timber, and land rights constantly violated by the Mexicans and whites living around the borders of their reservation.[2]

In rendering his impressions of the people of Isleta, Garland shows his usual concern with the impact of the Anglo and Mexican cultures upon these Southwestern people. In the conflict of cultures, the writer finds himself faced with an essential paradox: admiration for the primitive life style of the Isletans accompanied by condemnation of the white man's encroachment upon the Indian's life style; a sense of "the terrible solvent power of the white man" coupled with pride in his "wonder-working" power. Ultimately, Garland is intensely conscious of the change that has come to Isleta and regrets that life there, as he saw it in 1895, was "doomed soon to disappear and be quite swallowed up."

As is customary, Garland gives careful attention to detail. His enthusiasm for his subject is most apparent in his treatment of the threshing, which is one of his most vivid and graphic descriptions of the American Indian.

---

[1] Frederick Webb Hodge, ed., *Handbook of American Indians North of Mexico*, Pt. 2, pp. 622–623.

[2] *Ind. Commiss. Annual Report, 1895*, pp. 220, 570–571.

2. A Day at Isleta[3]

The Te-wan Pueblo of Isleta[4] lies but twelve miles from Albuquerque, New Mexico, in a region of blinding sunshine where rain seldom falls, and it was burning noon of an August [day] when the painter, the sculptor,[5] and I stepped from the train at the station and looked about us. At first glance nothing was to be seen but the depot, the section house and a water tank, but presently we made out a cluster of adobe houses sleepily crouching in the sand, unstirring, in the fierce glare of the desert. Toward these low walls we took our way.

It was our first contact with the Pueblo peoples and each of us acknowledged a feeling of timidity — not knowing how we might be received. To give ourselves the air of having business in the village we asked for the Padre. A small brown boy with shrewd face replied to my query in comprehensible western American, and we promptly suborned him as our guide. With an act of proprietorship he led us up a curious narrow street between low blank-faced mud walls, under the edge of flat-roofed fortress-like houses and turned a corner — and behold we were in a foreign land — a land as remote as Morocco, as sun-smit as the Soudan. Low walls of gray mud shut out the world we knew — the world of the gringo. With incredible swiftness we retreated into the past. It was as if the boy were some mighty conjurer.

A tall, powerful and graceful woman met us in the street. She carried a huge jar of water on her head. A thin white mantle covered her head and shoulders. A short black skirt belted at the waist with a vivid red sash draped her knees. Her feet were clad in tiny moccasins, while about her ankles bound linen formed a sort of white boot or legging. She moved largely, with free step, like a strong man. A little farther on we met a young girl similarly dressed, very pretty, very graceful and much abashed, who passed us with head held down, her hand covering her eyes. Nothing could have been further from our common American life than these figures.

A hush seemed to lie over the town as if its citizens were in the midst of a profound siesta, and these two women were all the pueblans we saw until we

---

[3] Item 435, Hamlin Garland Collection, University of Southern California Library, Los Angeles, published by permission of the University of Southern California Library and Constance Garland Doyle and Isabel Garland Lord. This document, edited in a slightly different manner, appeared in *Southwestern Historical Quarterly,* 78 (July, 1974), 45–68, and is reprinted with permission of *Southwestern Historical Quarterly.*

[4] Garland is in error here. Isleta is a Tiwa pueblo, as are Taos, Picuris, Sandia, and others. The Tewan pueblos are San Ildefonso, San Juan, Santa Clara, Nambe, Tesuque, and Hano. (Hodge, ed., *Handbook of American Indians North of Mexico,* Pt. 2, pp. 737–738, 747–748.)

[5] These men were Charles Francis Browne and Hermon Atkins MacNeil, respectively. (See Essay 1, notes 5 and 32, for identification of these men.)

stepped in on a small barren plaza before a ruined old church beside which the padre's house was set — so said our guide. The ancient building[6] showed sadly under the pitiless midday light. Its yard, once filled with flowers, was hard and bare and brown, with strange dusty weeds growing in the corners of the crumbling adobe fences. The cloister roof had fallen long before and little remained of its excluding walls. In the absurd little green steeples set on the mud towers of the corner, bells still hung, our guide assured us. It must have been an attractive place once with its cool interiors, its gardens, its fountain. Now it was disconsolate, a place for bats and spiders, its remotest corner graceless and hot as the street itself.

At the padre's house everything took place with the theatrical surprises of a medieval romance. As I pulled the bell outside the green lattice door a parrot far within screamed and a peacock uttered a harsh cry, precisely as if operated by the wire of the knob. The bell jingled remotely; a dog awoke with deep bay — menacing as a lion. After a second warning and another wait the gate opened and a middle-aged hard-visaged serving woman showed herself. She was not given to smiles, but answered quite civilly: — No, the padre was not at home. No, he would not soon be home. Certainly we might enter and procure a drink of water.

To go from the sun-smit pavement into the padre's garden was like slipping suddenly into some interior town in Spain. A long low portico trellised with vines bounded one side of the tiny court. Over the other the ruined church peered. Flower beds and fruit trees filled all the space of the garden with only narrow — very narrow — foot paths running between. In the center, however, stood a sadly utilitarian American windmill, whose office was to water the garden — a discordant note — as offensive to the eye as its dolorous *creak-crack* was to the ear.

The peacocks posed in the flower-beds, the parrot, amiably, garrulously chattered, and a big dog sniffed about our heels, as we entered the delicious shadow of the portico. A multitude of doves coo-ed and fluttered about the roof, adding the final touch of peace and serene enjoyment. American business and its railroads seemed very far away indeed as we rested in delicious shadow, looking out upon the fresh greenness of the peach and plum trees.

The serving woman spoke excellent French,[7] and she visibly softened under our diplomatic treatment, but did not go so far as to offer us a dinner,

---

[6] Isleta is said to be the only pueblo in which the church is the most prominent structure around which the rest of the village has grown. The first mission in Isleta, dedicated in 1629 in honor of San Antonio, was destroyed in the 1680 Pueblo Uprising. These were the ruins Garland saw in 1895. Fourteen years later, San Agustín de Isleta Mission was constructed on the same site. Several times remodeled and restored, this church has endured more than 250 years of continuous use. (Earle R. Forrest, *Missions and Pueblos of the Old Southwest*, pp. 152, 155 and Stanley A. Stubbs, *Bird's-Eye View of the Pueblos*, p. 14.)

[7] The woman's knowledge of French might be explained in more than one way. A resident priest in the early 1880s had been Father Clemente Peyron, a Frenchman, who was ordained in 1868. He was at Isleta as early as 1881. Also resident at Isleta were Joseph and Josephine Tondre. Tondre, a trader, was postmaster when an office was established there in 1882. (Lansing B. Bloom, ed., "Bourke on the Southwest, XIII," p. 195; Charles H. Lange and Carroll L. Riley, eds., *The Southwestern Journals of Adolph F. Bandelier, 1883–1884*, pp. 20–21, 361–362.)

in which we stood in growing need. Therefore, after drinking our glass of water each, we passed once more into the sun-bright streets hungrier than we came.

Observing a number of men and boys perched a-top the wall of a corral filled with horses, we took our way languidly thither, listening to their earnest discussion in confidence that something of interest was about to happen. Our dinner must perforce wait.

Just as we reached the spot an old man, dressed in white cotton trousers and a sort of white smock, jumped into the corral, a boy opened the gate and the ponies trotted out into the open.

I asked a boy what they were about to do and he said: "Thresh wheat."

"With these ponies?"

"Yes."

This was glorious! We were to see the trampling of wheat, a process as old as the hooked knife — as old as pharoah. I felt at the moment an elation, the exultation of the dreamer permitted to explore the past and stand beside [the] beginnings of agriculture.[8]

Out on the little hill to the south of the village stood a number of little circular pole corrals filled with unthreshed sheaves. Two were clean and empty — one held a pile of threshed but still unwinnowed grain. Into one of the corrals heaped with sheaves, the compliant horses were driven and the bars built up.

Then the driver burst into a shrill quavering cry and the ponies began their round, while the lithe young driver in white thin garments lashed after them with his whip, urging them round and round the narrow enclosure. His call was as singular as his occupation, ending with a quavering, rolling note, very shrill, but quite musical, and never for a moment did he cease his swift trot. Around the edge of the corral an older man walked with a fork to toss the grain back under the horses' hooves, and a handsome smiling girl with a bunch of willow twigs for a broom swept the scattered kernels into the straw. She wore the same dress as the two women we had met earlier, a blue black skirt, belted with a broad red band, white leggings and soft buck-skin moccasins.

They all answered our greetings pleasantly enough but kept on with their work, precisely as if we were their neighbors. The horses kicked and lunged and shook their heads, but the vigorous young man plied the whip relentlessly and round and round they swirled. The dust rose, the sweat streamed down his cheeks, but his cheering cry resounded with undiminished power. His swift feet seemed tireless.

Near by another family was similarly employed, and merry shouts and jests passed from corral to corral. The men were of kindly countenance, and

---

[8] U.S. Indian Agent N. S. Walpole had a different view toward the threshing methods of the Pueblo Indians. In his 1898 report, he asked for financial aid to offer the Indians new methods of threshing grain. He said that after the cows, horses, goats, and burros had trampled the grain, it was usually mixed with animal excrement, requiring untold labor to clean. The cleansing was "accomplished by picking foreign substance out with the fingers, throwing it up from baskets that the breeze may blow away the chaff, and washing it repeatedly in the water of a near-by ditch." Walpole recommended that "a fanning mill be furnished each Pueblo . . . to clean their grain quickly and in such manner as to render it salable in the surrounding markets." They received "only about half price for grain which was usually damaged by trampling, washing, and improper cleaning." (*Ind. Commiss. Annual Report, 1898,* p. 206.)

University of Southern California

Garland himself took this photograph of the primitive threshing process at Isleta Pueblo. His camera case and equipment can be seen in the foreground.

their voices rang with companionable jocularity. I longed to talk with them, to exchange farm-lore with them, but my interest seemed not returned. They tolerated us as prying Americanos — no more.

The family at the first corral consisted of two men and two women. One of the men seemed middle-aged, the other hardly more than a boy. The younger woman was nearly six feet in height, with a supple and graceful figure, whose every attitude was sculpturesque. She moved about the corral, passing an occasional laughing word to the young driver, and though she went round the fence occasionally to sweep the grain back, it was her duties that were voluntary. It was plain that her presence gave pleasure to the men.

The other woman, a serious matron, was busily winnowing the grain from a large shallow basket, and paid no attention whatever to us or to the people jesting about her. In the vivid pink bloom of the horse-mint near by a shy brown baby stood, half-concealed, roguishly eyeing us ready to flee at a word. The old woman alone was grim, silent, and intent — all else was fine, cheerful, companionable.

There lay in all this a certain incommunicable significance. The powerful southern wind swept up over the plain. The yellow chaff glittered as the men tossed it into the air. The girls laughed, and their white teeth lighted their pleasant dark faces. Their gay cloaks fluttered in the wind as they stood braced against it, and their powerful pliant forms were not merely more graceful but more impressive than those of the men. The shouts arose, the whips cracked, the horses whirled in snorting protest before the sweating driver's hissing lash and again [we felt] a sense of its remoteness, its simplicity, its solidarity. It was like something seen in dream.

I turned to my companions finding them as absorbed, as exultant as myself — held in admiration of the "material" in these figures, their attitudes. Here was the most primitive method of agriculture in the world. A man with a flat piece of wood for a spade was tossing wheat into the air to be sifted by the wind! There stood a woman, as alien to our day as Ruth, shaking from an up-lifted basket a stream of grain upon a spread blanket while the breeze caught and carried the chaff in a glittering veil over the grass. Here was grain which had been sowed by the outflung hand and reaped with an iron hook, being trampled by the feet of horses, and would be ground by the women rubbing the grains between two granite slabs to be baked at last on a piece of slate, while not a half mile away thundered "the vestibuled limited" — America's pride and characteristic achievement! And to me at last came the thought, Why disturb this peace — why "civilize" these kindly folk?

Shortly after this the horses were turned out of the corral, for a huge storm cloud was sweeping up the valley. And shouts of warning arose. The swift and graceful young women seized forks and spades and took vigorous hand in heaping and covering the grain, laughing at the wind and dust while the young men called cheerily from threshing floor to threshing floor. The strong blast pleased the threshers, for it swept the chaff away at one toss, leaving the clean hard plump wheat behind. I never expect to see a more peaceful, pleasantly suggestive farm scene. It was as though the golden past, the imagined peace of the dawn of our own race had been revealed to me.

As we walked down toward the gardens on the flat we could see others of the citizens, both men and women, digging companionably among vivid green trees and luxuriant vines, their white blouses shining. The whole effect was that of a happy, contented and peaceful people. I could not see that we had anything to give them. Why disturb them? Why harass them with our problems? About a thousand men, women, and children live here in this pueblo and its fields, and as the afternoon wore on, the streets thickened with singular figures. Along the sun-bright walls tall women in strange garments came and went like pictures, silent as shadows — men with huge hoes, or sickles, and girls with jars of water or sacks of grain upon their heads. And there was something powerful and primitive in their movements; even the old crones were erect of pose and athletic in step, resolute of action.

The houses so far as I could see were a succession of clean, white-washed rooms with folded blankets lying on the raised benches which circled the wall, and all looked cool and comfortable, though furniture was scarce.[9] Their barren whiteness was better than cheap plush and yellow varnish.

---

[9]The homes were single-story adobes. Typical houses of the pueblo consisted of two dirt-floored rooms, each about eight feet by twelve feet, and seven feet in height. They were neat and well-ventilated. (Bloom, ed., "Bourke on the Southwest, XIII," pp. 193–194.)

At six o'clock the smell of supper rose. The streets became thronged with men and burros and wagons returning from the more distant fields. A white man drove a small threshing machine through the streets — so it appeared that some of the progressive ones had made trial of yankee ways.[10]

Hunger began to gnaw upon our vitals, and accosting the man on the threshing machine, I asked aid. He directed us to the house of a woman who "boarded the school-teacher." And he even went so far as to introduce us to her.

She proved to be one of the brightest women of the Pueblo — a very attractive young woman, dressed (as all the Isletan women were) in native costume. We sat down within her yard while she prepared us supper. There was a well at her door, and a constant stream of women came and went through the gate, each with a jar of water on her head. Children shy as squirrels peered at us, through the doors. The daughter of our hostess, a child of ten or twelve, was dressed in American dress, but the change was not pleasing.[11] She was awkward, and her step heavy and heedless. "Why should she be stripped of her own pretty costume?" asked my artist friends.

Our hostess, too modest to look us in the face, smiled with downcast eyes as she called us in to a supper of eggs and bread with coffee and sweet corn. It was the best she had, but a cordial good-will sweetened it and made up for lack of napery and silver.

As we went out through the kitchen a maiden of eighteen or twenty stood at a table with her back to us to hide her embarrassed face, but she made a splendid picture. Her blue-black skirt, her white boots and yellow moccasins, her red under-waist and her gay little blanket — all stood out against the gray-white of the wall like a painting on a panel by Fortuny. She did not look up, but murmured "good bye" as we passed her. The painter glanced back regretfully as if he were losing the chance of a life time.

Taking seats in one of the little plazas we watched the sky grow flame-color and the walls richen from pink-gray into purple in the shadow, while the painter with his paint box on his knee sketched rapidly, surrounded by dogs and children.

Not far away, in the center of the village, on a mound of dirt, rising as high as the roof of the tallest house, several of the village fathers had gathered to smoke and talk in quiet tones. One stood with folded arms looking out across the plain — a figure of bronze against the evening sky. In such wise his forefathers had sentinelled Isleta generations ago, looking out for the Navajo or

---

[10] The Pueblo Indians at this time made their livings chiefly by producing crops of corn, wheat, oats, and vegetables and occasionally had for sale a surplus above their own needs. At some of the pueblos fruits were grown successfully; the agent stated this might be the case at nearly all of the pueblos if the Indians had not been too poor to purchase young fruit trees. (*Ind. Commiss. Annual Report, 1895,* pp. 220, 586.)

[11] According to the agent's report in 1895, of the 8,536 persons in the nineteen pueblos under his jurisdiction, 200 dressed entirely in the Anglo mode and 3,500 dressed that way in part. Bullis wrote, "Every year more of the Indians are adopting citizen dress, and in other ways conforming to the usages of their more civilized neighbors." (*Ind. Commiss. Annual Report, 1895,* pp. 220, 586.) Poverty played a part in this process of acculturation; the Indians often were too much in need to refuse free government-issue clothing, whatever the style.

the Apache, or the mercenary Spaniard. They had considered themselves pro-
tected by the desert, by the dry sand, by impassable cañons, by the ill-omened
cactus plant (which seems somehow to succinctly express the inhospitality of
the desert).

But all these had been no barrier to the terrible yankee whose far-reach-
ing eye had overlooked and mapped a thousand miles of waste as if it were
his garden. Seeing distant mountains and dreaming of gold-fields, he marched
westward. The western sea beckoned him, and so he had driven his plows
across the scoriae mud and planted poles, and laid iron bands and had sent
his monstrous "Cay-voi-yo" howling past the Pueblo of Isleta.[12]

He had built a city near by, this white man, and was casting greedy eyes
upon the Te-wan land and a lustful gaze upon the Te-wan women. He was
now determined to steal their children with intent to instruct them in ways of
life strange to their parents. He was a devil's child, this white man wicked
and wary.

In this way part of Te-wan thinks. Another part welcomes education,[13]
but fears the encroachments of the land-seeker.[14] The boys are going to school,
the girls are learning to read and to sew and to cook. The Pueblo is undoubtedly beginning to feel the terrible solvent power of the white man. That which
neither the Navajo nor the Ute, nor the Comanche could do, this restless, relentless wonder-working white man is doing. In the mighty solvent of his passion
all the old things give way.

As I walked out of the village past the men on the look-out, past the
women on the roofs, past the old men in the doorways, it was made known
to me that this life so stable throughout century after century, so beautiful
and kindly in many of its phases, is doomed soon to disappear and be quite
swallowed up, even as the night engulfed it as we turned to look back upon
it, sighing regretfully to think we might never see it again.

---

[12]Garland refers to the Denver and Rio Grande Railroad, whose route from Durango
to Albuquerque passed by Isleta Pueblo. (Robert A. Morton, *Territory of New Mexico
Map*, 1896.)

[13]Bullis wrote in 1895, "year by year parents are learning to appreciate the value of
education for their offsprings." At that time twelve schools were connected with the
Pueblo Agency: four were government schools and eight were Roman Catholic contract
schools. In addition, there were two Presbyterian day schools, one at Sciama and one in
Zuni. The number of school age children was 2,323; however, only 587 attended school in
1895, "a gratifying increase over the previous year," according to Bullis. Some 800 persons
could read English. (*Ind. Commiss. Annual Report, 1895*, pp. 220, 570.) Figures for school
attendance at Isleta are available for 1897. There were fifty-six children between six and
sixteen, of whom forty-six were enrolled in school (forty-four boys and two girls), aver-
aging seven years old. The agent reported an educational clash with the Isleta parish priest,
who was preventing the transfer of the day school students to the government boarding
schools. (*Ind. Commiss. Annual Report, 1897*, pp. 195–196.)

[14]Throughout the 1890s, the Pueblo agent reported that he was constantly occupied
with the settlement of disputes between the Indians and Mexicans and Americans living
on the reservation borders. In 1895 Bullis wrote: "Their water rights are often invaded,
squatters get on their land, their timber is cut, and their stock stolen." (*Ind. Commiss.
Annual Report, 1895*, p. 221.) In 1896 the story was the same, but some relief was seen
in 1897, when the Department of the Interior employed a lawyer to serve as counsel for
the several pueblos in land and other matters. (*Ind. Commiss. Annual Report, 1897*, p. 214
and *Ind. Commiss. Annual Report, 1898*, p. 94.)

Up at the station the boys and girls, the advance guard of the new order, were gathered waiting for the train, with melons and apples and pottery to sell.[15] The boys were playing about the water tank, wrestling and shouting in the dark, reminding me of the games we played at "school-meeting" in my boyhood. Others sat talking quietly.

One bright boy of sixteen told me he had been to school one year and that he wanted to go again.

"My fodda he no like me go to school. I like. I go two t'ree years. I like Melican man. No like live in mud-house."

So the world-wide, life-long struggle between the new and the traditional, the young and the old goes on here in these mud walls under the wide sky as elsewhere while the glories of moon and sun and stars fall as ever into the heart of youth, breeding the unrest which bids fair to reduce all the world to the same complexion of interest. There is sorrow before both man and maid, but my voice is for youth — my feet are set his way and my hand-clasp is for him.

I left Isleta in the deep night and it seems now like a dream — a fantasy, born of my reading, not of my actual living. Yet I know it was real and the eyes of the ambitious boy turned toward me in the dim starlight will not leave me, and his face more than any other thing, enables me to comprehend the awaking life of Isleta and to forecast some part of its future.

---

[15] The inhabitants of Isleta have made no painted pottery since about 1700. The pottery called "Isleta" is almost exclusively the product of Oraibi, a small settlement of conservatives from Laguna that "joined Isleta after splitting with the progressive faction at the old site." This pottery is brick red with white slip and black and red design. (Stubbs, *Bird's-Eye View of the Pueblos,* pp. 35, 38.)

Background

Garland's encounters with the Navajo Indians were widespread because of the vast area occupied by those people. The main body of them have resided on a large reservation originally set aside for them in northeastern Arizona and northwestern New Mexico in 1868 and later modified to include land in southern Utah. However, great numbers of the Navajo live outside the reservation. The tribe is basically Athapascan, but groups of other linguistic stock were absorbed into the group from time to time, in some cases bringing about linguistic changes and, in others, a diversity in stature and appearance.

Traditionally nomadic herdsmen, the Navajo were also historically a warring people. For nearly two centuries before the United States acquired the Southwest from Mexico, the tribe had made successful war against their neighbors. They were not subdued until 1863, when Kit Carson and his troops invaded their lands and killed their sheep. Starvation forced the tribe to submit, and most of them were held at Bosque Redondo near Fort Sumner until 1867, when they were given back their land and had their sheep replaced. The Navajo lived in peace after that time.[1]

When Garland saw these people in 1895, they were maintaining their livelihood as herdsmen, as they had traditionally done. The year before, their herds had numbered a million sheep, a quarter of a million goats, 100,500 horses, and 1,200 cattle. However, drought during that and the previous year had resulted in the starvation of much livestock as well as the failure of what crops the Navajo planted. Thus Garland visited the tribe during a time of economic stress. In 1895, there were some 20,500 persons under the jurisdiction of the Navajo Agency. Of that number, only 500 dressed in part in the Anglo mode and none dressed entirely that way.[2]

Although "Glimpses of the Navajo Indians" is a general commentary on the Navajo, it offers some interesting specific insights into their character, dress, occupations, and amusements. Most of the time, Garland's comments regarding these matters are cast in terms of Anglo-Indian relations, and, as usual, the writer emphasizes the fact that he is describing aspects of an adulterated culture.

Perhaps because of the economic distress he witnessed among the Navajo, Garland favored more white intervention in behalf of these people than he had with other tribes he visited in 1895. He complains that those with "the sensibility and the imagination to understand the Indians" did not remain with them long enough to learn their language. He lays upon the white man the responsibility of leading the Navajo to a "securer" and "better life."

---

[1] Frederick Webb Hodge, ed., *Handbook of American Indians North of Mexico*, Pt. 2, p. 41.

[2] *Ind. Commiss. Annual Report, 1895*, pp. 118, 582–583, 1008–1009.

3. Glimpses of the Navajo Indians[3]

Everywhere I went in southwestern Colorado, in California, in New Mexico, I saw the Navajo. As a matter of fact, I circumnavigated his reservation without entering it more than a few miles at any one point. It lies in northern New Mexico and extends over into Arizona, and contains nearly 20,000 people, for the Navajos form one of the largest distinct tribes now remaining on United States soil.[4]

I came upon them first at Durango — thin, alert, muscular fellows, wearing baggy cotton trousers and a calico overshirt, with fillets of red or green around their abundant black hair. They came to trade, bringing the justly celebrated blankets, which their women weave, and silver work which would please William Morris for its hand-worked quality.[5]

At Ignacio, on ration day for the Utes, they are often to be seen riding in to trade and to feast with their better-fed neighbors. The Navajo has no annuity;[6] he is obligated to hustle for a living; therefore, wherever is feasting and chance to barter he is to be found. He is not always welcome, but he is treated respectfully by his neighbors.

They are to be seen in Santa Fe and Taos and Isleta and Acoma on feast days. They infest the land of the Zuni with herds and flocks. They come riding gravely into the pueblo villages, followed by their women, who sit astride and ride extremely well. They always look the same — the men red-bronze in color, sinewy, rather grave of countenance, but not sinister; the women plump, dark and shy, with shining, perfect teeth. They dress in calico and their hair is carefully tended.

---

[3] Item 441, Hamlin Garland Collection, University of Southern California Library, Los Angeles, published by permission of the University of Southern California Library and Constance Garland Doyle and Isabel Garland Lord. This document, edited in a slightly different manner, appeared in *Journal of Arizona History*, 13 (Winter, 1972), 275–285, and is reprinted here with permission of *Journal of Arizona History*.

[4] The Navajo has become the largest tribe of American Indians.

[5] William Morris (1834–1896) was a well-known English poet, artist, and social reformer. Garland's reference to Morris is an apt one because his revolutionary work in decorative designs went far in dictating Victorian tastes. He also worked hard at reviving the applied arts, and in 1861 established a firm which advertised as "Fine Art Workmen in Painting, Carving, Furniture, and Metals." (*Dictionary of National Biography*, 22:1068.)

[6] Article 8 of the 1868 treaty with the Navajo, in place of an annuity, provided "articles of clothing, goods, or raw materials . . . as the agent may . . . estimate . . . not exceeding in value five dollars per Indian — each Indian being encouraged to manufacture their own clothing, blankets & c.; to be furnished with no article which they can manufacture themselves." ("Treaty With the Navaho, 1868," in Charles J. Kappler, comp. and ed., *Indian Affairs: Laws and Treaties*, 2:784.)

The Utes braid their hair — at least, the men — but the Navajo puts his up in a little pug somewhat like a spool of thread in shape. The women wear their hair in the same way, but part it smoothly in front, like Quaker girls. This gives them a demure, domestic look, quite different from the Ute women, who wear their hair cut short and hanging over their faces. The Ute women also retain more of the tribal dress. The Navajo men and women are rapidly taking on American dress.[7] The Navajo women wear almost invariably a calico dress of red and brown. They are to be seen at Zuni, at Wingate, at Holbrook. All along the Santa Fe route they come to trade. They are not, as a tribe, loafers; they are herders. They have sheep and goats and horses to look after, corn to plant and corrals to build. They come in once in a while to trade, and, as in the lives of many country white people, it is an event — picnic. Out of so large a population the loafers are comparatively small.

And let me say right here that I did not see a drunken Indian in all my coming and going among them. I did not hear an angry word or see a blow struck. True, I did not see a caress, except between child and parent, but so far as my observation went, they were calm, kindly, dignified; ready to smile at a joke, ready to yield to the demands of a child.[8]

On my way to Walpi I spent several days at a little trading ranche, practically in the Navajo reservation. It was forty-five miles from the railway, and the Indians there were as distinctly untouched by the towns as if they were in the reservation proper.

I came upon my first settlement of Navajos early one morning. I was riding alone up the trail in the midst of a singular landscape — a streamless land of tall, grotesquely carved buttes of red stone. There were no trees, with the exception of gnarled junipers. It had been raining, so that the land was at its greenest, but it was easy to see that it was a region of rainless summer and of snowless winter.

It was a strange and solemn land — a place of unusual hills, green and orange in color, carved fantastically or crested like eagles. There were enormous stretches of red soil, with sparse bunches of grass and greasewood. Suddenly, I rounded a height and came upon a little village of Navajo *hogans* set round a field of struggling corn. The light of morning filled the land till every blade of grass shone, and on the valley floor, and streaming up the slopes were flocks of sheep and goats, white and black, the white gleaming like rosy snow, the black like beads of topaz. A boy was chanting to them as he urged them forward.

There was something old and primitive in it all. I felt it to be a scene out of the pastoral life of all peoples, elemental and unchanging. These mud

---

[7] Dress statistics quoted in the introduction to this essay make it clear that the agent would have disagreed with this statement. He noted in 1895 that not one Navajo dressed entirely in the Anglo mode. (*Ind. Commiss. Annual Report, 1895,* p. 118.)

[8] Captain Constant Williams, acting agent, said of the Navajos in 1895: "The Navajos are cheerful, lively, and talkative, exceedingly generous to one another, and they are not quarrelsome. There is great affection between parents and children, and the latter are rarely punished. . . . There are many industrious men among them who set a good example for the rest, and as a rule the men do their share of the work." (*Ind. Commiss. Annual Report, 1895,* p. 118.)

huts, this herdsman in his covert of branches, the woman with her loom hung up on the trees, had their counterparts in Arabia, in Galilee, in the hill countries of Tibet and China, and in the Saxon swineherd of the time of Caesar. The dogs were such as fought under the table of Cedric the Saxon.

The Navajos live thus: five or six hogans set round a field of corn. They have no towns, no large villages.[9] They have their summer hogans and their winter hogans, and their residing places depend upon grass and water. As feed changes they move with it. They have no rulers in the sense in which chieftain is used in some tribes. They have a head man in each village called *the hosteen,* but all power resides in customs and superstitions. Their long peace and their scattered pastoral lives have made them democratic to a singular degree.[10] They have at present, I believe, not even a nominal chief.[11] Each man is the equal of his neighbor.

It was pathetic to me to see the interest these Navajos took in the white man. They wanted to respect him and they were eager to talk with him ever so little. They came to this little store because it seemed somehow to have a little touch of the great white man's world in it. There were pictures on the cans and wrappers of the groceries. There were curious pictures posted on the wall.

They sat there looking at me, seeing everything I did, reading every line of my face, and I wished I could read their thought, feel for a moment as they do toward this white race. It is not all suspicion with them. They do meet an occasional man who does not damn them in their hearing and seek to outrage their women. They are thinking, those grave old fellows, pondering on the power and plans of this white man.

There came a young woman to the store for supplies. She was shy as a partridge, and stood for a long time peering round the corner of the shanty, ready to run if any of the strange men looked at her. She got her piece of calico and mounted her horse and rode away to her village miles away.

There was one superb young fellow whom Mr. Browne,[12] the painter, sketched. He was dressed in a hickory shirt and a pair of blue overalls. He had the bearing of the proudest athlete as he leaned with folded arms against the wall. The hosteen of the village gravely smoked, exchanging an occasional word with the trader or with one of his sons. There was something rugged and strong in his face; something almost Scotch-Irish in character.

---

[9] Kluckhohn and Leighton suggest that in the old days the band was the basis of social grouping, for some local groups have retained the character of a band and have a headman each. (Clyde Kluckhohn and Dorthea Leighton, *The Navaho,* p. 117.) When Garland refers to the "village," he means local groups.

[10] This system of leadership has been preserved. The headmen had no coercive power, nor could they institute community policy without the consent of the people. They were responsible, however, for such things as looking after the interests of the needy in their groups. (Kluckhohn and Leighton, *The Navaho,* p. 120.)

[11] Manuelito was the last "chief" of the Navajo, elected in 1855. When peace came, Manuelito took command of the Indian police force, established in 1872. He died in 1893, two years before Garland's visit. (Hodge, ed., *Handbook of American Indians North of Mexico,* Pt. 1, pp. 802–803.)

[12] See Essay 1, note 5, for identification of Charles Francis Browne.

While we were there a tremendous shower came up and the land was covered with water. At the first lull the young Navajos stripped to their waist and rolled their trousers to the knee, and seizing spades, made off down the hill to drown out the prairie dogs. It was a fine sight to see them running through the rain, lithe, swift and graceful. They dug trenches leading into the prairie dog holes, and when the little fellows came out to breathe they killed them with the spade.

The old hosteen smiled gravely as if to say, "Let the boys have fun," and went on smoking. An hour later they returned with a blanket full of wet, dead bodies. They are undoubtedly as suitable eating as a squirrel, and no more of a dog than a rat, and no more of a rat than a gopher. There is no reason why they should not make an excellent fry. They have a way of baking them, however, under the ashes, I believe, somewhat as the negroes cook a 'possum.

Another thing remains to be said, and that is this: All the Indians I saw were ready to do anything they knew how, to earn a little money, and also that they kept their word. The trader hired the old hosteen for a small sum — too small, I felt — to take our horses back to Holbrook. I said to the trader: "Aren't you afraid to send out an Indian on such an errand?"

"No! If a Navajo says he'll take a thing to a certain place, or do a certain thing, he'll do it."

At another time I had some baggage to send a distance of fifty miles. The trader arranged with an old man to take it. He said: "I don't know this Navajo; he lives inland, somewhere, but it won't make any difference; it's just as safe as if you were with it yourself." And this trader, it may be said, does not profess ordinarily to believe in the Indians.[13]

At Keams Cañon trading post the Navajos were also to be seen, for "Willie," as they call the trader, was raised on the reservation and speaks Navajo with perfect fluency.[14] Each night after the store was closed they could be seen climbing the rocky walls like goats, their bright garments coming and going behind the rocks like sparks of fire. Or in the early morning they might be seen coming down in single file mounted on their spirited and sure-footed little ponies.

I thought of them coming out of their little *hogans* miles away, coming to spend a day at the store, hoping to have a word with the white man, to see his house, to get, perhaps, a taste of his food or a whiff of his tobacco — coming with quite the same desire for diversion which a backwoodsman shows as he comes to the crossroads in an Arkansas forest. And it was all so meagre.

I do not wonder that they say, "White men all liars!" I do not wonder that they are suspicious of a first kindness. When they come to believe in a white man they will go hundreds of miles to see him. His word is law with them.

---

[13] For Garland's attitude toward reservation traders in general, see his essay "The Red Man's Present Needs," which appears later in this book. The kind of trust which the trader reflects here is a basic part of the theme in Garland's short story, "Joe, the Navajo Teamster," which appeared in *Youth's Companion,* November 18, 1897.

[14] An account of the life of T. V. Keam, owner of the trading post at Keams Canyon from 1881 to 1902, appears in Lynn R. Bailey, "Thomas Varker Keam: Tusayan Trader," pp. 15–19.

They love to be silently in his presence like an intelligent dog.[15] One such man, unofficial in every way, can do more than a regiment to civilize the Indian.

Unfortunately, it seldom happens that men with the sensibility and the imagination to understand the Indians ever remain with them long enough to learn their language. We have our own taboos, the Navajo his. We date ours from Moses. The Navajo does not know when or where he was forbidden to eat bear meat or wild turkey. He does not know why he may not touch the hand, even the garment, of his sister, but he obeys, and he should be honored for obeying.[16] He should be taken for what he is, and little by little helped to a securer life, and then to a better life.

The Navajo is a natural herder, horseman, and çattle raiser. He should be instructed in those things, so that his sheep may be bred properly and his wool be of better quality. He should be aided in making wells for watering his stock and guided in his selection of time and place for planting. He is keen, alert, never stupid. He will learn and learn quickly when properly approached.

He has his faults, his vices, like the rest of mankind, but he also has conspicuous virtues. I was impressed strongly by his evident desire to learn, to meet the white man in a friendly manner, and by his keen intelligence.

---

[15] This is an unfortunate comparison, typical of the sort used by the white man to describe less "civilized" people during the nineteenth century. As Garland became more familiar with the Indians, he dropped such figures of speech.

[16] The Navajos could not kill coyotes, bears, snakes, and certain birds. Neither could they eat fish or most water birds and animals. Physical contact, even of no more import than walking down the street or dancing together, was forbidden with members of the opposite sex of one's own clan or of that of one's father. (Kluckhohn and Leighton, *The Navaho*, p. 201.)

Background

The Hopi ("Moqui" or "Moki" as they were popularly called) of north-eastern Arizona had their first contact with whites in 1540 when Coronado, then at Zuni, sent emissaries to visit the seven villages of the "Province of Tusayan." Five settlements which the Spanish recorded as inhabited included Oraibi, Shongopovi, Mishongnovi, Walpi, and Awatobi. The last named was destroyed in 1700, and the first is the only one which possibly has retained the same location it had when the Spanish came.

The first mission was established among the Hopi at Awatobi in 1629, and later churches were built at the other villages. The missionaries were generally unsuccessful, and in the Pueblo Uprising of 1680, they were killed and the missions destroyed. A church was reestablished at Awatobi in 1700, and the other villages were so angered that they attacked it at night, killing many, and forcing its abandonment. At the time of the rebellion, Walpi, Mishongnovi, and Shongopovi were in the foothills, and they were probably vacated about this time.[1]

When Garland visited the Hopi in 1895, the seven villages of the "Province of Tusayan" were as follows: On First or East Mesa were Hano, Sichomovi, and Walpi; on Second or Middle Mesa were Mishongnovi, Shongopovi, and Shupaulovi; and on Third or West Mesa was Oraibi. The people of Hano were Tewa who had come from near Abiquiu in New Mexico at the invitation of the Walpians in the early eighteenth century. Walpi occupied two different sites in the foothills before being moved to the mesa. There were no efforts to Christianize the Walpians after the village was moved. Oraibi was the largest of the Hopi villages and the seat of the most conservative Hopi society.

In 1895, the population of the Hopi villages was 2,029. Of that number, 105 could speak enough English for ordinary conversation, and 200 dressed partially in the Anglo mode. Most of this number were probably students at the industrial school at Keams Canyon. They numbered 108 in 1895. Some had to be turned away that year because of a lack of space at the school. Their main industry in 1895 was agriculture, their basic crop being maize. In addition they raised peaches, vegetables, and cotton, also maintaining sizable flocks of sheep and goats and small herds of mules and horses.[2]

The best-known ceremony among the Hopi was the snake dance. Observation of that ceremony was Garland's object in visiting Walpi. His description of it in "Among the Moki Indians" was one of the earliest popular accounts of the rite. His perspective in the essay is interesting. Since he was not permitted a first-hand observance of some parts of the ceremony, he had to rely on his reading on the subject and on his imagination. Thus, he held the position of an outsider for whom the pageantry and mystery of the ceremony was heightened because of the obscurity in which it was cloaked.

---

[1] Frederick Webb Hodge, ed., *Handbook of American Indians North of Mexico,* Pt. 1, pp. 560–562.

[2] *Ind. Commiss. Annual Report, 1895,* pp. 359–360, 564–565, 582–583.

4. Among the Moki Indians[3]

Imagine a wide land, a magnificent sky, a land lonely as the sky, spotted with cedars, and green and gray with sage-brush, soap-weed, and scant grass; a land which is a high plateau, in which ancient waters have cut deep wide valleys with precipitous sides; a mysterious, lonely, empty land, like the Bad Lands of Dakota, in which no sign of life can be detected. This is the land of the Hopituh or Moki Indians[4] — "The most ancient province of Tusayan."[5]

I entered it at sundown. To the west and south, on the rocky points of mesas, which stood like promontories out into the misty valley, certain regular rocklike piles could be seen. These forms, seemingly of the rock itself, were the pueblos of the Moki Indians. These cities, which secrete themselves, like turtles on the bare rock, by adaptation of color and form, are the homes of two thousand people.

It came upon me with great power, the thought that for three hundred and fifty years there had lived here, as on an island in untraversable seas, a race of people, subsisting by their own labor, knowing nothing of the world, shut close upon their island of rock by the Utes on the north, the Navajos on the east, the Spaniards to the south, and cut off by cañons of terrible depth to the west.

It is this isolation, enforced and complete, which now makes the villages of Walpi and Oraibi so interesting to the archaeologist,[6] for they have preserved traditions and customs of enormous antiquity, little influenced as yet by the great nation of which they are an unknowing part. They were here when Columbus set sail from Spain. Coronado saw them in 1540, and left them to their desert. They were here in 1776, fighting their own battles. They were watching the Navajos and the Utes while Lincoln was meditating the freeing of the negro, and the American flag was unknown to them.

To reach them to-day is to cross more than one hundred miles of dry plain,[7] beaten to quivering heat by the sun — a region of dry rivers and scanty

---

[3] Reprinted from *Harper's Weekly*, 40 (August 15, 1896), 801–807.

[4] Hodge says that *Hopi* is a contraction of *Hopitu* (peaceful ones) or *Hopitu-shinumu* (peaceful all people). *Moqui*, or *Moki*, means "dead" in these people's own language and, as a tribal name, seems alien in origin. (Hodge, ed., *Handbook of American Indians North of Mexico*, Pt. 1, p. 560.)

[5] "Province of Tusayan" was the Spanish name for the Hopi villages collectively.

[6] Garland probably alludes here to the well-known archaeological investigations of Matilda Coxe Stevenson (1881), Jesse Walter Fewkes (1890–1895), and Frederick Webb Hodge (1895).

[7] First Mesa is approximately seventy miles north of Winslow, Arizona.

[89]

grass. I felt everywhere the absence of water, and felt it with double thirstiness for the reason that I was but just down from the green and purple mountains of Colorado, where the grass grew thick and sweet to the highest peaks, and rills of cold sweet water foamed in every cañon.

I looked across the wide valley, at those promontories on which these ancient villages stand, unable readily to believe they existed. At a distance of six miles they seemed still without sign of life. A Navajo war party might easily pass them by, so perfectly do their flat, mud-colored buildings impersonate huge stacks of sandstone. In the valley we[8] soon came upon fields of corn set waist deep in sand (or in water) — poor, pathetic little fields, watched by an old man beneath a shade of cedar boughs, and surrounded by scarecrows.

It seemed hard to see corn, short and scant for lack of rain, suddenly submerged by a flood; but such are the implacable moods of this land. The sky was magnificent, the wind cool, but the sun fell with terrible power upon the sand, withering everything but the sage-brush and the grease-wood.

As we came nearer, three distinct villages[9] appeared upon the lofty mesa. At the right of the last village, and cutting deep into the mesa's backbone, was a chasm, which manifestly strengthened the position of the towns. It took fear of man to set these homes upon that bare sun-smit mesa, and they were glad of the chasm, which widened year by year, making the coming of the Ute and Navajo ever more difficult.

At the foot of the mesa we came upon many little adobe houses with red roofs.[10] They were the houses given by the government to entice the Mokis down from the rocks. Around these cabins were melon-patches and many peach-trees, also knee-deep in sand, which drifts there like snow.

The trail rose rapidly — merely a foot path. The cliffs became precipitous; enormous boulders broken from the mesa's walls lay beside the way. Below were little sheep corrals of stone looking like pools of dark water.

Suddenly I came upon the village of Ha-no. First a rush of wolfish dogs, next a group of naked brown babies, then a woman with a child slung at her back in a shawl, and a maiden with huge rolls of hair above her ears. Then a youth[11] in American trousers, who called to me. "This way — my home." He was our guide.

---

[8] As on the trips described in Essays 1 and 2, Garland is traveling with Hermon Atkins MacNeil and Charles Francis Browne. See Essay 1, notes 5 and 32, for identification of these two men.

[9] Walpi is located on the southernmost part of First Mesa. (Stanley A. Stubbs, *Bird's-Eye View of the Pueblos,* p. 95.) In 1895, First Mesa was most accessible by the northeastern trail, the one Garland took. (Hodge, ed., *Handbook of American Indians North of Mexico,* Pt. 2, p. 902.)

[10] Lieutenant E. H. Plummer, acting agent for the Hopis, wrote that the plan of building houses in the valleys for these Indians, with the view to persuade them to abandon their overcrowded pueblo dwellings on the high mesas, did not seem to be as successful as desired. Many of the houses built in the valley were unoccupied the greater portion of the year. Lieutenant Plummer commented that the Indians' habits, customs, and general mode of living were so intimately connected with the conditions of life on the mesas that it was doubtful whether anything less than compulsion would cause them to abandon their pueblo dwellings. (*Ind. Commiss. Annual Report, 1894,* pp. 100–101.)

[11] This was Percy, a Tewa youth from Hano. (Hamlin Garland, *Roadside Meetings,* p. 295.)

I turned into a narrow way between adobe walls, which led to a door in another wall, and I was "at home" in a Moki village.

The brown boy said, "My mother, my sister."

Two women met me. Little Quang, so Japanese you could not believe her to be Indian; her hair combed into great whorls[12] at the side, her eyes black as melon seeds, her hands slender, her naked feet small and brown. The mother, with her hair falling over her face, with gown of coarse blue cloth belted with a wide red belt and covered with a white over-blanket,[13] equally strange.

They did not speak, but they smiled their greeting in good full terms of white teeth.

I entered the house[14] which was on the ground-floor, and which consisted of one long room and a loft. In the left-hand corner was a pretty fireplace; in the other, three bins for grinding meal. At one stone a handsome young woman in Tewan (Tay-won) costume was working. In the middle of the room sat a stove. In the left wall two small windows and one large one filled the room with light. The whole room was freshly whitewashed, and looked very habitable — with this exception, there were no tables, no chairs, and very few pieces of kitchen-ware.[15]

I looked out of the window upon the little plaza. Behold a strange America. In the center of the plaza was a pool of water. In this pool a dozen comical little brown babies were paddling like ducks. Under the shade of adobe walls women with bare feet and bare arms, their bodies draped in scant gowns, were baking pottery or making bread. On the flat roofs other women, robed in green and black and purple, were moving about. A man in blue and pink, belted with a string of huge silver disks, was unloading an enormous dead wild-cat from behind his saddle, his pony waiting with bowed head. A peculiar smell was in the air.

The little ones, seeing a strange face, cried, "Pa-ha-no!" (white man), and came running up — lithe little boys with thick, bristling black hair, and fat pot-bellied little girls, with equally black hair, and equally unabashed nudity. Their coloring was of warm bronze. Dripping with water, they glistened like otters, and all stared shrewdly, not stupidly, and eventually (as nothing happened) went back to bob and bubble in the muddy pool.

Little Quang was about fourteen, and was a maid, as the whorls of her shining hair testified. Hèli was the house-owner, and was about forty-five — a straight, active, and pleasant-voiced woman. Percy and Quang had been to

---

[12] On reaching puberty, the girls dressed their hair in whorls at the side of their head in imitation of the squash blossom, the symbol of fertility. (Hodge, ed., *Handbook of American Indians North of Mexico*, Pt. 1, p. 564.)

[13] Hodge names the same clothing as Garland does here. (*Handbook of American Indians North of Mexico*, Pt. 1, p. 565.)

[14] The average size of a room in the Hopi village was ten feet by twelve feet by seven feet high. (John G. Bourke, *The Snake-Dance of the Moquis of Arizona*, p. 115.)

[15] Samuel L. Hertzog, superintendent of Keams Canyon School, described the new government houses in the valley as being furnished with stoves, bedsteads, dishes, and some chairs, an obvious enticement from the barren dwellings on the mesas. (*Ind. Commiss. Annual Report, 1895*, p. 564.)

school,[16] and could talk a little English. Hèli knew no word of English, but she seemed to be proud of the attainments of her children.

I went out into the street, along the edge of the lofty cliff, which we at once called the "lake-front." It swarmed with merry, nude children, quaintly dressed maidens, old men in shirt and trousers merely, younger men in American trousers slit to the knee, and young fellows with bare heads and wearing necklaces of turquoise, and with fillets of red or green circling their black hair. There was much laughter and chaffing. The voices were all pleasant, with a decidedly Chinese inflection. The Mongolian type was very common.

They all smiled at my salutation, "How-dy-do?" with the word "Lolla-mai," which means "good," "very well," "how are you?" and some other things. The house doors were open, and I could see the women grinding corn and stewing pots at the fireplace. On the roofs the young women took care of the babes and gossiped with their neighbors.

Back at Hèli's house we sat down flat on the floor to eat our supper, which consisted of tea, flat corn cakes (tough and heavy, but also sweet and nutritious), and small bits of fried mutton.

On the white walls hung dolls made in the image of the gods of rain and thunder.[17] From the ceiling hung prayer emblems made of feathers and bits of cottonwood. In the corner two old women were rubbing a flat stone up and down a slanting granite slab, grinding meal. A young man, with shining black hair bound with a fillet of green, looked in at the window to see the *pahanos,* and a naked boy stood in the door.

I spread my blankets on the floor that night, for beds are not common in Ha-no.

Darkness came early, for these people use little oil. Hèli pattered about in her bare feet, coming and going from loft to cellarway; the door to the cellar was an incredibly small space for a grown person to enter; a mere cat-hole it looked.

She hunted up a lamp somewhere in the town and placed it near me, and went over to her grinding slab in the corner. Preparations for bed under such circumstances were simple, and when my blankets were ready I placed the lamp near her and went to my blankets. She worked on busily. Her short black hair fell over her eyes, as she scrubbed with monotonous motion, keeping time to a low song.

I found the sound of the stone soothing and fell asleep listening to it, and to the low song with which she cheered her long, hard task.

---

[16] They probably had attended the Hopi industrial school at Keams Canyon. In 1886, twenty Hopi headmen had requested the federal government to open this institution near the trading post of Navajo agent Thomas V. Keam. (Byrd H. Granger, ed., *Will C. Barnes' Arizona Place Names,* p. 243.) An excellent account of Keam appears in Lynn R. Bailey, "Thomas Varker Keam: Tusayan Trader," pp. 15–19.

[17] These are evidently the celebrated Kachina dolls. According to Dozier, in all of the pueblos there is some notion of a cult of supernatural beings, the most complex of which is among the western pueblos. Masked and elaborately costumed dancers represent the beings, called Kachina, at ceremonies in these pueblos. Children are led to believe the Kachina are real. "Rain and fertility are the functions associated with the cult, although Katcina ceremonies are believed to bring about general well-being to the pueblo as well." (Edward P. Dozier, *The Pueblo Indians of North America,* pp. 155–156.)

The intimacy of the Hopi dwellings, which so impressed Garland, can be seen in this view of the village of Walpi in the 1890s.

It was an unforgettable event to go to sleep here on the floor of a Ha-no house, with mysterious blanketed people passing the open door, with a woman grinding corn with a stone upon a slab, singing a mystic chant. Just under my open window a family of six laid itself to sleep, after much frolicking among the children. On the roof others were moving about, spreading blankets for their beds.

It takes a strong and very specific purpose to bring a city dweller to such a place. My own motive was the desire to see these people perform "the snake dance."[18] Once in two years[19] they are said to set aside about fifty of their number to perform a strange and complicated ceremony, which lasts ten days, culminating in a public dance, wherein snakes are handled and carried in the mouths of the priests. Each year four days were set aside for the snake hunt, and the second day's hunt was in progress when I arrived.

I was awakened the next morning by the movement of Hèli as she came

---

[18] Garland claimed to have read several accounts of this ceremony. (Garland, *Roadside Meetings*, p. 293.) He was perhaps familiar with Bourke's *The Snake-Dance of the Moquis of Arizona*. Garland's 1896 account of the ceremony was followed in 1900 by an article by George Wharton James. This author asserts essentially the same attitude as Garland: "The Snake Dance is a solemn and dignified act of worship, participated in by serious-hearted, devout-souled people, with earnest sincerity of purpose. . . ." (James, "The Hopi Snake Dance," pp. 302–303.)

[19] The Snake Dance was held at Walpi during August of the odd-numbered years. (Earle R. Forrest, *Missions and Pueblos of the Old Southwest*, pp. 347–348.)

in. It was not yet light, but she placed her bowl of corn beside her and began work again upon the grinding-stone. When I awoke again it was sunrise, and the Snake-priests had passed to their hunt.

After a breakfast of bread and mutton and coffee, without butter, milk, or potatoes, I went out to see Walpi under the morning light. Every one was astir. The men were riding down into the fields in every direction but one, the world quarter in which the snake hunt was in progress. All work was prohibited there, and I was told I would "swell up and burst" if I went to watch the Snake-men catching snakes.

It so happened that Dr. Fewkes[20] was excavating in the very world quarter in which the hunt took place, and while visiting him I saw the Snake-men at their work. The doctor had suspended work out of respect to the priests, whom he knew, and no citizen of Walpi was at work in the fields. Every one was on the lookout for the snake-hunters.

That they were coming we were made sure of by the nervous action of the Moki boys. They stared with round eyes in the direction of the mesa, and refused to go for water even upon stern command of the cook, whose iconoclasm astonished them.

"*The Snake-man!*" cried one, pointing at a slim brown figure which had suddenly silently appeared among the grease-wood. It was a Snake-priest, naked, with the exception of a breech-clout and moccasins. He carried a little bag in one hand, along with his snake-whip, which is composed of two forked eagle feathers tied to a short stick. He carried also a pike or hoe with which to dig out the snake.[21]

Soon other black heads appeared above the hill, and other slim, graceful, brown-bodied men were grouped among the grease-wood clumps. The brown bodies glowed like bronze in the sun, and the float of the eagle feathers, and the lines of their staves against the sky was very fine indeed, primitive, and of the unploughed spaces.

They were trailing a snake, and their erect bodies and bent, intent heads were both alert and graceful. Every two years this four-day hunt takes place, and from sixty to a hundred snakes are gathered in to take part in the ceremony, because [in] the principal myth of their history it is said that "the elder

---

[20] Distinguished ethnologist Jesse Walter Fewkes was secretary of the Boston Society of Natural History when Garland made his acquaintance in 1895. At that time Fewkes was in charge of ethnologists studying the Hopi. In 1891 he published the first scientific study of the snake dance in the *Journal of American Ethnology and Archaeology,* of which he was editor. Among Fewkes's outstanding achievements were excavation and repair of the Casa Grande ruins in Arizona and the Sun Temple in Mesa Verde National Park in Colorado. (*The National Cyclopaedia of American Biography,* 15:32.)

[21] The equipment of the snake priests is interesting. The hoe is significant because it was the most important implement used to plant the Hopis' precious corn. Some authorities have offered a natural explanation for the snake-pacifying effect of the eagle feathers on the snake-whip. When an eagle swoops down upon a snake, it warily avoids striking directly but brushes the prey with his wing. The angry reptile, striking at the wing, spends his venom idly, and the next moment the talons grasp the snake just behind the head. When a pair of snake priests found a snake in the open, they mimicked this pattern. The escaping reptile was brushed rapidly upon the head with the feathers on the whip. This action subdued the snake instantly, and with a lightning-like dart of his hand, the snake priest seized the snake just behind the head. (R. B. Townsend, "Snake-Dancers of Mishongnovi," pp. 432–433.)

children of the Snake-woman," wife of "Tee-yo" (the snake hero) were metamorphosed into snakes.[22]

When they find a snake, Dr. Fewkes told me, they say "Elder brother," and the snake replies, "My younger brother." They have never allowed Dr. Fewkes to see the ceremony over the snake in the field, but they have told him that after the greetings they sprinkle corn meal upon the snake's head, and then put him in the little bag which they carry in their hands. They fold up a rattlesnake like a ribbon. They are, for the time, not snakes, but elder brothers, called in to take part in the great drama of the Snake Myth.

Back in the three villages of Ha-no, Si-Chom-avi, and Walpi the women were plastering the walls with thin mortar of clay, which they spread on with their hands. They all smiled pleasantly as we passed. We called "Lolla-mai," the only word we knew, and they smiled back with pleasant show of teeth.

It was startling to see the naked little imps of children playing on pinnacles of rock on the very edge of the cliff. A white mother would have died of terror to think of her child walking along the path, while these little creatures ran wild as goats over the entire "island" (as we called it). One little fellow, slender and graceful as a fairy, stood balanced on a rock which overhung the sheer cliff; seeing us look at him, he stood on one leg and gleefully clapped his hands.

It is said that a Navajo fell off the cliff once and was killed, and we passed by a little stick with attached eagle feathers set in the rock at a point where a Moki child fell and was badly injured. These were the only accidents we heard of. Generations of life on these dangerous heights have produced children with the fearlessness and certainty of action of acrobats or wild-cats.

The babes climb up the ladders before they can walk, and the dogs and chickens follow them. The copings of the walls of the lower houses reach to the upper chambers, and the babes come and go on these perilous stairways.

The mesa of Walpi is a bare promontory of rock, which narrows to barely twenty feet in width between the middle village and Walpi proper. The feet of thousands of men and women, dead and absolutely forgotten, have worn deep paths into the bleak, wind-swept rock. For hundreds of years all water used in these villages has been carried by complaining, grieving old women up the steep trail from "Kanilba spring," and others less accessible.

There are three villages upon this rocky height — Walpi (most ancient), Si-Chom-avi, and Ha-no. The first two villages are Ho-pi (Hopee), "Peaceful people" (they never call themselves "Moki"). They speak the same language, but Ha-no, the nearest the trail, is Tewan, and its people speak the language of the Rio Grande pueblos.[23] Polaka, the leading citizen, told me how they came to be there:

"My people came from the East. Ho-pee say: 'You stay here; alee time keep trail; fight. Navajo no come, Ute no come. We give you land, we glad you here!' "

---

[22] A similar account of the background of the Snake Dance legend appears in Townsend, "Snake-Dancers of Mishongnovi," pp. 429–30.

[23] Although the Tewa of Hano had intermarried with the Hopi, they retained their native speech and many of their distinctive tribal rites and customs. See Hodge, ed., *Handbook of American Indians North of Mexico*, Pt. 1, p. 560.

So for many, many years Ha-no has kept the trail. They speak the Ho-pi tongue now, but they keep up their own language, and their women dress like the women of Isleta and Acoma. They are also more progressive, readier to take on the white man's manners and ideas. They wear more of the white man's clothing, and more of them go down to live in houses on the plain.

Some of the leading men of Ha-no look upon the Snake ceremony with a sneer, but mainly the Ha-no people, and even the Navajos look upon it with respect, and many come long distances to see it.

The second day of my stay in Ha-no was the sixth day of the ceremony, and the fourth and last of the snake hunt, and I was determined to see the Snake-priests come in. I stationed myself on the eastern edge of the mesa, and searched the "world quarter" from whence they were to come. It was after five o'clock before I perceived the first one of the returning priests. He was far on the main mesa, outlined on the sky like a minute brown pin. Down on the plain soon others appeared, small as ants, now seen, now lost behind the rocks. Mysteriously, silently, a score had appeared, and were centring slowly and through devious paths toward the trail.

In the village there was suppressed excitement. The roofs grew thick with people. The word passed along, "The Snake-men are coming!" I hurried back to the narrow point between Walpi and the middle village in order that the men should pass very near me. I wished to study their faces at close range.

Soon they came, a red-brown slow serpent, winding slowly over the trail. They were thirty-three in number. They came in silence, led by Kopeli, the handsome high priest. His beautiful body was a splendid thing to see and his handsome face was grave and reserved. They all had a serious and intent air, and the old men were very weary. Their feet made no noise on the bare rocks. Their naked limbs glowed and glistened, and their splendid hair flowed in dark masses down their backs. All carried snakes in little buckskin bags, which they held in their right hands. The snakes made no noise. As they passed, the people all fell silent, out of respect for the hunters and their great office. At the kiva of the Snakes they laid down their sticks and hoes, and retaining the snake-whips and snake-scripts,[24] disappeared one by one into the cistern-like chamber. It was just sundown; the wearisome hunt for snakes was over for two years — one day to the north, one to [the] west, one to the south, and this to the east.

As I stood watching them enter the kiva an old man on one of the roofs suddenly rose and stood against the sky, and began to call, in a measured voice like a New England town-crier words which meant: "Let all the people of Walpi listen. The Americans are coming to the snake-dance, therefore sweep and clean out the dirt, that we may not be ashamed. The snake-dance is now but three days off. Let everybody prepare."

All along the street of the cliff young women were already raising a dust. The men were returning from the fields with burros laden with juniper branches,

---

[24] No source consulted on the snake ceremony makes any reference to the term *snake-scripts,* which is likely a misspelling of snake-scrips, or sacks, the buckskin bags containing the reptiles, which the snake priests did in fact retain along with their whips.

and also with corn and meat. Old women were toiling slowly up the paths with wood or water on their backs.

As I turned and looked back upon Walpi it was like some city at the end of the world. Out of the narrow, rocky ridge it rose in square piles, bristling with long ladders and peopled with dim alien figures. A purple mist was between it and me; beyond it a sunset sky, built of orange and flame-colored clouds, glowed with dull diffused fire. The great dim shapes of the San Francisco Mountains rose in the west, shadowy, blue, and soft, and over them Venus burned in sudden light.

The town looked time-worn and steadfast as the cliff itself, and as strange as the shadowed side of the moon. In no other place could the mystic rites of the Snake service be. Here it all seemed fitting and proper.

We ate our supper again upon the floor, and then we sat in the plaza, while the light went out in the sky, and the people came out upon the roofs, bringing their blankets to make their beds. The air was soft and cool, without being chill, and in the sky the stars thickened. The soft laughter of girls, the romping of children, continued until nine o'clock; then all voices ceased. Save the dogs'! The dogs — there were millions of them. They tore the air to shreds with their sharp wolfish yelping and howling. Just as the sweet silence was sending us off into sleep, some wakeful pup imagined he smelled a white man, and his yelp brought millions and other millions of yapping whelps to cry out and circle about the plaza before our windows. They wore out at last, and sleep came.

In the white-yellow dawn I heard a clear cry four times repeated. It was the crier in Walpi announcing the Antelope race, which was to take place at sunrise on the east side of the mesa. I dressed hurriedly, and reached the cliff edge in time to see the brown runners start from a point far down in the dim valley and come up the trail to the kiva. Then I went back to a breakfast of bacon and coffee and bread, which I ate on the floor in company with the sculptor and the painter.[25] The village was still quite free from white people, for the dance at the sacred rock was still three days away.

Meanwhile, in the secret underground chambers, mysterious and solemn rites were being carried forward.[26] An emblematic altar was being drawn in colored sand upon the floor of the kiva — a series of intricate symbols which set forth the fundamentals of their religious ideas, and in the Chamber of the Antelopes the story of Tiyo, the tribal Siegfried, was being dramatized. One

---

[25] Garland here again refers to his traveling companions, Hermon Atkins MacNeil and Charles Francis Browne.

[26] Dr. Fewkes, who informed Garland of the secret proceedings, was one of the few white men who had been invited to see the ceremony. (Garland, *Roadside Meetings*, p. 296.) In 1911, former President Theodore Roosevelt also was admitted to the sacred kiva at Walpi. He described his experience as follows: One end of the kiva was raised a foot above the rest. Against the rear wall lay more than thirty rattlesnakes, most of them in a twined heap in the corner. A dozen more lay scattered along the wall. A pot contained several striped ribbon-snakes, too lively to be left at large. Once when a rattlesnake glided within a yard of me, I motioned hastily to the snake-watcher. The watcher calmly extended his snake-whip and guided the reptile back to its position at the end of the kiva. (Theodore Roosevelt, "The Hopi Snake Dance," p. 369.)

of the most mysterious of these ceremonies is the dance of the Bear-man, to the accompaniment of a swift, strong chorus. This takes place with the Antelopes as spectators, and is an impressive and splendid grouping of the devout priests. Of its meaning little is known.

Dr. Fewkes thus describes it. "Kopeli sat at one side of the room muffled in a Navajo blanket, over which was thrown a white buckskin. For some time all present preserved the most profound silence, the Snake-priests holding their whips in a vertical position. Kopeli said a short prayer, after which the rattles were taken up, and for a few moments nothing was heard but the noise of these instruments. As this continued all began to sing, at first in a low mumble, then the voices increased in volume until they broke into a wild song.

"Wiki, who sat near the entrance to the dressing room, threw a pinch of meal across the floor to indicate a pathway for the strange actor, who immediately emerged from behind the screen. . . . He hobbled into the room, assuming a squatting posture, and swaying back and forth like a bear on its hind legs. He wore a great bunch of red feathers on his head and smaller tufts on his shoulders, and his face was covered with paint. . . . He went up to Kopeli in a squatting posture and drew a vine-stalk from under the Snake-chief's blanket. He then went from one to another of the novices, thrusting the stalk in their faces. The wild song continued while he danced back toward the screen and disappeared. He appeared a second time with almost the same actions, save that he drew from bèneath Kopeli's blanket a live snake." During all this time Kopeli sat like a statue, silent and motionless.

In the story of Tiyo,[27] its adventurous youth, is found the reason for the use of snakes in the ceremony. Tiyo (so the tale runs) was a wonderful hunter, who long ago went down the Grand Cañon of the Colorado to the ocean in order to see where the waters ran to. His going was sad and wonderful, his return triumphant. Therefore he is remembered by his people as the Saxons remembered Beowulf. In his long wanderings he was wed to two sisters. The children of the elder wife were turned into snakes. No special reason is assigned — it just happened so. Therefore the Hopi people dramatically continue to call the snakes "elder brothers." Therefore also they go forth with much labor to bring them in to participate in the dance.

There is no snake worship in this: it is doubtful if the snake is considered (by the younger priests) to be other than a beast, but they respect him because he is a part of a story which they love to celebrate. Most of them regard him possibly as a messenger. Generally they avoid killing him, but they do sometimes crush the rattlesnake, I was told by the young men of Ha-no.

In the Antelope kiva, the sixteen weird songs were sung at noon as upon other days, and I sat in the shadows of the house walls to listen to them.

They began on a low, humming key and passed to abrupt upward-leaping cadences; then fell to a deep, stern snarl. A rattle was shaken in time to the first series of eight, but was silent at the beginning of the second series. Between the ending of the first eight songs and the beginning of the series which followed,

---

[27] For similar accounts of the legend, see James, "The Hopi Snake Dance," p. 306, and Townsend, "Snake-Dancers of Mishongnovi," p. 431.

a boy came out, with head held down and eyes squinted as if at sight of a bright light. He was deeply excited by it all, very much oppressed with the responsibility thrust upon him. He was, in fact, the impersonator of Tiyo. Each song ended on a low key, a deep nasal hum, and began again on a higher key. The sounds of the opening were apparently these: *Ha-a-aa-hay-ee. Ha-aa-hay-ee* — passing then to other more complicated phrases.

Suddenly, in the midst of the tenth song, a whizzing, booming sound, like wind and thunder mixed, was heard in the kiva, and an old man came out and gravely swung two whizzers, each made of a flat piece of wood suspended on stout cords. He succeeded in making a sound which undoubtedly typified wind and rain and thunder. In the twelfth song no tapping was heard. In the fourteenth and fifteenth the shaking of the rain rattle began again, ominous, slow, quickening as the song proceeded, becoming slow and solemn again as the series of songs ended on a low, slow, throbbing strain.

The courier, a magnificent young man, emerged, dressed in ceremonial garments and carrying in his hand several *pahos* or prayer sticks. He looked neither to the right nor to the left, but started on a run down the mesa to the north, circled to the south, and so to the east. At the south we saw him running swiftly along the trail to a rock about half a mile from the foot of the mesa. Here he stopped, knelt down, lifted a stone, sprinkled some meal within a cavity, placed the *paho* there, replaced the stone, and remained kneeling in prayer. It was an impressive thing to see this fleet, strong young fellow kneeling there in the sunlight in memory of some ancient of days. He arose, swept like a hawk's shadow round the end of the mesa to the east, placed his third *paho* in the eastern shrine, repeated his prayer, and so to the north. This part of the ceremony is a beautiful and touching one.

For seven successive days this courier is sent out, bearing the prayers of the priests and the personal prayers of those who care to send a private *paho* with him. On the first day his circuit is nearly twenty-five miles in extent. The next day his circuit is a little nearer, until on the seventh day the circuit is within the limits of Walpi itself. The first circuit is outside of all the cultivated fields, and the idea is to toll the rain clouds in upon the fields, each day nearer, until at last they are to cover the town itself.

The courier wears his black hair flowing down over his shoulders, "because the rain clouds wear their tresses so." He makes the wide circuit "in order that the rain clouds which live far away may hear the prayers of the people and come nearer." Then when they have heard the prayers of the people they will certainly not refuse to visit the fields, and so, on the days following, he brings them to the peach orchards, and at last to the slopes of the mesa in order that the springs and the wells may not go dry.

I would not have this man or the priests who send him forth lose faith in the efficacy of his prayers. Certainly it is all beautiful and not more absurd or artificial than many of the customs and ceremonies of more civilized peoples.

The morning of the eighth day grew to a beautiful, happy, sunny, and breezy forenoon, like a September day in Iowa. The men did not go to work as usual. The women were very busy making *piki* (a sort of blue bread, thin as tissue paper) and making stews and bringing fruit from the storehouses. They built fires in the ovens, and spread the thin dough over a flat piece of stone which served as baking-pan. In this way great sheets of thin, crackling bread were baked and piled high on the floor inside of every kiva. They came into my room with armfuls of this pastry rolled into long sticks and corded up like cob houses, which they stacked away in the inner room, ready to be carried to the feast at sundown.

The children put on their school clothes. The women were all freshly washed, their heads glistening, their hair nicely dressed. The children went about eating boiled corn in celebration of the day. A roaring wind swept up from the south, swirling sand and the smoke from the fire-pots round the rocks.

On the plaza in Walpi a *kisi,* or sacred tent of cottonwood boughs had been built, and before it an oblong hole was being dug by the men. After it was almost two feet deep, a board was set in. Then a couple of stones and a second board, the latter being covered with dirt, was made level with the ground. In the *kisi* were placed corn and vines and rushes. The *kisi* was bound with a canvas sheet. Anciently a buffalo skin was used for this purpose.

At about a quarter to six the Antelope-priests came out in procession from their kiva and passed four times around the plaza, singing as they marched. They were fifteen in number, including two little children. Each man, as he passed the board[28] set in the ground, stamped upon it with vigorous action, and the little novices cunningly did the same. They were dressed in archaic ceremonial garments and carried rattles. At the end of the fourth circuit they ranged themselves on each side of the *kisi,* still continuing their low singing. The Snake-priests now came in, thirty-three in number, and also circled four times around the plaza, stamping hard upon the board as they passed. They then lined up before the Antelope-priests, and facing each other thus, the Snakes kept time with their rattles to the singing of the Antelopes.

The song, though without special passion, was strong and manly, with many deep falling cadences. It had the movement of a march. During this part of the ceremony I could not but feel the dignity and earnestness of the whole scene. The Snake-priests shook their whips in quivering action in time to the rattles, and stamped with the right foot. Suddenly the asperger stood before the *kisi* and flung some mysterious liquid to the four cardinal points. Then Kopeli and the priest who stood next him locked arms and approached the *kisi.* They stooped, and when they rose Kopeli carried in his mouth a stalk of corn. Thus they danced forward and back before the *kisi.* Kopeli dropped the corn, and changing places with his Antelope companion, once again danced before the *kisi,* the Antelope holding a vine in his mouth. Meanwhile the Antelopes continued their song.

After passing several times before the *kisi* in this way, the two priests returned to the head of the line, the Antelopes sang another song, and the

---

[28] Townsend also renders this description the same. He wrote: "In front of the Kisi a piece of board was set into the ground, and this board was the door to a hollow place beneath, which symbolised Shipapu, the mysterious abode of the spirits of their ancestors. Up to the door of Shipapu slowly pranced the Antelopes, men and boys ... And as each one in his turn came to the door of the spirit world he raised his right foot and stamped loud and hard upon the board. It was a call, a summons to the spirits to bid them attend." (Townsend, "The Snake-Dancers of Mishongnovi," p. 435.)

Garland recorded a detailed description of this part of the Walpi snake ceremonial. At the far right stands the cottonwood-bough tent called the kisi, *where the snakes were kept. The men are working on the board-covered hole to be stamped upon during the ritual.*

Snakes rapidly circled the plaza, striking the board as before, and after the fourth circuit passed out and entered the kiva. The line of Antelopes, still singing and shaking their rattles, made the circuit of the plaza and also passed out, leaving the old man with the whizzer to follow.

This is the corn dance which always precedes the snake dance. When one comes to understand the significance of all these little ceremonies they grow more and more pathetic. Corn meal is their sacred offering. Cottonwood-trees are precious in their eyes because they belong to the watercourses. So turtle-shells and water-worn roots of trees or stones are kept as if sacred. The need of water is ever present with these people, and their ceremonies all pray for rain upon their corn and vines. The decorations upon many of their garments and utensils are made up of conventional symbols representing rain clouds, falling rain, and lightning.

Early in the morning of the ninth day an Indian boy looked in at my window and said, "Better get up; mans go run; much mans."

When I came out into the trail on the bare ledge between Walpi and the two other villages, the landscape was ablaze with rose-pink, purple, and yellow-green; the ledge was like the prow of a ship sailing in a sea of glorious color. Young girls in gay shawls and fresh clean blue-black skirts were filing down the steep paths to the north of Walpi. They were accompanied by little boys, naked, and painted, like the Snake chiefs, in symbolic designs. Some of the lads carried cornstalks of delicious greenness; others bore melons and flowers. The girls were empty-handed.

I scrambled down the trail, which wound among huge rocks of sandstone that in some far time had tumbled from the cliff. At one point it dropped through a chimneylike crevice and came out at last on low rocky hills covered sparsely with greasewood and skunk-weed.

On either side of the trail the young people were drawn up, the little lads shivering and excited, the girls chattering among themselves. The girls wore their hair either drawn forward over the forehead in a peculiar horn, or flowing loosely down their backs. None of them wore it as on days before — in side whorls.

There came past me a magnificent youth of about eighteen years of age, naked with the exception of moccasins and a decorated loincloth. He was one of my neighbors in Ha-no. He recognized me with a smile, though I could not be sure I recognized him in the midst of his paint and finery. He wore bracelets of willow twigs about his arms, was painted with clay, and carried a bell at his belt. He also carried in one hand a splendid squash flower, and in the dark hair of his forehead a wild sunflower shone like a golden star, magnificently decorative in effect.

The shivering lads were jumping to warm themselves as I came up. The sun had risen and had struck across the beautifully mottled valley floor, and had lighted into burning gold the second mesa, Mashongnavi, but it had not yet taken the chill from the air. Above on the high cliff, looking like swarming midgets, the villagers and their visitors were assembled. Their chatter could be heard faintly.

A long, echoing, musical cry arose. It was the man at the goal announcing the coming of the racers. The lads sprang up. The girls laughingly ranged themselves along the trail. As the runners came, uttering joyous cries, their brown bodies shining, their long hair flowing, the maidens sprang before them in the trail and sought to wrest from them the corn branches which they bore. The runners dodged in the effort to escape, until a favorite maiden met them, whereupon they allowed themselves to be robbed, notwithstanding their struggles and apparently fierce outcries, sped on empty-handed up the precipitous trail.

They came in a long, straggling file, nearly forty of them. They had rushed four miles at top speed, but they mounted the trail toward Walpi with incredible celerity. As they passed me their long hair waved up at the sides in a peculiar and beautiful fringe. I have never seen anything finer in the way of motion. As they reached the summit other shouts arose, for other maidens were waiting to set upon those who still bore their corn stalks in triumph.

The laughter died away; the crowd scattered; the slower runners crawled up the path, bringing up the rear; the maidens from Ha-no, with backward glances, made off toward the north, bearing the trophies they had wrested from the young men.

There was something superb in all this — something natural, strong, and wholesome. The bodies of the racers had the rich coloring of bronze lit by flame. They ran with the chest thrown out and with a light step, which only three hundred years of daily climbing to and fro on this cliff could give. It was like seeing one of the old Greek games. There must also be some special meaning in the action of the maidens in snatching the corn from the runners. Perhaps, as in the old Roman games, it was an earnest of fertility and prosperity.

Up at the kiva, in the middle of the day, the wonderful ceremony of washing the snakes took place. This ceremony is the most secret and sacred of all. It has been witnessed by few white men.[29] It was impossible, therefore, for me to do more than to sit near the kiva and to hear the singing and the wild shouts accompanying it.

The ceremony began with the low sound of rattles, then a low, guttural chant arose — a peculiar, nasal, booming chant. The words of this song, as of many others in the ceremony, are archaic; their meaning is not known even to the singers. At times there came a pause, during which the rattle made a sound like the patter of rain or hail falling on dry leaves. Then the voice of an old man sounded alone, in a high, weird cadence; then all the voices together, with one voice reciting in the midst of it. At intervals the song rose to a deep, wild outburst, followed by fierce shrill yells like the yelp of a pack of wolves. It was at this point, as Dr. Fewkes informed me, that the snakes, caught up by the naked hands of the priests, were dipped into the medicine bowl and hurled upon the dry sand of the altar.

After each outburst the music sank again to the low guttural chant. Within, Dr. Fewkes sat among the shouting and singing priests, watching nearly a hundred snakes as they were hurled across the sand altar, or as they writhed and coiled in the hands of these wonderful men. This is perhaps the most complete survival of the olden days to be found among American Indians.

A solemn voice recited a prayer. Then the singing began again and died to a low murmur, and the continuous soft shaking of the rattle announced the completion of this ceremony, more wonderful even than the public dance with the snakes on the plaza. When all was silent below, an old man came up from the kiva holding a bowl in his left hand and a bear's foot in the other. He dipped the bear claws into the bowl and sprinkled the four quarters of the globe.

Over beyond, the plain lay with its warm, russet grass, its deep blue peaceful hills, and the tender sky was filled with white and rose-purple clouds. Below men sat to mix this strange potion in the dark, in the reek of the effluvia from a hundred reptiles. Such is the power of the past over men. Dr. Fewkes came up a little later bearing the marks of clay upon his face, which they had given him in token of their acceptance of him among their order. He told me that they handled the snakes with perfect freedom and with seeming carelessness, though many of the snakes were rattlesnakes.

And yet, sitting there, with those strange flat-topped houses round me, with naked brown men coming and going, it all seemed natural and historical — a fact in the midst of the town and the people. All about, the children

---

[29] One such man was Roosevelt. His description is one of few accounts of the snake washing ceremony and, therefore, is valuable. Too detailed to be quoted here, it can be found in Roosevelt, "The Hopi Snake Dance," pp. 371–372.

romped with apparently small regard for the priests or the snake terror; and yet it was noticed they did not disobey the command of the priests to keep away from the roof of the Snake chamber.

At five o'clock the plaza surrounding the sacred rock was heaped and piled with people. There were representatives from the other six villages; there were cowboys from southern Colorado and from Holbrook; there were Navajos from the great reservation to the east; there were reporters for Eastern papers; there were scientists from Boston, New York, and Chicago; there were teachers from the Moki school at Keams Cañon.

Upon every cornice, every roof, every adobe balcony, the Mokis themselves were gathered, attired in the most brilliant and the quaintest costumes. The building rising against the deep blue cloudless sky covered with these barbaric colors, made a picture worthy the brush of the finest artist. As a painter said, "It was a Salon picture." Nothing can be compared with it except possibly the final feast of Holy Week in some interior Mexican town. The white people laughed, the dogs and children made tumult, while the crowd waited patiently the incoming of the Snake-men. Below on the valley floor the cloud shadows floated like boats on a yellow sea.

As I stood near the *kisi* of cottonwood boughs a man passed me with a bag containing something heavy; for an instant I could not realize that the bag contained snakes; he handled it as if it contained sand, and the reptiles made no noise. So matter of fact were his actions, few observed his entrance. I returned to the kiva and waited the coming of the priests. Two children emerged first from the Antelope kiva, little tots hardly more than five or six years of age, striped like their elders with kaoline, with little chins whitened and foreheads blackened, with string of beads looped about their necks and rattles in their hands. The little fellows ranged themselves up near the corner of the nearest house and waited the coming of their elders. It was wonderful to see with what dignity these chubby little babes bore themselves. They did not allow themselves to smile nor to notice the other youngsters about them.

The asperger came next, an old man carrying a bowl of charm liquid. While the rest climbed out behind him, he busied himself in sprinkling the way to the Snake kiva; the other Antelopes following scattered from their right hand a pinch of meal into the open door of the Snake kiva. The rear was brought up by the whizzer, an old man dressed in completely archaic costume, carrying two small pieces of board attached to strings. These he whirled sharply, making a sound resembling thunder and wind.

After they had all passed through the narrow street out upon the plaza, the Snake-priests came up from below. They took down the sign[30] which hung upon the ladder, and which was always present during the last four days of their occupancy of the kiva, and slowly formed into line. Each man had the upper part of his face blackened and the lower part of the face whitened. Each

---

[30] This sign, the "natchi," consisting of two eagle-wing feathers tied to a short stick, was placed in some matting at the hatchway of the kiva. The sign was effective in keeping the superstitious, yet curious, Hopi youth away from the sacred kiva. (James, "The Hopi Snake Dance," p. 304.) Roosevelt stated that on the ladder leading to the entranceway hung a cord from which fluttered three eagle plumes and three small animal skins. (Roosevelt, "The Hopi Snake Dance," p. 369.)

carried a bunch of eagle feathers in his hair, and from his belt behind streamed the complete skin of a fox. Each wore a short cotton kilt, ornamented with a figure of the Great Plumed Serpent. Many of them, if not all of them, wore upon the right leg a small turtle shell rattle. Their whole dress was splendidly barbaric, and their faces were very intent, almost solemn. There was, however, no sign of abnormal excitement. They talked among themselves in low tones, and ranged themselves in line. There were no signs of hypnotism, and no sign of the strain under which they had been laboring for nine successive days.

At a signal from the leader, Kopeli, they entered the plaza in single file, on a rapid walk, and after circling the plaza, ranged themselves in a slightly curved line before the tent of cottonwood boughs in which the snakes were placed, and on each side of which the fifteen Antelope-priests stood in line singing a wild and guttural chant. It was almost a repetition of the corn-dance of the day before.

Standing thus, the Snake chiefs took their snake-whips with a peculiar quivering action, in time to the rattles and the chanting of the Antelopes, stamping also with the right foot. The whole line swayed rhythmically as they rose and fell in this measured step from the right foot to the left. The song changed to a deep, musical, humming sound; the asperger stood before the *kisi* asperging to the cardinal points. The Snake-men did not sing at any time.

A wilder hum arose, a portentous, guttural, snarling sound, which passed soon to a strong, manly, marching chant, full of sudden deepfalling, stern cadences. Then Kopeli, the Snake chief, and the one second to him joined arms and danced slowly down before the *kisi*. They stopped, and when they rose Kopeli held in his mouth a snake. His companion[31] placed his left arm over the Snake chief's shoulders, and together they turned, circling to the left. The snake hung quietly from the Snake-priest's mouth.[32] It was held at about nine inches from the head. Behind him walked the third man, the snake-gatherer.[33] They passed with a quick, strong step, one might almost say with a lope, in time to the singing.

Immediately behind came another group, the snake-carrier holding an entire snake in his mouth, the head protruding about an inch. These two were

---

[31] This person was called the "hugger," whose duty was to stroke the snake's head with the snake-whip to keep the snake from striking the carrier's face and eyes. (Townsend, "The Snake-Dancers of Mishongnovi," p. 436.)

[32] In his notes, Garland says that the priests whispered messages for the snakes to take to the supernatural gods of the underworld while they held the snakes in their mouths during the dance on the plaza. (Hamlin Garland, "Walpi," n. p.) While visiting First Mesa in 1881, Bourke picked up a piece of "medicine," which the snake priests chewed before carrying the snakes around the plaza. He thought the "medicine" was pure clay, creamy-white in color and even in texture. He said that the clay was not chewed as an antidote for venom, but rather it seemed to fill the mouth and the angles of the teeth. Thus, when snakes were grasped in the priest's mouth, the danger of irritating the reptiles would be minimized. (Bourke, *The Snake-Dance of the Moquis of Arizona,* p. 146.)

[33] The gatherer followed the carrier and the hugger and caught each snake after it had been carried around the plaza and dropped to the ground at a certain spot. The gatherer stroked the snake in an effort to get the snake to uncoil and to attempt an escape. At that moment he could catch the snake easily. The gatherer continued to catch the snakes until his hands were full. (Townsend, "The Snake-Dancers of Mishongnovi," pp. 436–437.)

followed by a third man, the snake-gatherer; and soon the entire line of thirty-three Snake priests had broken into eleven groups and were circling the plaza, one man in each group carrying from one to three snakes in his mouth. The singing continued, stern and swift like a strong stream, and although at times the dancers lost step to the music, in general they may be said to have retained throughout all the rush of movement a tolerable accuracy of rhythm. A group of women stood near and threw sacred meal upon the men as they passed. They kept far from contact, I observed. The excitement of the spectators increased. I pushed close to the circle of dancing priests to study their faces.[34]

One man passed with an enormous bull snake in his mouth. Its tail hung down to his knee. Each snake carrier danced with his eyes closed and his chin thrust forward. The reasons for this were obvious. The little snakes were the most vicious, and struck repeatedly at the eyes and cheeks of the priests. Several of them seized upon the skin, and held on until brushed away by the whip of the "hugger." In every case which I observed the rattlesnakes hung peaceful, and without any action whatever, from the mouths of the dancers, and only struck or coiled to strike after falling upon the bare rock. Their coats seemed dry and dusty.[35]

One man went by with two large rattlesnakes in his mouth. Another held a rattlesnake and two larger bull snakes between his lips; and a third priest, to silence all questions of his superiority, crowded into his mouth four snakes! The gatherer who followed him held in the fingers of his left hand six or eight snakes, strung like pieces of rope. In fact, they all handled the snakes precisely as if they were skeins of yarn, with the single exception of the moment when they snatched them from the ground.

Once or twice there was a brief struggle between the snake-gatherer and the fallen snake. In every case which I observed, the snake-gatherer brushed the snake with the feathers of his snake whip until he uncoiled and straightened out to run. After the gatherer picked him up he was as helpless as if dead.

As the dance went on, the excitement grew. The clink of metal fringes and the patter of rattles filled the ear. The snakes dashed into the crowd, shouts and screams and laughter rose, but the wary snake-gatherer in every case caught the snake before it passed out of reach. In one or two instances when a rattlesnake ran toward the women with their basket plaques of meal, they broke into wild screams and ran. Evidently they feared the rattlesnakes quite as much as any of the white women. At last, so deep was my interest to see, I lost all sense of hearing. They all moved like figures in a dream.

During all this time, whatever the outcries among the spectators, whatever the screams or laughter among the women with the meal, the Snake-priests, intent and grave, showed no trace whatever of excitement. It is absurd to speak of hypnotism or frenzy of any kind. They were not in the slightest degree moved either to fear or laughter, or even to the point of being hastened or retarded by the presence of the white man. They had a religious duty to per-

---

[34] Garland describes the stern and serious faces of the snake priests in *Roadside Meetings,* pp. 296–297.

[35] The snakes were dusty, probably because a short time prior to the actual dance on the plaza they had been washed in the sacred water and hurled across the kiva to the floor of the altar. (Roosevelt, "The Hopi Snake Dance," pp. 371–372.)

form, and they were carrying it forward, intent, masterful, solemn, and perfectly silent. Incredible, thrilling, savage, and dangerous as it appeared to us, to them it was a world-old religious ceremonial.

At last, when all the snakes had been carried, and when each snake-gatherer held in his hand huge bundles of the apparently inert serpents, the Antelopes and the snake-gatherers formed a swift circle. As they waited, Kopeli drew a circle of meal upon the ground, and all the snakes were thrown in a tangled writhing heap within this circle. Then the women rushed timorously forward and scattered meal over the writhing mass. Then, most wonderful of all, before the swiftest serpent could escape, the priests snatched them up in handfuls, and started with them down the sides of the mesa. In an incredibly short time every snake had been whipped from the ground and was in the hands of these runners. Each man carried from eight to twelve, indiscriminately snatched up. This whole action of heaping the snakes within the circle, covering them with meal, and snatching them up again was all done in the space of a few seconds.

The snakes, "the elder brothers," had taken part in the dance, their heads had been sprinkled with meal, the prayers to the gods had been whispered to them: they were now to return to the fields to carry the messages of the Snake-priests to the gods of rain and of plenty.[36]

Down the southern side of the mesa I stood to watch two of these marvelous runners. They ran with the speed of goats down the precipitous slopes and out over the sandy foothills. At a distance possibly of half a mile from the foot of the mesa, under a huge rock, they knelt down, uttered a little prayer, and released the snakes. In returning they mounted the steep paths with almost undiminished speed. Other runners went to the east, to the south, and to the west. In twenty minutes from the time the Snake-priests had ranged themselves before the *kisi,* a hundred snakes, half of them rattlesnakes, had been carried around the plaza, recovered by the snake-gatherers, thrown into a heap, sprinkled with meal, snatched up by eight men, and carried back to the open country. During this time no one had been bitten,[37] no smallest snake had escaped in the crowd which closely crowded upon the Snake-priests, and, so far as could be told, no ill thing had occurred. This was the climax of the incredible, and I could not believe it had I not witnessed it. As I look back upon it, it is akin to the sense-defying action of dreams.

Meanwhile the Antelopes had calmly finished their singing and had marched back to the Antelope kiva. The remaining Snake-priests had also

---

[36] Roosevelt gives a similar rendering of the proceedings of the snake dance on the plaza and of returning the snakes to the desert below the mesa. (Roosevelt, "The Hopi Snake Dance," pp. 371–372.)

[37] Townsend stated that the priests drank an herbal solution which served as an antidote to venom. (Townsend, "The Snake-Dancers of Mishongnovi," pp. 432–433.) Roosevelt offered other explanations. First, he stated that the bites of desert rattlesnakes were usually not fatal, as were those of the huge diamondbacks. In answer to those who claimed that the fangs were removed, Roosevelt noted that even if this were so the dangerous venom still would be loose in the rattlers' mouths. The former president also noted that some persons asserted that the snakes were drugged, and one priest even told him that the snakes had been given medicine. Roosevelt did not know for sure if this were so, but he did believe that the priests either naturally possessed or had developed the same calming power over snakes that certain people have over bees. (Roosevelt, "The Hopi Snake Dance," p. 373.)

retired to their kiva, and were divesting themselves of their snake-whips and rattles, and other removable parts of their regalia.

There now occurred a singular scene on the north side of the village, on the edge of the cliff. This was the vomiting of the priests.[38] It has been called a ludicrous sight; certainly it is an unusual thing to see thirty men drinking an emetic at the same moment. But I felt little inclination to laugh, for it showed how severe had been the strain upon the devotees. It was no joke. They had been fasting for thirty-six hours. They had been forced to live for five or six days with a hundred snakes in a close underground chamber. They had held the writhing bodies of from five to twelve snakes in their mouths. They may have been bitten by the snakes. Whatever the purpose of this retching, certainly it was a grim and heroic treatment. They passed through it with so much of dignity as any man may. They make no talk among themselves or to those standing about. As in all the other ceremonies, they were composed, serious, and intent.

This, however, was the final and severest part of the ceremony. They were now permitted to drink copiously of clean water. They also immediately unbent. They smiled and greeted their acquaintances standing about. And now a pretty custom intervened. There came into their group five or six young girls, daughters and sweethearts, we may suppose, to help the priests wash the paint from their bodies. It added a fine touch of clean, sane domesticity to the scene. The girls had no sense of false shame. They laughed and chatted as they splashed the water over the glistening brown bodies of the men. It would be impossible to see elsewhere in America another such scene. It humanized these people. It took away all feeling of savagery from these men. They were priests. They were performing in a traditional ceremony. The ceremony itself had in it something of the barbarity of the olden time, but their pleasant and smiling faces as they received water from the hands of their women had no trace of ferocity left.

The fitting close to this remarkable and in many respects beautiful drama and religious ceremony was the procession of women bearing gifts of bread and meats to the kiva. They came with seriousness and reverence, carrying in their uplifted hands steaming stews, piles of blue piki bread, and golden mush. This disappeared down the kiva mouth, enough provision to last a hundred men a week. As it was passed down, the name of the donor of each basket or basin was called out. The scene reminded me of a "donation party" in School District No. 7.

It took away all the horror and much of the grimness of the snake-dance to see the smiling priests surrounded by these gentle women and their fragrant loaves and stews. The observer who rides up to the mesa at five o'clock to see the snake dance, and after it is over rides back and away, carries with him an absolutely false idea of this dance and of these men. We who had lived with them in the village, and who met them after the war-paint was washed from their faces, know them for what they are — a pleasant, laughter-loving, simple-minded, and peaceful people.

---

[38] This scene is rendered similarly in James, "The Hopi Snake Dance," p. 310.

Even the dance itself to me was neither disgusting nor in any way unduly exciting. It proceeded as a matter of course, and not in a frenzy. I admired their skill, and I had no fear of results. When they threw the snakes in the swarming heap I stood within two paces of them, feeling not the slightest doubt but that every snake would be secured, and that the priests would carry them back safely to the plain. For had they not been doing this for a thousand years? And had not the skill been transmitted from father to son with the same absolute certainty which marks the action of the eagle or the panther?

In the evening the air rang with merry shouts as the young maidens carried forward the game which was now to continue for three days — that is, the capture from the young men of whatever piece of calico or melon or pottery they might carry. It rounded out and completed the day. It made an idyl of the ceremony. It was, indeed, the poetry, and the drama, and the history, and the religious tradition of this people.[39] The right interpretation of this peculiar ceremony will not leave out its solemn and beautiful and tender phases. It was impressive, it was exciting, but it was not revolting at any point.

Originally a prayer for rain, it has come at length to include something of drama, of story, and by allegory contains hints of the wanderings of the people hundreds of years ago. It is also a festival and a time of smiling for these patient souls, to whom water is more precious than pearls, and green leaves beyond beaten gold. There is no reason why the snake dance should be interfered with or condemned.[40]

The night came, soft and radiant, filled with the laughter of girls, the shouts of the young racers, the hum of neighborly talk upon the roof-tops. A little later groups of young Navajos, encamped high on the houses, began a mysterious singing, wherein the voices of wolves and owls and wild-cats intermingled; in their silent intervals young Hopi singers replied in sweet, quavering, timorous song. At ten o'clock the town was quiet, and overhead myriads of stars flamed in majesty.

There are few unpleasant recollections of Walpi Mesa and its brave and cheerful people.

---

[39] Townsend's companion was a churchman who argued with the Indian agent regarding the importance of the snake dances. He said: "If you break up these dances of the Indians you destroy what never can be replaced. . . . It is of immense importance to us to have them to compare with primitive religions in the rest of the world. It is only within the last quarter of a century that their value has been understood, and the scientific method applied to their study. But civilisation has destroyed them over the greater part of this continent . . . ; the few that still survive are inestimable treasures." (Townsend, "The Snake-Dancers of Mishongnovi," p. 441.)

[40] The Indian agent in 1904 set forth an attitude typical of that of many governmental officials at that time: ". . . these people have souls, and to my mind it matters a million times more to preserve their souls from hell fire than to stock your museums with some miserable relics of heathendom. These things that they do are straight-out devil-worship, and the men who do them are heathens living in sin. . . . And the older Indians utilise them to draw the young ones into their net. Once they go into the dances we can do nothing with them. The only hope for them is that they shall be taught English at school while they are small, and then taken away and brought up in boarding-schools, absolutely apart from the vicious influences of the pueblo. . . ." (Townsend, "The Snake-Dancers of Mishongnovi," pp. 441–442.)

Background

The Zuni pueblo Garland visited in *1895* was the only permanent settlement remaining of what was once a complex of seven flourishing pueblos. These were what Coronado was led to believe were the Seven Cities of Cíbola. The pueblo was first called Zuni by Antonio de Espejo, who visited them in *1583*. By that time the Zuni were occupying only six pueblos. The first mission to the Zuni was established in *1629*, and one existed there, intermittently, from then until the nineteenth century.

The Zuni participated in the Pueblo rebellion of *1680*. At that time they occupied only three towns: *Halona, Matsaki,* and *Kiakima.* The Zuni killed their priest and fled to their stronghold on *Taaiyolone,* where they stayed until New Mexico was recaptured in *1692.* By that time the pueblos had fallen into ruin. At the site of Halona, on the north side of the Zuni River, they built a new pueblo, the one Garland visited in *1895.* A church was built there in *1699,* and the pueblo was the site of a Spanish garrison for a brief time in the early eighteenth century. The church was allowed to fall into ruin, the priests visiting it only occasionally. When the Southwest became the possession of the U.S., the Zuni had been abandoned and remained so for several years thereafter. When missionaries returned to the Zuni, they had little success.[1]

Once more, in describing his experiences at Zuni, Garland is aware of the economic stress which this group of people were experiencing as a result of the previous year's drought. Their extreme poverty touched the writer deeply, and he bitterly attacks those whites who would rob Zunis of their land and buy from them, for a mere pittance, their last treasured possession. He also attacks those who idly watched the Indians suffer and those who lied to them. Garland's comments in this respect have grown more caustic as his journey has progressed, as he has gained first-hand experience of the result of Indian-white relations.

The essay suffers from a lack of detail when compared to some of the others Garland produced at the time. That is probably due to the absence of the Indians and the writer's subsequent lack of subjects to observe.

---

[1] Frederick Webb Hodge, ed., *Handbook of American Indians North of Mexico*, Pt. 2, pp. 1016–1018.

5. A Day at Zuni[2]

Zuni is not the inaccessible place it was when Frank Cushing[3] first wrote of it. It lies forty miles south of Gallup, a small town on the Santa Fe Route — an easy day's drive.

The road rises steadily for the first fifteen miles and leaves behind the dry hills and barren soil with the lower altitudes. At an elevation of about eight thousand feet the trail enters upon a superb region of pine forest, glorious in August with wild asters, sunflowers, gramma grass and wild oats. The rains had been abundant and the whole plateau was deliciously green and fragrant — a marked contrast to the hot sand of the road to Walpi. At about four o'clock we began to descend. Buttes thickened round us and the swales became sandy washes.

A thunder storm was crashing round Zuni as we came in sight of it, a small yellow-brown mound in the center of a wide valley. Coming fresh from Walpi with its rugged walls and precipitous trails, my first glimpse of Zuni was a disappointment. Then, too, Cushing had left such an impression on my mind of its remoteness and inaccessibility. I was scarcely able for the moment to believe that this village in the valley was really the scene of his exciting discoveries.

We passed by a ruined town on the right[4] and farther on a high mesa

---

[2] Item 436, Hamlin Garland Collection, University of Southern California Library, Los Angeles, published by permission of the University of Southern California Library and Constance Garland Doyle and Isabel Garland Lord.

[3] Ethnologist Frank H. Cushing (1850–1900) represented the National Museum on an 1879 expedition to New Mexico. He remained there for three years, living as a Zuni and studying these Indians' habits, history, and language. In 1882, Cushing accompanied a party of Zuni headmen to the Atlantic coast to secure water from the "Ocean of Sunrise," thus promoting universal interest in the Zuni. Later he translated and recorded the Zuni myths and legends. As head of the Hemenway Southwestern Archaeological Expedition, the ethnologist excavated many long-buried Zuni cities, then undertook fieldwork which uncovered the remains of the "Seven Cities of Cíbola." (*The National Cyclopaedia of American Biography*, 11: 26–27.)

[4] Garland here refers to the site of the old pueblo of Halona, which fell into decay during the Pueblo Revolt in 1680. After the reconquest, it was rebuilt and all of the Zuni concentrated there. (Stanley A. Stubbs, *Bird's-Eye View of the Pueblos*, p. 91.)

almost as inaccessible as the enchanted mesa at Acoma was pointed out to me as the site of ancient Zuni.[5] In fact this whole land from Zuni to Socorro is full of these dead cities. While it is probably true that there never was an immense number of people living in any of the valleys, still one can but feel that a busy and numerous population has been at work here for centuries struggling against drouth and savage neighbors, patient, primitive.

As we approached the town it looked silent, deserted. There were few people or animals to be seen. No thickly moving figures on the roof tops as at Acoma.

Unlike Walpi, Zuni sits beside a shallow river,[6] which crawls silently over the sand like a flattened serpent. We crossed this stream and drew up at a long low building built of stone — conforming in general type to the pueblo architecture. This was the Hemenway headquarters wherein Cushing and his successors lived and worked during their studies and excavations.[7]

It is occupied at present by Mr. D. D. Graham, the trader,[8] who welcomed us at the door and made us comfortable for the night. The thunderstorm boomed around the cliffs but did not cover the village, and the sun sank in the most gorgeous and splendid illumination of clouds.

Mr. Graham explained to us the condition of affairs. The people were all at their summer villages in Nutria, Ojo Caliente and elsewhere,[9] and only a few of the women and half a dozen old men remained in the town. He walked with us over to the village after supper and showed us the doors sealed up and the windows plastered over, closed as if for a lifetime.

The bridge which crosses the river is a primitive affair at best, and the city council[10] had taken the planks up for fear they [the planks] might get washed away during their absence, and it was rather skittish crossing. I saw several women come down to the bank, roll up their leggings and wade across rather than trust to the bridge. I do not imagine a Walpi babe would have troubled himself that far, but the Zunis are no longer cliff dwellers.

---

[5] Cushing, testifying on April 19, 1880, about the site of the old pueblo of Zuni, said the location was on a high table land, three miles in a southeasterly direction from the modern village of Zuni. (*Ind. Commiss. Annual Reports, 1898*, pp. 93–94.)

[6] This was the Zuni River.

[7] The Hemenway Southwestern Archaeological Expedition was generally acclaimed by ethnologists who sought to preserve the antiquity of the American Indian. There were governmental Indian agents, however, who criticized Cushing. One stated, "He [Cushing] was an evil influence among them; he encouraged them to go on in their wickedness. There is no tribe of the pueblos today where witchcraft and killing for witchcraft, and all the rest of its attendant evils, are so rampant as in Zuni ... that is Mr. Cushing's work." (R. B. Townsend, "Snake-Dancers of the Mishongnovi," p. 442.)

[8] Douglas D. Graham opened a trading store at Zuni in March, 1881, and sold out in 1898. (Frank McNitt, *The Indian Traders*, p. 240.)

[9] For example, Pescado and Tekapo.

[10] The Spanish called early for the appointment of civil officers in each pueblo. These various officers' duties were to represent the pueblo when dealing with outside authority, to assist the governor and to act in his absence, to maintain law and order, to assist the priests, to maintain discipline in the mission, to act as ditch superintendents, and to provide warriors to go against Indian enemies and to lead them in the field. This basic governmental organization has persisted in most pueblos. (Edward P. Dozier, *The Pueblo Indians of North America*, pp. 189–190.)

The village as it stands covers about ten acres and is built in the usual manner of a pueblo, one story above another, the roof of one serving as the door yard of the one above, etc.[11] There is a little plaza and a ruined church[12] near it and a minute grave yard where the people are buried so thickly, every burial exhumes a half dozen others. The men lie all on one side, the women on the other.[13]

One curious development which I did not see at the other pueblos was the plot of tiny gardens south of the buildings.[14] Each little garden was surrounded by a mud wall and was laid out in little square beds a foot or two in diameter, each bed with a tiny dike around it. These gardens of onions, chile and beans were watered by the women who carried water from the river on their heads in great jars. There were dozens of these little toy gardens lying wall to wall, each carefully closed up with a gate made of sticks and cobblestones, an elaborate contrivance which must take a half an hour's time to put up or let down.

"They're an industrious people," said the trader. "Of course they cling to old manners and tools, and yet they are ready to improve. There is a gradual use of American tools.[15] We have a blacksmith and wagon-maker here — a native, oh, yes, he's a Zuni."

Mr. Graham speaks their language fluently and knows them intimately. He was here before Cushing. As the dusk fell on the pleasant green and yellow plain and the turkeys gobbled about us, he told us many things of the people and their ways.

"They are sun worshippers," he said. "Sometimes I see them as they come out to sprinkle meal at sunrise. They come and pray to the water at night and scatter meal upon it. They are a curious people — no doubt of that. See that little heap of stones just beyond my barn? — that was put there to mark the center of the world."[16]

---

[11] At one time the houses of Zuni may have risen to a height of five stories around a central plaza. (Stubbs, *Bird's-Eye View of the Pueblos*, p. 91.) When Garland saw Zuni the houses were probably not more than two stories high. The site of Zuni appeared higher than it actually was because the village was built over the ruins of the former pueblo.

[12] The mission was established in 1699 and completed in 1705. It had a precarious existence for the next century and was abandoned when the Franciscans were expelled from New Mexico in 1823. The Americans did not begin efforts to Christianize the Zuni until the 1870s. The Zunis were the least affected by Christianity of all the Pueblo Indians. (Earle R. Forrest, *Missions and Pueblos of the Old Southwest*, p. 184.)

[13] In early times the dead were cremated and their ashes thrown into the river, but later they were buried in the churchyard with their heads to the east. (Fred Eggan, *Social Organization of the Western Pueblos*, p. 159.)

[14] The stone-walled garden plots, so distinctive of this pueblo, were laid out to the west and southeast of the old section of the pueblo. (Stubbs, *Bird's-Eye View of the Pueblos*, p. 94.)

[15] These Indians were self-supporting, the government issuing only the "deserving" Indians articles of husbandry and tools, such as farming implements and fence wire. (*Ind. Commiss. Annual Report, 1894*, p. 210; *Ind. Commiss. Annual Report*, 1895, p. 220.)

[16] The most sacred shrine in Zuni was *Hep-ah-teen-ah,* the "Center of the Earth." It was a hole in the ground covered by a pile of stones, just southeast of the pueblo. According to Zuni legend, the Zuni people came upon the earth through this hole, long, long ago. (Forrest, *Missions and Pueblos of the Old Southwest*, p. 187.)

"That's primitive enough, I'm sure. Oh, I don't know. There are a hundred towns that think they are the center of the earth.[17] The psychology of the Zuni isn't so widely different from that of the theologian who thinks the earth and its people the special care of the creator. To the physical eye the earth is the center of the solar system."

The doctor[18] asked, "Are they increasing in numbers?"[19]

"I think they are — very slowly though."

"Is there much sickness among them?"

"Not much — less than you would expect. Lack of food and bad ventilation are their chief enemies. They're pretty good doctors. They keep pretty close to the hot rock and herb treatment. I think in spite of all they hold their own."

At supper that night we were waited on by a stalwart man with dark skin and black mustache. We took him for Mexican but Mr. Graham said, "Pat, aren't you from Isleta?"

"Yes, I'm Isleta," he replied.

"No Mexican?" I asked.

"No Mexican."

"What a name for an Indian," remarked the doctor.

"Pat is short for Patriceo," the trader smilingly replied. "Pat's a good hand, too. He can cut wood or fry eggs as need be."

The next morning as we started toward the village we met a bright looking man of middle age who greeted us in a sort of English. We fell into talk with him and found him to be quick-witted and courteous. He became our guide in our round of the village.

"Where you from?" he asked as we walked toward the bridge.

"Washington," we replied, because to an Indian any place far to the East is Washington.

"Mrs. Stim'son, you know her?" he asked.

"Stimpson. No, I'm afraid not," said the doctor.

"Mrs. Stim'son, she my fliend. She live my house. She send me letter."

"He means Mrs. Stevenson[20] who writes on pueblo matters," said the doctor. "Yes we know of Mrs. Stevenson."

---

[17] Dozier writes, "The Pueblo Indian is quite ethnocentric about his pueblo, and considers it the 'center' of the universe. Language, appearance, ceremonials, anything that may be compared or evaluated is at its best in one's own pueblo." (Dozier, *The Pueblo Indians of North America*, p. 209.)

[18] Theophil M. Prudden, head of the Department of Bacteriology at Columbia, became Garland's traveling companion when he left Walpi.

[19] In 1898, the first accurate census taken of Zuni Pueblo in over a decade set the population at 1,796. (*Ind. Commiss. Annual Reports, 1898*, pp. 209–210.)

[20] Matilda Coxe Stevenson (1850–1915) accompanied her husband James Stevenson, an explorer and one of the founders of the U.S. Geological Survey and the Bureau of Ethnology of the Smithsonian Institution, on various expeditions to Arizona and New Mexico. In 1879, she went with his expedition to Zuni and assisted in collecting artifacts. Soon after the death of her husband in 1888, she became a member of the Bureau of Ethnology and devoted a number of years to valuable field research among the Zuni. (*The National Cyclopaedia of American Biography*, 20: 53–54.)

The adobe-walled garden plots described by Garland can be seen beyond the village in this 1879 view of Zuni.

"She good woman — she my fliend. Me knew Cushing. You know Cushing? He come, dig, find much bottery."

Up at the village we found a few people stirring, but mainly the houses were closed. Dick took us into his own house first, a nicely white-washed room with some American furniture.

"Take chair," Dick insisted and would not let the doctor sit on a box. He was proud of his chairs.

Dick's little children were bright little scamps with considerable Zuni soil on them — good wholesome dirt, however. Dick took us back through small doors into inner rooms, store rooms dimly lighted, and showed us old, old treasures. [One was] an old war club — of which he said, "Long time ago Navajo him bad. Him fight Zuni. So war chief he make um club. Mebbo so hit Navajo." He handed us the club to look at. "No use 'em any more. Navajo no fight Zuni any more, allee same trade."

There were also the ceremonial dresses which the men and women use in their dances, and old hunting fetishes and old bowls. "*Too* old," Dick called them when he showed them to us, meaning of course *very* old. Curious places, those store houses, full of things which epitomized an immense period of their lives.

When we saw so few men in the village we said, "Dick, why aren't you out farming?" He laughed. "Me no farm. Me all time make beads." He was an artisan, not a common hand.[21]

"Let's see you make beads."

He took us back into the main living room and there he laid out a box of shells, a little bag of turquoise, a box of little disks chipped out of shells and a drill of his own fashioning. He clipped a disk with his pinchers; then with the curious and very well-working drill, he bored a hole in the disk. He was very adroit and proud of his trade.

"Navajo like 'em — trade blankets — pay ten dollars string."

We went into other houses, for when it was known that we were buying pottery and that we had candy for the children, the people came over the housetops like goats across the rocks, asking us to come and see what they had.[22] There were a few plump, laughing girls, some old men and the rest were women of middle age.

We saw Dick's father, so crippled that he walks on his hands dragging his legs along the ground. He had a resolute, intelligent and uncomplaining face. We saw a little sick baby looking pathetically wan and limp, and a girl with a badly burned foot. In one house we came upon an old woman — old as a gray boulder — old and thin as a gnarled dead gray cedar tree. She sat by the open door and held her head in the streaming glory of morning sunshine. She had but one garment, and her skinny arms and legs looked hardly human.

I bought a bowl which sat beside her and put the money into her hand, and the doctor gave her some candy.

She lifted her head as though this unusual kindness had given her new life, and peered at us as if she would remember us forever. She lifted her hand to be shaken and I shook it and said "Way-no." She then kissed her hand to us in token of her gratitude to the strange white man who had done what her sons had probably never done, remembered her age to her honor. For that is a strange thing among these generally kind people — the old are neglected.[23]

Ah, but they are poor. As we went through their homes buying a little pottery, we saw all their poor pathetic possessions. Their bowls and blankets, their extra robes, their one or two battered chairs, the coffee lithographs on the wall, the children robed in old salt sacks — and yet men plan to rob them! Men want to take their land — to grow fat off their trade — no wonder the white men are wolves to them.

---

[21] Metal and stone work, principally in silver and turquoise, has become a chief industry among the Zunis. Zuni has come to be almost a single-guild town, with hundreds of persons turning out fine silver and turquoise jewelry and accessories. (Stubbs, *Bird's-Eye View of the Pueblos*, p. 94.)

[22] Pottery that Garland saw was probably chalky-white slip with sharply contrasting designs of red and black. However, pottery-making rapidly declined as a Zuni craft during the twentieth century. Stubbs records how in 1930 a curio dealer stored a large lot of modern Zuni pottery in a warehouse. This cache became the only large collection outside museums to testify to the once-flourishing ceramic art of the Zuni. (Stubbs, *Bird's-Eye View of the Pueblos*, p. 94.)

[23] See Essay 6, note 22, for discussion of the fact that anthropologists writing on these Indians do not support Garland's observations about mistreatment of the aged.

Last year they had no crop. They were forced to eat their faithful burros, their dogs. They were forced to sell everything that men would pay five cents for, and they sat in their cheerless houses and endured hunger and cold with the patience of martyrs, and the white people sat by and saw it and did little. One man, ever-lasting shame to him, gave an old man copper cents for his necklace and told him they would buy a bag of flour. Such are the tales they tell of greed.

This year they have a good crop, and so they are smiling. I should like to have seen them when they came together for their harvest home dance and festival.

As we came to say good-by to Dick I said, "Dick, I'll send you some shells when I get back. Mebbe so ten days and ten days. Mebbe so one month."

"Good," said Dick. "Me need much shells, make 'em beads, sell 'em Navajos."

"All right, I'll send some."

"One time," began Dick impressively, "man say, me send 'em shells. Me go home me send 'em shells." A pause. "He liar. He no send 'em shells."

There was no misunderstanding this broad hint, and I joined the doctor in a laugh. "Well Dick, you see, I'm no liar."

I understood the other man's case. Someone had said on the impulse "I'll send ya some shells, Dick," and then had forgotten it in the complexity of his city life. But there is no complexity in Dick's life, and he remembers every word the white man speaks. I sent those shells, and I would have done it at any cost. I could not have Dick An-tinni-he think me a liar. A man should keep his lightest promise with an Indian.

Looking back on Zuni I saw once more how it secrets itself on the plain as Walpi hides upon a rock. It lay behind us there, a low red hill in the midst of the wide sun-filled valley. Around it purple sands lay, and a slow river crawled by it. Far away on all sides great mesas towered a thousand feet above the valley floor.

As we rose we came again to radiant vistas of sunflowers, which ran to great scooped and carved walls of sandstone. Pine trees began again and grass and flowers, a beautiful wilderness.

We spent the night in the camp of a trader about twelve miles from Zuni. We were awake at dawn and saw the sun blaze into sudden splendor in the heaven. All through the cold white half-light a coyote cried — uttering a liquid whistling wail — so sweet and wild it made that dawn forever memorable to me.

A young man cooked our breakfast, a Zuni helped him, a Navajo horseman waited outside. Columbia College was represented in the doctor who was out studying the ancient pictographs upon the rocks — and I, I listened in ecstasy to the mystic shrill wail of the coyote, and watched the sun flare up the sky and thought of this wonderful coming together of men in the bush.

Background

"The Most Mysterious People in America" presents Garland's composite reaction to his 1895 travels among the pueblan peoples. Aside from a brief piece on the Acomans, this essay represents, as well, his most substantial statement on Acoma and Laguna.

Acoma, a Keresan pueblo located about sixty miles south and west of Albuquerque, New Mexico, was first visited by whites in 1540, when some of Coronado's men went there. At that time, they were a much-feared, hostile tribe. The first permanent mission was established among them in 1629. The inhabitants participated in the Pueblo Uprising of 1680 and did not come under Spanish control again until 1699, when the name was changed to San Pedro. Like most pueblans, the Acomans were farmers and herders. It was the harvest dance that attracted Garland to them in 1895, and he recorded his reactions to the ceremony in a brief, unpublished essay titled "The Harvest Dance of the Accomans," to be found in the Hamlin Garland collection at the University of Southern California.

Laguna, also Keresan, located about forty-five miles west of Albuquerque, was established in 1699. The people were of mixed linguistic backgrounds, principally Keresan, Tanoan, Shoshonean, and Zunian. In the early 1870s, the inhabitants began taking up permanent residences in what had been summer villages, so that the population had dwindled considerably[1] by the time Garland visited the village with his friend, Colombia bacteriologist Theophil Prudden.

In 1895, the entire population of pueblans numbered well over 8,000. They made their livings chiefly by raising corn, wheat, oats, and vegetables and occasionally had a surplus above their own needs. The acreage under cultivation by them in 1895 was 5,500, on which were produced 11,500 bushels of wheat, 8,250 bushels of oats and barley, 2,000 bushels of corn, and 5,750 bushels of vegetables. Fruit was also grown at some pueblos. In 1895, 200 pueblans dressed entirely in the Anglo mode, and 3,500 dressed that way in part. Twelve schools were operated among them. Of the 2,323 children of school age, only 587 attended. Eight hundred pueblo Indians could read English.[2]

As usual, Garland shows here his strong interest in the impact of the Spanish and Anglo societies on the Indians. And, as typical of his thinking at this time, he prophesies the destruction of the Acomans' once "stable" cultures by the changes in environment brought about particularly by the Anglo influence. He laments the rapid disintegration of civilizations that took centuries to build.

---

[1] Frederick Webb Hodge, ed., *Handbook of American Indians North of Mexico*, Pt. 1, pp. 10–11, 752–753.

[2] *Ind. Commiss. Annual Report, 1895*, pp. 220, 570–571, 586–587.

6. The Most Mysterious People in America[3]
The Cliff Dwellers and Pueblo People of Arizona

In passing from the plains of Eastern Colorado to the seaward slope of the Sierra Mountains, the traveller sees little else than sand, sage-brush, magnificent cliffs of red and green stone and distant mountain peaks.

It is an arid land. There is but one oasis of green in this mighty and resplendent desert — this is the San Francisco group of mountains. After leaving Albuquerque there are no towns on the Santa Fe line till Flagstaff, which is only a lumber village, then desert again and at last the Sierras and Los Angeles. There are stations and forts and Indian pueblos and Mexican towns in New Mexico, in Arizona scarcely forts or villages, only long rows of section houses marked 1-2-3 and so on and on.

The train rises and falls over enormous divides and winds down sunken rivers with violet-shadowed cliffs of mighty mesas on either hand; it seems ever climbing or descending. And yet, as a matter of fact, this whole land is a prodigious plateau from six to eight thousand feet above sea level. It is meshed by a thousand cañons with almost perpendicular sides and dotted by peaks rising from two to four thousand feet higher than the plain, attaining a total altitude of from eight to twelve thousand feet, a region of ancient mountains with sand-filled valleys.

All through this region of perpetual sunshine and of glorious atmosphere, in the valleys beside the slender rivers lost amid sands, on the mesas hundreds of feet above the valley, in the seams of cliffs a thousand feet high, in the cinders of extinct volcanoes are to be seen the homes of the most mysterious people in America — the cliff-dwelling Indians.

As you ride by in the train you may see them threshing grain at Santa Clara, urging their nimble ponies round and round the corral, trampling out the wheat as the Egyptians did of old.[4] At Isleta their boys and girls will enter the car to sell you peaches and melons, and at Laguna to show you jars and quaint clay figures. At Gallup, a Zuni will sit his horse among the Navajos and watch the train go by, and in the Grand Cañon the Suppai[5] young men will meet you with baskets of fruit. Assisting are the Navajos and the Apaches.

---

[3] Item 449, Hamlin Garland Collection, University of Southern California Library, Los Angeles, published by permission of the University of Southern California Library and Constance Garland Doyle and Isabel Garland Lord.

[4] Garland describes the threshing scene he saw at Isleta in Essay 2 of this book, "A Day at Isleta."

[5] Garland refers to the Havasupai Indians, whose reservation is in the Grand Canyon, several miles northwest of Grand Canyon, Arizona.

[119]

This whole blazing, arid, beautiful, and sinister land is the home of the pueblo man who is in fact the cliff-dweller and the mound-builder of still more inaccessible regions.

The cliff dweller was the pueblo Indian in times of trouble or of migration. To escape the Ute, the Navajo, the Apache or the Spaniard, he let himself down over the cliff and built a secret refuge for himself and his children. With incredible cunning he traced out a trail along the side of the cliff or hewed a stairway out of a pine tree or twisted a ladder out of horse-hair, and when his enemies ravined he fled to his cliff dwelling like a sand martin to its burrow.

You may see these caves and ruined dwellings high over the modern pueblo of Santa Clara and in the Cañon de Chelly and in the Little Colorado.[6] They look like swallows' nests high up there in the soft sandstone. You may find also, on "thunder mountain" and other enormous heights about Zuni, traces of ancient villages which were used in times when fortification was more needful than now. These are the stages. In time of greatest danger the cliff dwellings were built and temporarily inhabited. In times of less danger the towns were built, like Acoma and Walpi, on high precipitous mesa points. In times of peace pueblos were built in the valleys isolated by stretches of desert lands from friends and enemies as well.

In New Mexico these people have come down off their cliffs for the most part, but not entirely. Santa Clara, Isleta, Laguna, Zuni and many others are built on the valley floor, but Acoma still remains perched perilously upon an isolated table butte four hundred feet above the valley. A wonderful town this is, unforgetable as Gibraltar, as strange, as remote as Thebes.

In Arizona are to be found "The Seven Villages of Tusayan" all on heights nearly six hundred and fifty feet above the valley floor: Walpi, Hah-no, Seechúm-a-ver, Shum-ó-pa-ver, Mashong'-na-ver, O-raí-bee, Schu-paul'-o-ver.[7] In the Cataract Cañon the Su-pai people live three thousand feet below the rim of the cañon, and up and down their inhospitable valleys are innumerable ruins of older peoples — whose life was practically that of Walpi and Oraibi today. The cities in the cliffs are uninhabited now, save by bats and the mountain lion possibly.

The cliff dwellers are known to be not of enormous antiquity. Even in the cave dwellings of this region, pottery, tools and clothing almost identical with that of Oraibi and Walpi have been found. If we know how the people of Walpi, Zuni, and Oraibi live, we know how the cliff dwellers lived.[8] The traditions of the Hopi people (called the Mokis) tell of the wandering of their people from the southwest and that on these journeys they often built houses

---

[6] Santa Clara Pueblo is about twenty-five miles north of Santa Fe, New Mexico. The ruins which Garland mentions are probably Puye, a few miles to the west. He no doubt refers to the famous White House Ruin and others at Canyon de Chelly northwest of Window Rock, Arizona, and to the Wupatki group and others on the Little Colorado, northeast of Flagstaff, Arizona.

[7] Here Garland gives his own phonetic spellings of the names of the seven villages on the Hopi reservation.

[8] This is an over-simplification.

in the cliffs or on high mesa points. And Dr. Walter Fewkes[9] of the Smithsonian Institution and field workers under Major Powell's[10] direction have proved the truth of these traditions by excavating along the lines indicated by the Moki story-teller.[11] The Mokis are known to be cliff dwellers.

The origin of these people is quite another question. They may have come from the South — from Central America. They may have come from China. Probably they came from Central America. Certainly they are not closely related to the Northern Indian. To me they seem Chinese or Egyptian. I saw faces among them which were marvellously Semitic — while their speech, their "Pigen English" had the movement and the endings of the Chinese. They are dark bronze in color and mainly light and graceful and are matchless climbers and runners — which are necessities in cliff dwellers.

About one hundred miles north of the Santa Fe road and midway in the northern half of Arizona lies the Indian Reservation called *Tusayan* after the Spanish.[12] Within a few miles square there lie the seven villages named above — best known of which is Walpi. To reach them you must ride across a wild, shelterless land of sand and sage-brush — a land without water and with little herbage. You will pass by the Navajo *hogans* on the way, but no other roof save one ranch. Even in the "rainy season" it is necessary to sling a canteen of water to your shoulder. Grass is scanty, and your horse suffers for lack of water. It has little life save the rabbit, the prairie dog, the rattlesnake and the horned toad. And yet here in this lonely desert land some thousands of people live in cities known to be three centuries old. They have their own government, their own customs enormously old, their own dress and a language distinct from the Apache and the Navajo. Ethnologically they belong to the Shoshonean family.

In 1680 we have the first mention of them.[13] Coronado on an expedition in search of riches and wonders was lured across the desert by tales of a great city in the desert. He came with men in "iron clothes" and departed into the mysterious south. And then other men like unto him came and "men in long dresses" (priests) who taught the people many new things and brought them peach seeds and horses and mules and sheep, but also made the people captive

---

[9] See Essay 4, note 20, for background on Fewkes.

[10] John Wesley Powell (1834–1902), who reached the rank of major in the Civil War, led an expedition to explore the mountain region of Colorado in 1867. He led another expedition the following year, the purpose of which was to map the canyons of the Green, White, Yampa, and Blue rivers. On May 24, 1869, he and his party entered the Grand Canyon and became the first Americans to successfully descend the Colorado River. In 1881, Powell became director of the U.S. Geological Survey and later head of the Bureau of American Ethnology as well. (*The National Cyclopaedia of American Biography*, 3:340.)

[11] The Hopi villages, with possible exception of Oraibi, occupied other sites at various times in the past. (Hodge, ed., *Handbook of American Indians North of Mexico*, Pt. 1, pp. 560–562.)

[12] This is the Hopi Reservation.

[13] Garland is mistaken here. Coronado traveled among the Pueblo Indians in 1540. The date Garland gives is that of the Pueblo Uprising.

and forced them to build churches and drag great trees across the desert from the mountains to the west — also they interfered with the songs and prayers of the Hopi.

Then they went away, and the churches rotted down, and the Hopituh returned to their own beloved dances and ceremonies and songs. They were at peace for many years, but the Ute and the Navajo still threatened. Therefore, they kept to the high rock. Then at last came other white men, whiter than the men from the south. These men had no iron clothes. Their warriors wore blue clothes, blue as the jay-bird, and they brought priests and women who taught the children to look understandingly on white leaves. "This white man said to the Navajo, 'You no come to hurt the Hopi.' To the Ute, 'You keep on your own land.' Hopi people velly well like the Pahano."

It took fear of man to set these villages on these heights. As I approached Walpi,[14] I could hardly believe anything living was upon it. The houses — massive, dirt-colored, flat and square as rocks — secreted themselves upon the cliffs like turtles. The first evidence of life was a small field of corn set deep in the wash. Then an old man watching it seated beneath a shade of piñon boughs. Then some peach-trees knee-deep in sand. Then some red-roofed houses built by the government.[15] By this time I could see tiny figures moving about on the high ledges and on the roofs of the houses. Up the trail a man on a burro was driving a flock of sheep and goats. He wore light cotton trousers and a calico shirt. His legs were bare. On his head was a straw hat. Farther up the trail some old women were toiling with huge bottles of water slung upon their backs.

From the moment I entered the trail I was deep in the elemental past. Here was life reduced to its simplest form. Houses of heavy walls with interiors like cellars or caves sit for defense upon a cliff. Here were flat roofs thick to keep out the sun and to make a door-yard for the next tier of houses above. Here were nude children with tangled hair, wild as colts and fleet as antelope, dancing on crags as high as church spires. Here were dogs just one remove from wolves, dogs who could climb a ladder. Here were men and women seated upon the floor eating from plaques of willow and bowls of clay of their own shaping and burning.

It was all strange, remote, elementally primitive. It grew more so as I got deeper into their way of living. They war with drouth and sandstorms; therefore, they have but one crop, corn, one meat, mutton. Some few peaches and a sort of tasteless melon they raise, but their main food is corn, of which they make mush and a sort of tough, heavy bread, which is much better than it sounds, being very sweet and nutritious. Their mutton they roast and stew, and it is often very good. The corn is ground by the women, who rub a bar of stone up and down a slab, like a laundress today on a wash-board. In every

---

[14] The description of Walpi which follows is a condensation of a more detailed treatment of the subject in Essay 4, "Among the Moki Indians."

[15] See Essay 4, note 10, for commentary on these government-built houses.

house there is a corner set aside for the mealing trough, and almost any hour of the day the dull rasp of the *metate* can be heard accompanied by a low chant by the women.

The arrangement of each room is practically the same.[16] In one corner is the fire-place. In another the mealing trough. On the white-washed walls hang prayer emblems of feathers and willow twigs, and gay dolls made in the images of deities.[17] Fine jars and bowls stand about filled with water or meal or fruit. Navajo blankets are folded and laid along the walls. Bags stuffed with ceremonial dresses are suspended from the ceiling in the corners. In the back wall are openings to other rooms. One leads by a notched tree trunk to a dark chamber — a store room. The other, a mere cat-hole, leads to a sort of cellar where grain and fruit are kept. If the family is wealthy there may be other rooms connected in like manner.

It needs little elimination to get at the possessions of the cliff dweller of prehistoric times. Before the Spaniards came he had no sheep, no horses, no burros, no peaches. Corn, "the mother of all," he had, and clothing of cotton which he wove for himself.[18] In summer he required little clothing. In winter he had skins of deer, wild-cats, mountain lions and wolves. His house was nearly the same as now, only its windows were of obsidian (some of them in Zuni, in Oraibi, and in Walpi are still so filled) and his door was a skin or a hanging of willow matting. Even if built in a cliff side, the architecture was much the same.

He planted then and now by thrusting a wooden spear deep into the sandy bed of the valley and dropping the corn therein. With a bit of obsidian to reflect the sun he lured the prairie dog to the mouth of his burrow and pierced him with his arrow. He killed the mountain lion also with his bow and arrow. He made use of every edible thing in his barren region and lived almost as monotonously as the rabbit or the horned toad. His home was determined by the question of water. He built near a spring. If the spring dried up he moved. When it did not rain sufficiently to grow his corn he starved.[19]

For these reasons he came to hold in sacred care anything which pertained to rain or to running water. His prayer sticks were of water willow. A turtle shell was a priceless treasure — so also was the water-worn root of a cottonwood tree, which is always found by running streams in this dry land and often is the only tree. His ceremonial dress is made up of symbols per-

---

[16] An illustration of the interior of a typical house in a Hopi village appears in Walter Hough, *The Moki Snake Dance*, p. 43; see also, Bertha P. Dutton, ed., *Indians of the Southwest*, p. 14.

[17] See Essay 4, note 17, for commentary on Hopi Kachina dolls.

[18] The Spanish found many of the Pueblo Indians farming cotton. (Albert H. Schroeder, "Rio Grande Ethnohistory," p. 48.)

[19] In 1895, Captain Constant Williams, agent for the Navajos and Hopis, wrote that the latter "have been taught by experience to store up corn in good years, so that they suffered comparatively little for want of food last year. Their crops will be large this year." (*Ind. Commiss. Annual Report, 1895*, p. 118.)

taining to rain clouds, fruits, and grains. Meal is used in all ceremonies as the Hebrews of old used oil. It is cast upon the water as offering. It is sprinkled upon the ground in their dances and tossed to the four world quarters as a votive offering to the clouds. "Corn is life itself," they say, "for it comes from the heart of Ut-set. Were it not for the mother corn none could live."

The dancers of Acoma wear bracelets of pine or cottonwood boughs, so precious are green things. The women of Acoma in the harvest dance wear on their heads tall boards painted with cloud symbols ⌒⋁⌒⋀⌒ ⌐⌐ or rain symbols ⸪⸪⸪⸪⸪. Tad-poles are sometimes used. As they sing to this dance, the men of Acoma thank the deities of rain and thunder for crops, for good rain and for grain. In the great snake dance at Walpi this prayer for rain is a principal theme. The priests wear their hair flowing as the women of Acoma do in the harvest dance, "because the clouds wear their tresses so." They call upon the cloud-people to come and water the earth that their crops may be good.

On the kilts of the dancers at Walpi and Oraibi are drawn ∧⋁∧⋁ lines to indicate lightning and clouds. ⌐⌐ In the construction of dolls for the children, these symbols appear, and also on their pottery and blankets. There is something pathetic in all this — tragic indeed. It tells of death and drouth, of awful hunger and still more intolerable thirst, of unrequited toil — patient and cheerful.

These cliff-folk are a busy folk. The women grind meal and weave blankets and baskets and make very interesting and often beautiful pottery. The old men make moccasins very deftly, while the younger men go down from the cliff into the fields to tend the growing crops, to watch the struggling corn as it battles against drifting hot sand and against sudden floods. Such are the extremities of their climate. Each morning while I was in Hano I heard the men at early dawn go singing down the steep trail, down into the purple plain, their queerly minor songs floating up to me with strange beauty. Each morning while it was still dusk the women woke me by entering the room where I lay, to grind corn, and each night I went to sleep to the regular rhythm of the mealing stone timed to the mystical religious chant of the toiling women.

Let it be said that there is no woman slavery among these people any more than among the Navajos. The women are chief property holders. The house is generally the woman's, and descent is through her and not through the father.[20] The men are seldom severe in manner, and in Acoma, and Walpi, as well as in Laguna and Zuni, I saw the men taking care of the babies and doing it with great tenderness and smiling patience.[21] I saw no evidence of any severity except in case of the old women. They seemed to be the drudges of the household in Walpi and in Acoma, carrying wood and bottles of water

---

[20] For a discussion of household systems of the western pueblos, see Fred Eggan, *Social Organization of the Western Pueblos*, pp. 195–197.

[21] In Essay 1, "Among the Southern Utes," and in Essay 3, "Glimpses of the Navajo Indians," Garland notes that adults in these two tribes, like the Hopi, treated their children in a particularly gentle fashion.

up the steep trail — bent, withered, morose and complaining.[22] They alone of all these people seemed saturnine. They were not smitten with rods. They were merely ignored or ordered about by the younger women. Incredible endurance was in their skinny limbs, and the querulous malevolence of a vagabond dog was in their rheumy eyes. They were the exception. The other members of the village were very social in habit.

The good nature, the laughter, the singing was a surprise to me. The children played without clamor, and their voices were infinitely less sharp and wolfish than those of a group of white children. Under my window each night a family went to sleep on the ground of the open plaza. Their children chattered and romped and shrieked with laughter in an equivalent to a "pillow-fight" in which the parents took laughing interest. In summer they sleep thus in the open plaza or upon the flat roofs of the houses, and songs and merry-making resound. They go to bed with the chickens and rise at the first rooster crow.

The houses are heavily built of stone heaped together, sometimes four stories high with many inner rooms. This is for defense primarily and for warmth in winter. In Acoma the houses are built in long rows with a blank wall to the north. This throws the open doors and windows toward the sun in winter. Often the houses are built round an open court as in Hano. In earlier days the door-ways were very small so that upon attack the cliff people could hold at bay the Apache or the Navajo. Now they use wooden doors and American window sash. When they built in the cliff wall they conformed to the ledge, but the living room was much the same as now.

In Acoma they bake bread and meat in an outside oven shaped like a bee hive, which was derived from the Spaniards possibly.[23] In more ancient times they baked in the coals or on a slab of stone laid upon the fire. They boiled meat by dropping hot stones into vessels filled with water. It was a fine sight to see the women at Acoma baking for the Thanksgiving dance,[24] the light from the ovens shining redly over their dark faces and picturesque dress. They first filled the oven with hot fire; then when its walls were rosy with heat they raked out the fire and put in the bread or meat and sealed up the oven with a stone and clay. This was done with fine grace and celerity. Their fuel

---

[22] Garland also describes this lack of respect for older women in Essay 5, "A Day at Zuni." However, Eggan does not support Garland's contention that the old women were treated badly. (Eggan, *Social Organization of the Western Pueblos*, pp. 196–197.) Dozier says, "The women are the important members of the [household] unit; they own the house, are responsible for the preparation and distribution of food, make all the important decisions, and care for the ritual possessions of the family. The oldest woman of the household enjoys the most respect, and the members of the unit look to her for instructions and seek her advice in times of trouble." (Edward P. Dozier, *The Pueblo Indians of North America*, p. 137.)

[23] The idea for these ovens, mentioned as early as 1591, was possibly borrowed during Coronado's visit to the Rio Grande in New Mexico in the winter of 1540–41. (Albert H. Schroeder, "Rio Grande Ethnohistory," p. 53.)

[24] The dance spoken of here is probably the September 2 annual fiesta and harvest dance. For Garland's account of this celebration, see his unpublished essay "The Harvest Dance of the Accomans" in the Hamlin Garland Collection, University of Southern California, Los Angeles.

is juniper and grease-wood and dried sheep manure. The smoke of their fires is exceedingly malodorous and haunts the whole village.

The women are often very pretty as girls and some of them make stately young mothers. They work generally in groups of three or four — cooking, white washing, weaving or painting pottery. They seem to have a good deal to chatter about, and their smiling faces are very agreeable. They have most excellent white teeth. Their ceremonial dress is very picturesque, especially the costume of Acoma and Isleta girls. All burdens are carried by the women of Acoma, Isleta, and Laguna upon their head, and they have in consequence a magnificent carriage even late in life. The old women of Walpi on the contrary are bent and down-looking.

The everyday dress of the women consists of a sort of kilt, which is wrapped around the hips and fastened with a belt (a modification of the blanket or wolf-skin). Above this a sort of sleeveless chemise partly covers the bosom. Their hair is carefully tended but is worn in an ungraceful mode by some of the women. The women of Hano cut the hair in front square across about to the line of the lips while the back hair is gathered into a sort of billet. The front hair hangs down over their faces often concealing one eye. They have a pretty little trick of giving it a twirl with the fingers and a fling back from the face, which they make use of when they are interested and want to see more clearly. When they are abashed their hair falls like a trick veil over the entire face. They brush it with the short end of their whisk brooms, which are made of a bundle of splints bound tightly in the middle.

The unmarried women in Walpi wear their hair in a strange way. They coil it into two big disks just above their ears, the intent being to symbolize their youth and promise by imitating the squash flower. The matrons, correspondingly, dress their hair to symbolize the ripened squash. Some of the maidens were wonderfully Japanese in appearance. Little Quang, the daughter of Heli in whose house I stayed, was a most amazingly oriental type. Nearby was a girl of pronounced Semitic type.[25]

The women of Isleta, Acoma, and Hano wear a sort of legging formed by winding about the calf a strip of white cotton cloth; anciently it was buck skin no doubt. This gives their legs a heavy look, but their movements are full of dignity and power. They seem more muscular than the men and are indeed large and strong. It was marvellous to see them come and go up the perpendicular trail at Acoma bearing jars of water and baskets of plums up a trail so difficult I needed both feet and hands to feel secure.

The men are slender fellows, with rounded pliant limbs in youth, and even in age they seldom grow heavy or inactive. They wear their hair clipped in front like the women but confine it to their heads with fillets of red or green. "A stunning composition of color" their heads were to the artist. They are all great users of tobacco, and the first act after hand-shaking is to ask for "T-boc." They are mainly very pleasant of feature except when before a camera. They manage to look very awkward and very morose when being photographed. They also look darker than they are and coarser in type. In reality there is

---

[25] Garland's racial comparisons are of little modern value. However, they were perhaps useful to the popular audience of the 1890s as comparisons of the unknown with something familiar.

a fine glow of red-bronze in their faces and the hair falling over the face is not repulsive in life.

"The religion of the Hopitah like that of the Sia,"[26] according to Mrs. Stevenson,[27] "is not a religion mainly of propitiation, but rather of supplication for favors and payment for the same." That is to say it is a religion of rites and votive offerings and prayers to the people of the clouds to send rain and good health and prosperity. Always the cry of rain. Always the hope for water. So of the people of Acoma and Walpi and Oraibi. And these words occur over and over:

> "White floating clouds
> Clouds like the plain
> Come and water the Earth
> You father of us all. Great spider
> Call upon the cloud-people
> That they water the earth."

Some of them are sun-worshippers no doubt. The Zunis sprinkle corn meal or pollen on the river at sun-rise, chanting a mystical hymn the while. They also believe that a good much has been said of their [the Hopis'] uncleanliness, but it seemed to me they were as clean as could be expected of a village whose every drop of water had to be brought in jars from distant springs up the heavy trail. They were much more wholesome of life than the crowded quarters of our cities. The sun and wind aids them. The dry pure air, the splendid winds and the constant sun dries all refuse, and the wind sweeps it off the pass or ledge. Their method of cleaning is not to wash but to brush the dirt away. There is always a heap of refuse at the edge of the cliff, and that brings me to their burial customs.

They seem not to care much for the body after death. It is hurried away and thrown into some crevice in the rock or into the refuse heap. It is in such deposits that the pottery, the sandals, the ornaments and tools are found which have established the identity of the cliff dwellers with the Mesa dwellers.

They hold their land in gentes, not in tribes.[28] Each family, like "the Snake people" and "the Antelope people," holds land in common and divides products, but the Snake people do not hold land with the Antelope people. The unit is the gens, not the tribe. And in times of great hunger, which come often in this dry land, the gens also is forgotten and the family is fed first. Thus, the primitive unit is laid bare — the father, mother, and child united by love.

---

[26] The Zia, or Sia, pueblo is occupied by a small Keresan tribe and is located on the north bank of the Jemez River, sixteen miles northwest of Bernalillo, New Mexico.

[27] Garland quotes ethnologist Matilda Coxe Stevenson, whose background is outlined in Essay 5, note 20.

[28] Garland uses the Spanish *gente* and the French *gens* to designate the concept of clan, in this case matrilineal. Eggan says, "The clan is the major grouping in western Pueblo thinking. It has a name, frequently a central residence known as *the* clan-house, relations with sacred symbols, often control of agricultural lands or other territories. . . . The specific mechanisms for inheritance and transmission normally reside in the lineage; the clan is normally the corporate group which holds ritual knowledge and economic goods in trust for future generations." (Eggan, *Social Organization of the Western Pueblos*, p. 299.)

Spirits are in the earth for thence comes the green grass, and the corn, does it not sprout there? Springs, the best of all kings, come also from the earth as the Hopi people did long ago. Religiously, they are in a transition state. Part of their gods are below — part above. Some few of the men have reached a conception of one god "who sits in the heart of the sky." The six world directions still have mysterious significance to them. They address the mythical beings, the bear, cougar, the dark woman who dwells in the west or south or deep in the earth. They pray to the six world directions and sprinkle offerings in the same way and always from north to west and so round the compass. This strange use of the world directions seems to set them apart from other Indians — though it may be that a cosmogony equally curious and complicated was once held by the Sioux or Iroquois.

There are thirty inhabited villages of the pueblo dwellers. They may not all possess cliff dwelling ancestry, but most of them do. The larger part of them still dwell in fortified cities or fortress-like mesas. They are cliff dwellers, though not in the strict sense of the term as applied to the artificial caves in the Cañon de Chelly or the Mesa Verde or the volcanic cones of the San Francisco Mountains.

As cliff dwellers they will soon be gone. Stable throughout the centuries, they are now subject to new forces and environments. What the Navajo and Apache did, the whiteman will undo. As they come to trust in the white man they will come down from their cliffs and build on the plain. They are now doing this. Zuni is already a valley town. The Santa Clara people live in houses mainly of one story like the Mexicans. So do the people of Isleta. Laguna is on a low ledge and still retains the cliff forms of architecture — the houses piled one above the other. Zuni likewise retains these forms. Acoma still looms like a fortress, and there the people all retreat in winter but they too are building in the plain. Small offshoots like Acomita, near Acoma, and Nutria and Ojo Caliente near Zuni show the slow progress of disintegration.

It is very marked at Laguna. The people are coming more and more to make their summer homes their winter homes, also. And the town on the ledge is falling into decay. It looks like a ruin anyhow. This process will before long bring the people down from Oraibi and Mashongnavi and Walpi. Hano, especially, of the Tusayan villages is coming to dwell more and more in the plain. The young men care less and less for ancestral customs. They come to see the waste of effort in climbing the mesa. They take kindly to the government aid, and they go to school and the white people's ways are coming to be their ways.

It is the old, old story of progressive youth and conservative age. There is sorrow ahead for them all — but there is also enlightenment, and enlightenment, we are accustomed to hear, is worth its cost. Possibly to us — but it will not be altogether a joyous thing to see these kindly, quaint and fascinating folk become booted and hatted citizens of Arizona. Even now the girls and boys of Si-chum-a-vi are to be seen in mongrel dress to their great disadvantage.

Their isolation makes them the most suggestive people on the continent. The study of their manners and customs will throw a vivid light upon the early life of the Greek and Roman and German peoples as well as upon races less advanced on the scale of development.

Background on
The Jicarilla Apaches

The apparently despondent attitude and the poverty Garland observed among the Jicarilla Apaches in 1896 may well have resulted, in part, from the unsettled condition which had been their history. Akin in languages to the Mescalero and the Navajo, they considered those peoples as enemies and allied themselves by blood with the Ute and Taos peoples. They ranged from the mountains of southeastern Colorado and northern New Mexico into western Kansas, western Oklahoma, and northern Texas. In historical times they have been disliked because of their practice of theft as a natural means of support.

In 1853, some 250 were persuaded to settle on the Rio Puerco in New Mexico. When Congress failed to ratify the treaty, the Jicarilla went on the warpath and were subdued by the army in 1854. In 1870 they were on the Maxwell grant in northeastern New Mexico, but its sale forced their removal. In 1873 there was an attempt to move the tribe south to Fort Stanton, and the next year a small, temporary reservation was set aside for them on the Tierra Amarilla in northern New Mexico.

Trouble resulted from an 1878 Congressional act transferring the Jicarilla to Fort Stanton. When they refused to go, their annuities were cut off. Two years later the 1878 act was repealed, and a reservation was set aside for them by executive order on the Rio Navajo. There they remained until 1883, when they were removed to Fort Stanton. Finally, in 1887, the Jicarilla were given a larger reservation on the Tierra Amarilla.[1] It was here that Garland found them in 1896.

The Jicarilla numbered only 853 in 1896. Of those only forty dressed entirely in the Anglo style, and the remainder dressed that way in part. They had begun to adopt other white ways as well. They built thirty-four houses of log, lumber, or adobe in 1896. They owned 2,000 ponies, 3,000 sheep, and 500 goats. Anglo and Mexican ranchers on lands surrounding the reservation frequently allowed their livestock to graze on the Indians' land. Consequently, in 1896 the Jicarilla had 8,000 acres under fence, 7,000 of which was fenced during that year. Many were giving up their tribal beliefs and had begun eating formerly taboo foods. Excellent craftsmen in making baskets and beadwork, as well as in pottery and bow and arrow manufacture, they derived an income from their crafts in 1896 of about $2,000.[2]

Garland's account is thematically permeated with what he calls the Jicarillas' "desperate attempt to secure a living in conformity to the law of the awe-compelling white man." He also notes the Spanish influences upon them. Garland states his indebtedness to John L. Gaylord for his insights into Jicarilla beliefs. Much of the essay is direct quotation from this sensitive, good-natured BIA clerk. There is some humor here, too, but the humor is Gaylord's, not Garland's.

---

[1] Frederick Webb Hodge, ed., *Handbook of American Indians North of Mexico*, Pt. 1, pp. 631–632.

[2] *Ind. Commiss. Annual Report, 1896*, pp. 215–216.

7. The Jicarilla Apaches[3]

In the extreme northern part of New Mexico lies a small Indian reservation of which little is known by the general traveller. It is the present home of the Jicarilla or "basket making" Apaches. They were formerly a part of the Mescalero Apaches, but for some reason they objected to living in the Sacramento Mountains[4] and so were sent up to this lonely land.

The Jicarilla country is a part of the high plateau of the Rocky Mountains — a land of ridges and narrow valleys all pine clad. It is without streams for the most part and though a beautiful land to look at is very arid and uncertain of crops. In '95 the Indians had a fine yield of wheat; in '96 they were cut short — the whole land being burned brown and bare.[5]

The reservation is about twenty-two miles broad and thirty-four long and contains less than five hundred souls all told.[6] I rode through it in company with the clerk of the reservation, John Gaylord,[7] and I shall long remember the

[3]Item 448, Hamlin Garland Collection, University of Southern California Library, Los Angeles, published by permission of the University of Southern California Library and of Constance Garland Doyle and Isabel Garland Lord.

[4]The Sacramento Mountains were the dwelling place of the Mescalero Apache in south-central New Mexico. In 1879 James H. Roberts, the farmer in charge of the Abiquiu Agency for the Jicarilla Apaches at Tierra Amarilla, stated that the Jicarillas were content in northern New Mexico and did not want to leave because most of them had been born there and felt the country was their home. (*Ind. Commiss. Annual Report, 1879,* p. 112.)

[5]As indicated here by Garland and later by Gaylord, from 1890 to 1894, the crop yield on the Jicarilla Reservation was so small that many of the Indians were almost entirely discouraged with agricultural endeavors. However, 1895 was a good year, and abundant rainfall enabled the elated Indians to have large crops of grain and excellent grazing well into the hot part of the summer, when usually a drought had set in. (*Ind. Commiss. Annual Report, 1895,* 2, p. 221.) The growing season during which Garland visited the reservation, however, was exceptionally dry, with no rainfall from March 20 to July 5, 1896. Crops were expected to be a total failure. (*Ind. Commiss. Annual Report, 1896,* p. 215; Hamlin Garland, "Colorado, Ouray, 1896," p. 148.)

[6]Garland is mistaken here; actually the population of the Jicarilla Apaches during the years from 1894 to 1898 was well over 800 persons. (*Ind. Commiss. Annual Report, 1894,* p. 210; *1895,* p. 221; *1896,* p. 215; *1897,* p. 202.)

[7]John L. Gaylord began working at the Jicarilla Agency between 1891 and 1893 as a blacksmith and carpenter. In 1896, he was serving as the clerk in charge of the agency when Captain John L. Bullis was taking care of the affairs of the Pueblo Indians. Other Anglo employees included Edwin R. Fouts, physician; H. L. Hall, farmer; Robert Ewell, assistant farmer; Edward J. Mix, teamster; and William H. Gleason, blacksmith and carpenter. There were four Indian employees and eleven Indian policemen at the agency. (*Official Register of the United States, July 1, 1897,* p. 776.)

impression made upon me by this little settlement of men. I was fortunate in my guide, for Mr. Gaylord is one of the few whites who are able to speak the language of the Jicarillas, and more than this he has been made "blood brother" in their hunting parties and they love and trust him.

We left the agency,[8] which is a little village of low cabins, and struck across the hills to the south. In the valleys were little meadows of scant grass and on these the Indians were at work raking and stacking hay,[9] their fringes and braids streaming in the wind. We passed one young lad riding a hay rake and singing a wild native song as he drove his horse.

"It's hard," said the clerk, "to see these poor fellows put in a crop as they did this year and then see it burn up. Last year was a wonderful year. It rained just enough and the crop was large. They were all full of grit and started to put in large fields. It will be hard to get them to try again now."

Our trail led through pine openings and noticing large "blazes" on the trees I inquired the cause.

"The Jicarillas eat the inner bark of the black pine. It has a sweetish taste and is a great delicacy with them. They make a drink of it too."[10]

The people, so far as I observed, live in rude cabins of logs chinked and mud plastered. They fence with heavy pine logs laid on short cross pieces.

The cabins are in the valleys and quite widely separated.[11] The loneliness of the families was almost civilized in its painfulness — quite unlike the cheerful village settlement of the pueblos. It is hard to be so poor and so lonely too. One compensatory phase of most barbaric peoples is their community life.[12]

The men generally wore some part of the white man's clothing — blue denim trousers and hickory shirts, but retained some part of their native dress; doubtless they kept complete costumes for ceremonial occasions. Their hair was braided and drawn over the shoulders in two braids like the Utes, and the women had hair not unlike the Ute women. Most of them retain the leggings and the Gee-string, and when going away from home they still wear the blankets.

Like the Utes they use the tee-pee in summer but retire to their cabins in winter. In their cabins were tables and rude sleeping bunks. They have

---

[8] The subagency of the Pueblo and Jicarilla Agency for the Jicarilla Apaches was located at Dulce, New Mexico, 216 miles from Santa Fe. Once again Garland is traveling with Gaylord, hence the reference to "we."

[9] Hay was the chief crop of the Jicarilla Apache farmers. Production was 800 tons in 1894, 1,000 tons in 1895, 150 tons in 1896, 500 tons in 1897, and 600 tons in 1898. (*Ind. Commiss. Annual Report, 1894*, pp. 590–591; *1895*, pp. 586–587; *1896*, pp. 542–543; *1897*, pp. 502–503; *1898*, p. 210.)

[10] They made a drink of the pine bark during the summer, when a surplus of sap was in the bark. (Garland, "Colorado, Ouray, 1896," pp. 147–148.)

[11] The isolation resulted from the allotment of land in severalty. Lands were parceled in 1892 to 845 Jicarilla, but only 14% of the allotment papers were delivered, owing to the confusion of names or the neglect of the allotting officers. However, the agent reported in 1898 that the Indians were beginning to live on and improve the various pieces of land which they claimed the agents had allotted to them. (*Ind. Commiss. Annual Reports, 1898*, p. 210.)

[12] Garland makes the same point in a number of his works; for examples, see Essay 10, "Notes on the Cheyenne Country and Lame Deer" and Essay 8, "The Red Man's Present Needs."

only had machinery to work with for a few years. They are getting along amazingly well, but there is a hard future as farmers before them, for there is no way to irrigate the land.[13] No streams in its whole extent save the short incursion of the Florida river at one corner.

We passed the cabin where lived one of Gaylord's hunting companions, and we had a piece of long distance sign language.

The Indian was standing at his gate. He made a long sweeping horizontal gesture with his left hand. "Where you going?"

Gaylord replied by a gesture beginning back and ending forward. "Over that way."

The Indian made another sweeping gesture. "Come here."

Gaylord replied with a similar gesture. "Come with me."

The Indian pushed the palm of his hand downward toward his feet. "I stay here," and we rode on.

"Yes they can all talk it — at least all the old men," Gaylord said.

Once we met an Indian jogging along on his pony from the agency. He stopped and spoke with great earnestness to his "ta-ta" (father), as they call their agent. After he rode on I asked the subject of his conversation.

"He wants me to come and see what is the matter with his mowing machine. They have trouble with complicated machinery. They forget to oil it for one thing. They seem to think if it starts off all right it ought to keep right on."

They were all pathetically poor. The women were weaving baskets of willow, and they are capable of doing most excellent work, too. They pluck the willows at a certain time of year and save them for their spare time when there is no more work to do on the land.[14] The men seemed to be doing all the work in the hay, however.

The day was perfect, but the land was distressingly bare and dry. The beautiful valleys had no streams. The hay in the low lands was scant and yellow, and the people seemed dispirited and silent. They have some sheep and goats[15] around the few stagnant ponds of the reservation and even in the corner where the river runs. They all have ponies for riding and for use in their little fields.

---

[13] Since there was such little future in farming on the reservation, the agent suggested in his annual report for 1893 that he be permitted to sell $20,000 worth of pine timber from the Indian lands, to invest the money in sheep and goats, which seemed to do well on the land, and divide them equally among the Indians. Legislation was approved in 1894. (*Ind. Commiss. Annual Report, 1894*, pp. 84, 442.) However, the agent advertised the timber locally during November, 1894, and received no bids due to the inaccessibility of the forests and short period allowed for logging. (*Ind. Commiss. Annual Report, 1895*, pp. 96, 221–222.)

[14] The agent noted in 1896 that between 1500 and 1600 wicker baskets had been manufactured by the Indians and sold at from fifty cents to eight dollars each. The baskets were well made, and some were very artistic in design. (*Ind. Commiss. Annual Report, 1896*, p. 216; *Ind. Commiss. Annual Reports, 1898*, p. 210.)

[15] In 1894, the Indians had traded some of their well-bred ponies for 2,200 sheep and 200 goats. After the agent recommended the sale of timber in order to furnish all the Indians with animals, the 1895 report showed an increase to 2,400 sheep and 250 goats, and the 1896 report indicated there were 3,000 sheep and 500 goats. However, the drought of 1896–1897 reduced their herds to 600 sheep and 200 goats when they were forced to use their animals for food. (*Ind. Commiss. Annual Report, 1894*, pp. 84, 590–591; *1895*, pp. 586–587; *1896*, pp. 542–543; *1897*, pp. 502–503.)

They seemed to be making a desperate attempt to secure a living in conformity to the law of the awe-compelling white man.

During the ride I asked a thousand questions, and the clerk replied freely and in good measure, giving me most valuable accounts of these strange people.

They do not eat fish or fowl.[16] No matter how hungry they may be, they see the turkey fly by without thought of eating it — although one or two very progressive men do not hold rigidly to this rule. "One young fellow boasted of having eaten a duck, and he felt as puffed up as Ingersoll might after lunching upon the bread and wine of communion."[17]

"Fish they consider part of themselves," said Gaylord. "At least that's as near as I can come at it." They don't eat bear meat but they kill for the fur. They will sell the pelt, oil and meat. They never eat hog meat.[18] One year the government issued pork rations, and the Indians took it but they did not eat it. They sold it to the Mexicans and white settlers.

"I learned many of their traditions of hunting by experience," the clerk continued. "When I first came here I was unmarried and had nothing to keep me at the agency, so I spent a lot time hunting with the Indians. We soon got to be good friends. I slowly picked up the language and they became confident at last.

"They have a great many rules about hunting which must not be broken, rules about the camp and so on. I remember I found out one of their rules in a way I shan't forget for a while. We had been hunting one winter day and had just made a camp by wallowing down the snow. Our fire was burning up strong and I was just beginning to feel comfortable when I thoughtlessly stuck a knife in the fire. They got out o' there flying. I had made very 'bad medicine.' We had to set to work and make another camp. I argued but it was no use and when we got the new fire started they made 'good medicine' over it.

"They're a very religious people according to their ideas. Everything they do is done according to ceremonies, and they pray often to the Great Spirits for good luck. All the hunters carry some kind of charm, generally little stones with animals carved on 'em. They never hunt alone. One man kills deer for his companion. He does not touch it himself. They smoke and pray before going out in the morning and again at night after they return. If they have bad luck they pray and if they have good luck they pray."

"Did you ever hear of their having a sort of black art among them?"

"Yes and I've seen it, but it took me a long while to get at it. They are very careful not to let the white man see that. It's just like the jugglery they

---

[16] The agent noted in 1896 that the Jicarilla had begun to give up many of their former beliefs and were now using milk, butter, fowl, fish, eggs, and vegetables of various kinds, "which was something they have never before done." (*Ind. Commiss. Annual Report, 1896*, pp. 216, 542–543.)

[17] Robert Green Ingersoll (1833–1899) was a noted American lawyer who was famous for his agnosticism.

[18] Schoolcraft said that the Apaches generally believed in metempsychosis, which explained their respect for bears and other animals. Writing in the 1850s, he said that they would neither kill nor eat bears; they would not eat pork because they felt hogs were unclean animals. (Henry R. Schoolcraft, *Historical and Statistical Information Respecting the History, Condition and Prospects of the Indian Tribes of the United States*, Pt. 5, p. 209.)

tell us about among the East Indians. I used to hear of it occasionally. Sometimes the agency doctor would run up against it when some old medicine man was treating a patient, but for a long time I couldn't find anything but the medicine business, which is very common. One day Charley Marilla, who is my right hand man and partner on our hunting trips, began to talk of what his father could do, that he could make corn grow while you looked at it and made two birds out of one and so on.

"I laughed at him and told him I didn't believe a word of it. Then he said he could do some big medicine himself. After that I kept egging him on to try and one night when we were all sitting round the fire I got to laughing with him again about his superstitions and he braced up and said, 'Me show you.'

"He went into his tent and brought out a small trunk. Out of this he took the dried tail of a gray squirrel. Then he got a big oja or jar and turned it upside down beside the fire. He took some eagle feathers out of the trunk and after putting the squirrel's tail under the jar, he began to sing and dance round it. He made motions before the oja with the eagle feathers which he held in each hand. Finally he tipped over the oja and out came a live squirrel!

"Well, sir, it knocked me cold and the Indians all laughed fit to split. The squirrel ran up one of the tepee poles and looked down at us. There was no mistake about it. It was a living squirrel. Charley took it in his hands and put it back under the oja. I was watching with all the eyes I had. He sang and danced as before and finally kicked the oja out of the tent and there lay the squirrel tail again. It was a mighty smooth job and I never *did* figure out how it was done. They had the laugh on me sure.

"I never saw them make corn grow under an oja but Charley told me his father could do it, and no doubt they have a trick of that kind. I've seen some of their big ceremonies where the medicine men eat fire and knives.[19] Each man has his specialty that he is particularly proud of. One of the biggest meetings they have hinges on a queer belief they have that a lizard is a devil or evil thing and that your enemy can send one to eat your body when you are drinking or asleep and that after that you will waste away and die. A medicine man will give you a holy stone to ward off the lizard but sometimes that don't work and then the whole tribe comes together in a kind of camp meeting in an enclosure to make medicine and try to relieve the man who is bewitched.

"I attended one of these once. It was a wonderful show. A man had fallen sick and the medicine man had tried to heal him with his holy stone and finally made a dance and called on everybody to be there. The idea was to force a show down on the part of the man's enemy and make him ask forgiveness. The meeting was held in an enclosure, and all the people were there, most of them in their best dress. No one was allowed to go out after he had entered unless he left a pledge at the door.

---

[19] Many tribes had magic tricks in which they claimed to make plants grow. Some Navajos claimed they could make yucca grow, and some Zuni and Hopi claimed, respectively, that they could make corn and beans grow. Fire handling was also common among such tribes as the Navajo, Arikara, and Menominee. The Navajos were well-known for their arrow swallowing. (Hodge, ed., *Handbook of American Indians North of Mexico*, Pt. 1, pp. 784–785.)

"They had turned loose on their music when I arrived. They had their tom-toms a-going with flutes and a queer kind of contrivance made of raw hide as much like a wash board as anything I can describe. It was ridged with sticks covered with raw hide; the operator scraped it with a stick also covered with raw hide. It made hell's own noise — a kind of booming rattle. The men did all the singing.

"The old medicine man went through his paces, but I couldn't see him as well as I wanted to for he was on the other side of the fire. He would point at the moon and stars overhead, then grab at the fire and throw coals and ashes into the air — occasionally he'd catch the coals, throw them into his mouth, and chew them. Then he'd swallow knives and take them out of his side. It was all mighty fakirish. I couldn't see how it was done. They claim he was able to mark a spot on his side and let somebody shoot a bullet through him. I didn't see that.

"But the wildest performance of all was the appearance of thirteen men all naked and painted and carrying spears and knives. They were painted to represent devils with their hair dressed to stick up like horns. One man was painted black, with white stripes to represent a tiger. They came on dancing and imitating the trailing of a deer. They were after that enemy of the sick man, and it was their business to make him feel sick and I reckon they did. They made the cold chills run up my back, well as I knew them. They seemed to go clean crazy with the music and their own racket. If one of 'em eased off a little he'd take a sniff of a root he held and off he'd go again crazy as a loon. I don't know what the root was but it smelled like corditeen powders.[20]

"I don't know how it came out. It was in winter, and I got so cold I had to leave. I was obliged to drop my overcoat in the hands of the guards at the door too but I got home as soon as I could. The next day all was quiet. The enemy had asked pardon and the man was better. Sometimes these dances last three or four days.

"In their social dances the women select their partners. The men sit around the fires outside waiting. They seem to be bashful and when they see a squaw coming, they cover their faces with their blankets. They act just like so many young girls.

"Another of their curious ideas is they're afraid of the coyote. They seem to think he's a sort of magician. I didn't know this for some time, but one day while I was riding over the hills I shot and killed a fine specimen. I wanted his hide so when I came home I told Charley Marilla to go and get him. I noticed he went off mighty slow and he looked at me in a queer way. I didn't think much about it then but I did afterward.

"He was a deuce of a while getting back and when he came he was dragging that coyote at the end of his rope and the pelt was ruined. I pitched into him about it, and then he told of their superstition about a coyote. He had fooled away an hour or two figuring how to bring that coyote in without touching him. 'Him witch. Me no like touch.' He had rather brave the wrath of the

---

[20]Cordite was a smokeless powder made of nitroglycerin, gun-cotton, and mineral jelly. It was usually gelatinized by the addition of acetone and fashioned into cords resembling dark twine. *Corditeen* may have been a brand name.

tata than that of the powers represented by the coyote. It don't do to try to run cross ways of their superstitions. They are gospel with the older people."[21]

The Jicarillas seemed to me a peaceful and patient people as almost all the Indians I have met are. They bear much and silently. Doubtless it would be possible to provoke them to strike back. They live peacefully because their reservation is considered worthless and there is no reason for encroaching upon it.[22]

They are a dark people, more brown or black than copper colored. The sun asserts its dominion over them. They have been much influenced by the Spanish language and customs but seem to have been touched very little by the Spanish priests. They use many Spanish words, and their names are often "José" or "Juan."

One old man who visited the agency during my stay was supposed to be ninety-seven years old. He was a famous medicine man and looked like Father Time, so thin were his brown legs, so wrinkled his face, but his voice was marvellous, clear and of astounding sonority. Without apparent effort he spoke so that he could be heard across the valley. He was a mighty orator in his day, and he could speak yet with the dignity of a king. His rags were forgotten in such moments. So far as I could know he faced death with undaunted eyes. That he had lived long and in vain did not, I hope, come into his mind.

As I recall the glimpses I had of these people, it seems to me they are more sorrowful than the Navajos, for their lives are more solitary. The Navajos live in small communities, but these poor people are as lonely as the settlers on the Kansas plain, and even more poverty stricken and drouth accursed. They endure because they must, also because they can. May their dreams of the Happy Hunting Ground all come true.

---

[21] Garland's notes on these beliefs, as related to him by Gaylord, are extensive. (Garland, "Colorado, Ouray, 1896," pp. 138–155.)

[22] When the government moved the Jicarilla to the Mescalero Apache Reservation in southern New Mexico in 1883, it promised these Indians that they could return to the north if they wished. Meanwhile, about twenty Mexican families moved onto their reservation and took bona fide homesteads, claiming all the land fit for agricultural pursuits. When the Indians returned, they found very little land left that was suitable for farming. (*Ind. Commiss. Annual Report, 1894*, p. 211.) In 1895, the agent reported that the intruders were looking upon the Jicarilla reservation "with covetous eyes, and agency employees are scarcely able to keep them off...." (*Ind. Commiss. Annual Report, 1895*, p. 221.)

Background on
Notes on the Cheyenne Country and Lame Deer

The Cheyenne are an Algonquian tribe which before 1700 lived in what is now Minnesota. They were, at that time, an agricultural people with fixed villages, and they apparently made pottery. They gave up their agricultural pursuits and arts when the Sioux, who were retreating before the Chippewa, drove them westward. Lewis and Clark found them in the vicinity of the Black Hills on the headwaters of the Cheyenne River in South Dakota. With the Sioux still pressing them, they moved to the North Platte. After the establishment of Bent's Fort near modern La Junta, Colorado, in 1832, part of the tribe decided to make permanent settlements on the upper Arkansas while the rest stayed on the North Platte and the Yellowstone. In the treaty of Fort Laramie in 1851, the division of the tribe became permanent.

The Northern Cheyenne participated in border warfare after 1860. During the mid-1870s, they allied with the Sioux and participated in the Custer fight. By late 1876, the army had captured many of them and sent them to the Cheyenne-Arapaho Reservation in the Indian Territory. Discontented with the climate and weakened by malaria, Dull Knife and Little Wolf led a number of men, women, and children back to the north in what became known as the "Dull Knife Raid." Captured in October, 1878, they were moved to Fort Robinson, Nebraska, where they attempted an escape during which many of them were killed. On March 1, 1883, Congress provided for these and those Northern Cheyenne in Indian Territory to be removed to the Pine Ridge Reservation, South Dakota. However, since 1878, the Northern Cheyenne had immigrated to the Tongue River valley in Montana, and by 1883 numbered 575. A reservation was established there for the Northern Cheyenne in 1884.[1]

At that time, some Indians had made permanent improvements, but many were destitute. They made little progress in any respects during the following decade. Their boundaries were poorly defined, and there was constant friction between them and the white ranchers on their borders. The climate was too harsh for successful farming, and the government failed to fence their range and furnish them sufficient cattle to build their own herds. Such was their general condition when Garland visited them in 1897. During that year, the 1330 Northern Cheyenne had only 246 acres under cultivation and 2,500 acres under fence. They produced 488 bushels of corn, 627 bushels of vegetables, and 385 tons of hay. They had 3,686 horses, 68 hogs, and 329 domestic fowls.[2]

"Notes on the Cheyenne Country and Lame Deer" offers the reader Garland's first impressions of the Cheyenne. Their demeanor, the courtesy with which he was received, and the enjoyment they derived from their ceremonial dance seemed to refute the rumors of an outbreak which the writer had come to investigate. Garland uses the dance as a springboard for arguing against a pet theory of the assimilationists of the day: that the traditional ceremonies of the American Indian should be discontinued because they were barbaric and immoral, and, therefore, disruptive to the "progress of civilization."

[1] Frederick Webb Hodge, ed., Handbook of American Indians North of Mexico, Pt. 1, pp. 251–253.

[2] Ind. Commiss. Annual Reports, 1897, pp. 176–177, 502–503.

8. Notes on the Cheyenne Country and Lame Deer[3]

It was a beautiful July day, the day we rode across the divide, between the Crow country and Lame Deer. The trail led up the valley of Reno Creek down which Major Reno[4] had led his command to the Custer fight. It grew greener as we went upward, and on the higher hills were groves of pine, dark green and delicious to the eye. The grass became heavier and fresher. The water in the creeks lost its alkaline character and became cool and sweet. At the summit wild roses were still in bloom. Here we spent the night in the cabin of the government saw mill superintendent, and the next day we rode down into the hot, dry country of the Cheyennes. Here again was another Indian country upon which the sun shone piteously and the rain almost never fell. It is a hot red country, the walls of the canyons are of red rock, the grass is very short and dry, the streams are small and slow, and every indication is of a barren and difficult land in which to live.

The Cheyennes are a leaner people as we saw at once than the Crows or the Sioux. They reminded me of the Navajoes. The women were taller, however, and decidedly more lean than the Crows. Many trails lead across the hills, and at issue day the people come from every direction on horseback. The young men especially come whirling up the valley or filing down the hills in picturesque squads.

Around the pleasant agency yard and buildings[5] the Indians were working building fence, painting the roofs of the barns; others were grinding sickles. They seemed to be excellent workmen, quiet and methodical in manner. In fact, one of the very first impressions made upon me was that this was a strong and serious people. They have always been warriors, and they have the war-like virtues. They are progressive now and eager to learn the best that the white man can teach them.

---

[3] Item 450, Hamlin Garland Collection, University of Southern California Library, Los Angeles, published by permission of the University of Southern California Library and Constance Garland Doyle and Isabel Garland Lord.

[4] Marcus Albert Reno (1834–1889) was born in Greene County, Illinois, graduated from West Point in 1857, and assigned to duty in the West. He served in the Civil War and afterwards worked for the Freedmen's Bureau. In 1868 he was made a major in the Seventh Cavalry. As a result of the Custer defeat, he was dismissed in 1880, charged with cowardice and other misconduct during the battle of the Little Bighorn. (*The National Cyclopaedia of American Biography*, 4:526.)

[5] The Northern Cheyenne Agency was at Lame Deer on the Lame Deer River, a few miles above its confluence with the Rosebud.

The agent at the Lame Deer post, I found to be Captain Stouch,[6] a military man of admirable qualities. There had been some trouble with the white settlers in the Tongue River country, and there were several troops of cavalry camped upon the flat floor of the valley, their white tents glistening under the vivid sunlight.[7] Having letters of introduction to both Captain Stouch and officers of the troops, we were made at home at once, and began messing with Lieutenant Livermore[8] and Captain Cooper[9] of the 10th Regiment. The cook of the mess was a Chinaman, and his domination of the Captain and Lieutenant was a source of great amusement to us. He had a way of saying, "Have some meat" in the tone of a man who orders it, and he was very indignant if we were a minute late at the mess. He afforded me a very curious study of the Chinaman under modified conditions. He really bullied the Captain and Lieutenant until, ultimately, they were obliged to discharge him.

On the evening of the second day of our stay, we attended a dance[10] in the big dancehouse just south of the Agency. It was a big circular tepee of logs, or rather octagonal in shape with the logs interlacing at the corners. When we arrived the people were all seated around the inner wall, the Crows who were visiting the Cheyennes on one side and the men and women of the camp on the other side. Old Two Moon,[11] one of the principal chiefs of the Cheyenne people was the host, and right gallantly and courteously he bore himself.

---

[6] George W. H. Stouch, born in 1842 at Gettysburg, Pennsylvania, served in the Civil War and in the U.S. Army departments of Missouri, Dakota, and Gulf from 1864–1899. In 1893, he was Indian agent to the Sisseton Sioux in South Dakota. He was the Northern Cheyenne agent from February 1, 1894, to November 16, 1897. At that time he became agent to the Crows and, in 1899, to the Southern Cheyenne and Arapahos at Darlington, Oklahoma Territory. (*Portrait and Biographical Record of Oklahoma*, pp. 381–382.)

[7] These troops had been dispatched to Lame Deer as a precaution in the conflict between the Indians and the ranchers. Troops A and K of the Tenth (Negro) Cavalry, under the command of Captain Robert D. Read, Jr., arrived from Fort Custer on May 27. On May 31 and June 1, more troops were dispatched from Fort Custer and Fort Keogh. From the former came Troop E of the Tenth Cavalry under Major Stevens T. Norvell, and from the latter came Company E of the Second Infantry under Captain John Kinzie and Troop A of the Eighth Cavalry under Lieutenant John N. Morgan, as well as an assistant surgeon and a detachment of hospital corps. Total military personnel included 11 officers and 243 enlisted men. (Assistant Adjutant General Gilmore to Adjutant General and M. V. Sheridan to Adjutant General, May 29, 1897, Tongue River Reservation Consolidated File 45572.)

[8] This was Second Lieutenant Richard Larremore Livermore, Tenth Cavalry, Fort Keogh, Montana.

[9] Captain Charles L. Cooper, Company A, Tenth Cavalry, Fort Keogh, Montana, served as commander of troop stationed at Camp Merritt during 1897, when Garland visited Lame Deer.

[10] Garland used the scenes at this dance, including the description of the dancehouse, the little dancer, and the old dancer in a similar episode in *The Captain of the Gray-Horse Troop*. (Hamlin Garland, *The Captain of the Gray-Horse Troop*, pp. 189, 191.)

[11] Two Moon, born about 1847, was half Arikara, a Caddoan tribe from the Dakotas. He became a well-known chief who led a segment of the Cheyenne in the Custer fight. After he surrendered in 1877, he scouted for General Miles against the Nez Percé, then settled quietly on the Tongue River Reservation. (George B. Grinnell, *The Cheyennes: Their History and Ways of Life*, 2: 143; John Stands In Timber and Margot Liberty, *Cheyenne Memories*, pp. 227, 239.)

He greeted us pleasantly and invited us to a seat by his side, where an exchange of courtesies in the way of tobacco took place. In the center of the lodge was a huge fire, and the smoke rolling up through a large aperture in the roof was lighted gloriously by the flames beneath, while out of the shadow of the walls the bronze faces of the smiling people appeared.

At length, Two Moon arose, walked forward and spoke in a loud voice, in which he probably announced the beginning of the dance. The drummers who had been seated quietly around the drum raised themselves upon their knees, and then their leader began a high-keyed imitation of the howl of a wolf, the other joined in yapping chorus with hurried action and beat upon the drum and the whole company fell at last into a deep musical humming chorus.

At once the dancers, splendid in their dancing costumes and head dresses, advanced from their seats near the wall in splendidly dramatic steps. They imitated the action of the hunter on the trail, looking to the ground and then glancing at the sky with a powerful and sinuous and flinging motion of the head. The step was quieter than that of the Crows. A very dignified, almost gliding step with a singular snapping of the ankle. In general, however, the movement was like the dancing of the Crows. The Crows moved with a more impetuous and rebounding step, their feet seemed to spring up from the earth like a rubber ball, deft, quick and muscular. They all danced into the center and round the fire, uttering occasional war whoops without confusion and without crowding. In the midst of them was a little boy of about three and a half years of age.

This little fellow was dressed precisely like a warrior who had been through many battles. He was a slim and active little figure and danced with the greatest gravity and serenity of countenance. It was beautiful to see how careful the men were not to jostle him, not to embarrass him in any way. He had just as much right upon the floor of the dance lodge as any of the oldest warriors there, and was accorded equal space.

Nearly two thirds of the dancers were Crows, and Two Moon, as the host, had a great deal to do in making them feel at home. If he saw someone uncertain of finding a place or if some question of etiquette arose, if some visitor were trying to find another Crow, he rose to his feet as any hostess would do in a drawing room and set forth to make everybody comfortable and at ease.

The musicians crowded closely around the big drum which stood at the right of the door. The singing at times began quietly like that of the Crows, plainly an imitation of wolves upon the trail, but fell always into a deeper and more melodious strain toward the close. The fire roared up, filled with soaring sparks, and the smoke rolled away and was lost in the deep blue sky which could be seen through the roof. The Crows moved about with their superbly dramatic dance with violent stamping action, imitating the movement of men on the hunting trail or war trail, but each dance was short, wild and splendid, and it seemed it went forward with perfect decorum and rigid etiquette. After some minutes of dancing, the dancers took their seats again against the wall and lighted their pipes, while Two Moon returned to his seat beside his white visitors. In the intervals between the dance, gifts of horses and blankets were brought in and conveyed across the lodge to the visiting Crows. There was less of this giving away of goods among the Cheyennes, perhaps for the reason that they are poorer than the Crows and also because they do not believe in it so thoroughly.

An old man of the Crow people 72 years of age became very much moved by the dance and the singing and being a good deal of age arose and danced as best his stiff legs could, and was treated with laughter and applause. He ended with a peculiar rheumatic kick which amused them all very much indeed.

The giving of presents was preceded in each case by the separate dance of those about to make the present, holding in their hands a sort of head dress made of trailing feathers. This seemed to mark the willingness of the man carrying it to make a present. The presents were mainly horses and, as among the Crows, a stick represented the horse, and once the little boy was permitted to carry the stick across the big firelighted hall and present it to the Crow who was to be honored by the little boy's father.

Sometimes only two would be dancing, at other times four or five; again, just before a set, as country people would say, Two Moon arose and called out something in a loud voice. This was, undoubtedly, the notice that a certain society of young men were about to dance, for the dancers would appear from separate parts of the room. There are many societies among these people, and these young men were undoubtedly all members of such societies and perhaps of several societies at the same time.[12]

Heard from the outside, it would have seemed to a timid newspaper correspondent from New York a very demoniacal performance. Seen from the inside and from my position by the side of Two Moon, it was a very genial and interesting ceremony. Two Moon was a most gracious and charming host. He seemed to beam kindly hospitality. He was tireless in his attempts to make us at home. The swirling forms, the leaping fire, the vivid colors, the haughty fling of tall head dresses, the drumming feet, the tinkle of bells, the short shrill whoops, the furious beat of the drum, all these were superbly dramatic and had in them nothing more than drama and a social coming together of the people.

At times, men arose whose will it was to make speeches and tell what they had done in their olden days. They were not listened to very carefully, by the most of those sitting about, but the drummers in the manner of a hired clerk at the theatre, broke in upon every impressive period with a furious pounding of the drum. The speeches were of this character: "I am Eagle Feather. You all know me. I have been a great hunter (boom, boom, boom). I have stolen many horses from my enemies (boom, boom). In the old days I made war upon the Sioux, they were afraid of me, they ran before me so fast I had to beat my horse hard to overtake them (boom, boom, boom). They were like the long eared rabbits of the plain. They had no heart (boom, boom)."

The young men spoke of these men as old timers. Their bold deeds of olden times fell as indifferently upon young ears as do the tales of grandsire

---

[12]Among the Cheyennes, the most significant groups or societies are the family, kindred, band, military fraternities, women's societies, and the tribal council. (E. Adamson Hoebel, *The Cheyennes: Indians of the Great Plains*, p. 20.)

when he tells of being at Bull Run or Lundy's Lane or the Wilderness.[13] After one or two speeches of this kind, the dance again went forward. I remained until nearly twelve o'clock, listening to it, watching with eager eyes the splendid action of the lithe and powerful figures, fascinated by the ever-changing groups of forms and colors, but at last I rose to go, and as I did so, Two Moon rose, and with the finest courtesy shook my hand and bowed me out of the door.

There was nothing in the whole dance which could by any reasonable interpretation be called ferocious or demoralizing. It was their social gathering; it afforded them an opportunity of coming once a week together, quite in the manner of a dance in the country. It afforded the young men an opportunity to show their grace and power to the young girls, and afforded also an opportunity for the young girls to select from among the dancers those whom they most admired. These people are like any other people. They need recreation. They are very social, and they need something to bring them together. In the olden time they had many such social gatherings, many feasts, many festivities. It would be cruel to cut them off from this, their principal way of meeting in harmless amusement. The story-telling of the old men is no longer an incitement to daring deeds. There is no danger in the talk of the old timer.

---

[13] Bull Run and the Wilderness were battles of the Civil War. Lundy's Lane was the most sharply contested land action during the War of 1812. Garland probably alludes to them so readily because at this time he had just completed his biography of General Ulysses S. Grant, which he had worked on since January, 1896. (Hamlin Garland, "Notes and hints.") During 1897–1898, *McClure's* published the biography serially, and the Doubleday & McClure Company published the work as *Ulysses S. Grant: Life and Character* (1898).

Background on
A Typical Indian Scare

Indefinite boundaries of the Tongue River Reservation were a constant source of friction after its establishment in 1884. Both the western boundary between the Crow Reservation and the Rosebud River and the eastern boundary west of the Tongue River remained unsettled. Anglos occupied 1500 acres of the best lands on the Tongue River. The Indians complained that the ranchers allowed their stock to range over the reservation, and the ranchers charged the Indians with killing their livestock. In 1896, agent George W. H. Stouch, as previous agents had done, futilely suggested that the government survey the boundaries, purchase land owned by bona fide ranchers, and fence the reservation as a way of settling the questions.[1]

During 1896 and early 1897, authorities found three murdered men on land adjoining the reservation. Anglos blamed the murders on the Indians but could prove nothing. No serious conflict occurred until May 23, 1897, when a party found the body of John Hoover, a sheep herder for the Fred H. Barringer Ranch. The whites charged the Indians with the death and armed themselves to take revenge.[2]

Newspapers promptly reported an "outbreak" of the Northern Cheyenne, and warned that war seemed imminent. Stouch, however, feared no outbreak but sent to Fort Custer for soldiers. Two troops of cavalry arrived at the agency on May 27. In spite of having to thwart the violent intent of a mob of ranchers who invaded the reservation, Stouch succeeded in arresting one David Stanley (alias Whirlwind and Little Whirlwind's Voice), Spotted Hawk, Shoulder Blade, Sam Crow, Yellow Hair, and Little Whirlwind. The latter Indian seems to have escaped Garland's notice, for in his essay he makes no mention of him as a separate person, instead confusing him with David Stanley, who had two similar Cheyenne names.

Garland's ignorance of Little Whirlwind as a separate individual is surprising, since when the men went to trial, Little Whirlwind was convicted of second-degree murder and given a life sentence. Nor does the author mention Spotted Hawk, who was sentenced to hang until his attorney gained a new trial and, upon presenting the case to the Montana Supreme Court, obtained his release because of a lack of evidence.

David Stanley, or Whirlwind, had entered a plea of guilty to second degree murder and received ten years at hard labor, but the sentence was later reduced

---

[1] In 1892 Cheyenne agent John Tully charged that land officials in Miles City were allowing whites to stake homesteads and desert claims on tribal land. Tully attributed the white-Indian friction to a lack of established boundaries. (*Ind. Commiss. Annual Report, 1892*, pp. 302–303.) Stock losses also provoked and irritated the whites. Indian thievery became so bad on Calvin C. Howes' ranch that in October of 1896 he asked the government to intervene to stop the losses. Major Jacob H. Smith investigated and reported that the killing of cattle was being done "out of mischievous devilment of the young men who in spirit of bravado, play the cattle for Buffalo." (Report of Smith, December 7, 1897, Tongue River Reservation Consolidated File 45572.)

[2] *New York Times*, June 1, 1897; *Ind. Commiss. Annual Reports, 1897*, p. 81.

to five years. On October *19, 1899*, Stanley died in prison, having admitted that he was the sole murderer of Hoover. The other three Indians implicated in the case were released from custody.[3]

It was news of the so-called "outbreak" that brought Garland to the Northern Cheyenne Reservation. He interviewed the head men, the agent, and the military officers. From his interviews he wrote the following depiction of the incident. The account is not typical of the journalistic writings that followed the author's *1895* visit to Indian tribes in the Southwest. Instead, it is a report, agreeing in both substance and tone with Stouch's report to the commissioner of Indian affairs and with military reports. In it Garland defends the Indian as virtuous, speaks against frontier vigilante retribution, and advocates the military to preserve justice.

In *1900* the author planned a novel treating life on the Northern Cheyenne reservation. That work became The Captain of the Gray-Horse Troop (*1902*), the germ for which came from this *1897* report of the murder incident.

---

[3]Affidavit by T. J. Porter, July 20, 1897; Court Minutes, May and October terms, 1897, and May term, 1898, District Court, Seventh Judicial District, Miles City, Montana. The authorities released Shoulder Blade on November 5 and Sam Crow on November 13. Little Whirlwind was pardoned from prison on July 1, 1901. (*Ind. Commiss. Annual Reports, 1901*, pp. 161–163.)

9. A Typical Indian Scare: The Cheyenne Trouble [4]

The Cheyenne reservation is in Custer County, Montana, and adjoins the eastern line of the Crow lands. It is a dry country — this year pitilessly dry. It is watered by three small streams: the Rosebud River, and Lame Deer and Big Muddy Creeks. All else is arid. These streams can be made to irrigate a few small patches of bottom land — no more.[5] It must forever remain without cultivation. The whole tract is from four to five thousand feet above the sea and is composed for the most part of rugged hills covered with scattered pines.

On the east is a strip of land several miles in width which has been withdrawn from settlement by the Department of the Interior but which has not been added to the actual reservation. The eastern line of the acknowledged Indian lands has not been accurately surveyed, and out of this indefiniteness much of the trouble of recent years has arisen. Another and fruitful source of trouble is the presence of white settlers on the lands claimed by the Indians. These ranchers came into the country before the land was set aside for the Cheyennes, and they hold all the best sites and a large part of the water rights of the entire reservation.[6] Their interests are opposed to the Indians', and they are not philanthropists.

These settlers claim with justice that the Indians should either be removed or the government should buy out their claims. It is probable that they would welcome a purchase for the reason that ranching has ceased to pay. Many of the papers of the state are vindictively and unreasonably the enemies of the

---

[4] Item 459, Hamlin Garland Collection, University of Southern California Library, Los Angeles, published by permission of the University of Southern California Library and Constance Garland Doyle and Isabel Garland Lord. This document, edited in a slightly different manner, appeared in *Arizona and the West*, 15 (Autumn, 1973), 257–274, and is reprinted here with permission of *Arizona and the West*.

[5] In 1897 the Northern Cheyennes had 246 acres under cultivation and 2,500 acres under fence. They produced that year 288 bushels of corn, 627 bushels of vegetables, and 385 tons of hay. Their livestock included 3,686 horses, 68 swine, and 329 domestic fowls. (*Ind. Commiss. Annual Reports, 1897*, pp. 502–503.)

[6] As early as 1887, agent R. L. Upshaw reported there were at least ten white settlers on the reservation who claimed to have acquired rights previous to its creation. Their claims covered some of the best lands. (*Ind. Commiss. Annual Report, 1887*, p. 147.)

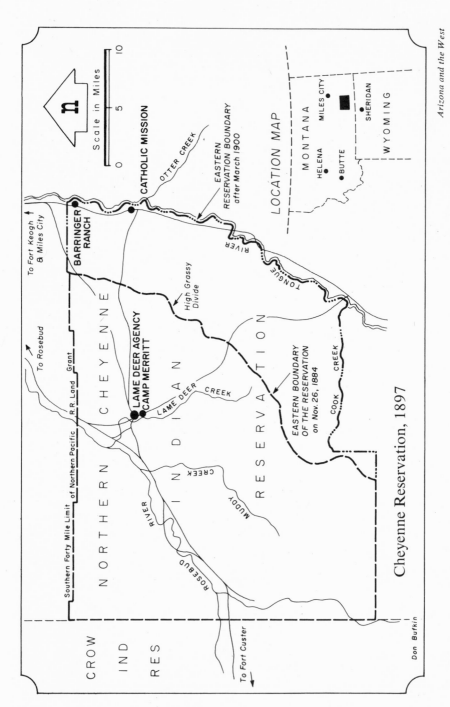

Cheyenne Reservation, 1897

LOCATION MAP

MONTANA

HELENA
•BUTTE

MILES CITY

SHERIDAN

WYOMING

Scale in Miles

0   5   10

BARRINGER RANCH

CATHOLIC MISSION

EASTERN RESERVATION BOUNDARY after March 1900

To Fort Keogh & Miles City

To Rosebud

R.R. Land Grant

Southern Forty Mile Limit of Northern Pacific

NORTHERN CHEYENNE INDIAN RESERVATION

LAME DEER AGENCY
CAMP MERRITT

High Grassy Divide

LAME DEER CREEK

EASTERN BOUNDARY OF THE RESERVATION on Nov. 26, 1884

COOK CREEK

TONGUE RIVER

OTTER CREEK

MUDDY CREEK

ROSEBUD RIVER

To Fort Custer

CROW IND RES

Don Bufkin

Arizona and the West

The land between the high grassy divide and the Tongue River was in constant dispute by the Indians and Anglo ranchers.

Indian and lose no opportunity to magnify or falsify reports of Indian trouble and attack remorselessly any one who dares to suggest that the Cheyennes should be justly dealt with.[7] A row between a white man and a Cheyenne is held to be an "uprising" and the state is advised to sweep the Indian from the earth.[8] Men who are reasonable in other subjects, who profess to be Christian gentlemen, give utterance to the most ferocious sentiments. Generally, however, the advice to "sweep the Indian off the earth" comes from those who are not ready to do the sweeping on their own account.

In spite of many provoking causes there has been very little actual violence. The prejudiced press of the state make numerous charges, but they are not sustained by competent investigation. The situation has been growing graver each year, and recently the dispatches sent out from Miles City have filled the papers east and west with news of "Another Outbreak of Indians," "Cheyennes on the War Path," etc.[9] Being on the ground, I here present a plain story of the affair as it has taken shape in my mind after interviewing the agent, the settlers, the officers at the camp and the Indians themselves.[10]

About the first day of May a sheep herder on a Mr. Barringer's ranch had occasion to leave his sheep to go to the Rosebud River, and another man took his place.[11] This temporary herder, so the Indians say, drove his sheep too near some meadow land on the territory in dispute, and two young Cheyennes saw him and told him to drive his sheep back. They fell into anger and the herder gathered up rocks and stoned the Indians away. Next day, Hoover, the regular herder, returned to his post and a few days later disappeared altogether.[12]

---

[7] The Miles City *Yellowstone* on May 7, 1897, warned that if the Cheyennes had murdered Hoover, there would be trouble. The settlers had "suffered long and if not patiently, at least doggedly," hoping that the government would settle the Cheyenne question.

[8] Garland's statement is reflective in tone and content of the later statement of the well-known novelist Oliver LaFarge: "It is typical of white men's thinking of the time that when General Custer and his cavalry were wiped out because they attacked superior numbers, it was called 'The Custer Massacre,' but when these Sioux with their women and children were murdered in their tents, it was called 'The Battle of Wounded Knee'." (Oliver LaFarge, *A Pictorial History of the American Indian*, p. 178.)

[9] The *New York Times*, on June 1, 1897, began carrying a full account of the incident. Citing an unidentified newspaper in Helena, Montana, it declared that the Cheyennes were "on the warpath and had already killed a dozen men, including five United States soldiers." The settlers were in arms and had sent their women and children to town for safety. The *Times* editor, however, admitted he could not verify that there had been an outbreak.

[10] For a reproduction of a page from Garland's original manuscript for this essay, see the Introductory Survey in this book.

[11] The Fred H. Barringer Ranch was near Geddes, Montana, and on the Tongue River. John Hoover, a young man and the son of Monroe Hoover of Everton, Missouri, had recently gone to work there. (*New York Times,* June 2, 1897; Billings *Times,* June 10, 1897.) Hoover's substitute cannot be identified.

[12] On May 17 Barringer wrote the Miles City *Yellowstone* concerning Hoover's disappearance. Hoover had gone to work at the ranch on March 14, herded sheep until April 26, taken two days off, and then returned to his camp. When a flock of sheep wandered into the ranch headquarters on May 3, Barringer and another man drove them back to Hoover's camp and found the herder gone. They could find no trace of him or his dog. (Miles City *Yellowstone*, May 21, 1897.)

On the sixth of May a man from Barringer's neighborhood[13] came to Captain Stouch (U.S.A.), acting Indian Agent at Lame Deer, conveying the news that Hoover and a valuable dog had disappeared and that Barringer had offered a reward for any news of the dog or Hoover.[14] He also told Captain Stouch that the settlers laid the man's disappearance to the Indians. The captain immediately called together White Bull (Chief of the Tongue River band of Cheyennes) and his headmen[15] and told them he wanted a search party formed. While the party was organizing, he wrote to Barringer asking for a guide. This note he sent by courier, and before the party was ready to move, the courier returned with a letter from Barringer stating the man had been heard from and that there was no further need of the search party.[16] This news the captain asked the criers to announce to the band, and the Indians were much pleased and the whole affair seemed ended.

In a few days it was discovered that the report was a mistake.[17] Hoover could not be found and on the 22nd a cousin[18] of the herder reported to the captain that a search party of citizens had been organized to start on the 24th, and that he would like the aid of the Indians. The white settlers had grown very much excited, but Captain Stouch sent his Indian police to join the party at once.[19] Before they arrived at the point of rendezvous, however, the body was found in plain view where the man fell a short distance off the land claimed by the Indians. It was also alleged by the settlers that three shells were found and signs of three horses, and that there was a carcass of a beef near.[20]

On the 25th Captain Stouch sent word to White Bull to bring his band in and camp near the agency,[21] and on the morning of the 26th they arrived. Captain Stouch had little faith in the stories of three murderers, for the reason

---

[13] This man may have been Walter O'Connell (see note 16 following).

[14] On May 13 the Miles City *Yellowstone* reported that a reward of fifty dollars was offered, probably by Barringer, for information concerning Hoover. The Indians would not hunt for him, believing that if they found him dead they "would be charged with killing him."

[15] Stouch asked White Bull to select only seven or eight men — particularly Badger, Spotted Hawk, and Two Bull — to come to his office that night. (*Ind. Commiss. Annual Reports, 1897*, p. 82.)

[16] Mrs. Samuel O'Connell sent her son Walter to inform Barringer that Hoover was at Bob-Tail Horse's camp near Hungry Woman Creek above the SH Ranch. Barringer doubted the report, for Hoover had recently come from Missouri and was frightened of the Indians. (Miles City *Yellowstone*, May 13, 18, 21, 1897.)

[17] R. P. Colbert and Ottway Jackson went to Bob-Tail Horse's camp, and were told that Hoover perhaps was at an Indian camp on Lame Deer Creek. (*Ibid.*, May 21, 1897.)

[18] Hoover's cousin cannot be identified.

[19] Stouch sent a captain and nine men to join the search party. (*Ind. Commiss. Annual Reports, 1897*, p. 177.)

[20] Stouch said that the searchers found the body on May 23 and buried it near the scene of the murder. (*Ind. Commiss. Annual Reports, 1897*, p. 81.) Barringer theorized that Hoover had come upon several Indians who had killed a beef and they had fired at him to scare him away. "It is a well-known fact," Barringer said, "that they shoot at every white man who comes onto them while killing a beef, though they may not always shoot to kill." (Miles City *Yellowstone*, May 21, 1897.)

[21] Because White Bull's permanent camp was in the vicinity of the murder, his band was immediately suspected as containing the guilty parties.

that nearly three weeks had passed and rains and the passing of many ponies and cattle made it improbable that any signs so definite could still remain. However, he was anxious to disprove the charge by a careful examination.

Early on the 27th of May, he sent for White Bull to come and see him. White Bull is chief of the Tongue River band of Cheyennes, and the captain felt that if Indians committed the murder, they were in White Bull's band. White Bull is one of the most powerful men in the reservation and is heartily in sympathy with the agent. He is a tall old man, dark, rugged and wrinkled of face. He listened in silence to the agent's story but his face showed great concern. "Now go home," said Captain Stouch, "and tell all your headmen to come down and see me tonight at my house."

About two o'clock[22] a band of armed white men rode into the agency yard from the east, and a few minutes later another band rode up the valley from the north, making in all about twenty-five heavily armed men. Their coming was sinister, but the agent met them as pleasantly as possible and inquired their business. He was answered by the sheriff.[23]

"We are a committee, appointed by the settlers now at the inquest of the murdered man, and we have come to demand the murderers of you.[24] I came to satisfy the crowd who hold the Cheyenne tribe responsible for this murder."

The agent saw the danger in this armed mob's invasion of the reservation but he did not lose his head. "Have you warrants?" "No." "Do you know the names of the Cheyennes who did the deed?" "No." "Do you *know* that they did it?" "We know damn well they killed the man and we're going to hold the whole tribe responsible for the murder and if they don't give the men up we'll wipe the tribe off the face of the earth."

Talk grew loud. One man said, "There is three hundred men from Sheridan ready and a hundred from the Rosebud.[25] We've stood this just as long as we're going to."

Some more sensible men struck in. "Go slow boys; we'll fix this matter up."

Another said, "Yes it'll be fixed up just as it has always been and no one will answer for it. It'll end right here."

"Not by a damn sight," struck in another. "If you back out I'm goin' on. With ten good men I'll clear out the whole cussed tribe."

In such wise these patriots and law-abiding citizens fumed and boasted. Without warrants, without the faintest evidence to convict any individual, they invaded the lines of an Indian reservation with the design to begin an exterminating war upon the Cheyennes. Captain Stouch was not at the moment in a

---

[22] This mob actually arrived at 2:00 on May 28, not on the 27th, as Garland implies.

[23] The sheriff was John Gibb.

[24] Over one hundred people came to the inquest. (*New York Times*, June 1, 1897.) Sheriff Gibb said he had difficulty in keeping the crowd from invading the reservation. His group included four deputies, a committee of twelve men representing those at the inquest, and men who volunteered to help seize the murderers. Stouch did not record his dialogue with the visitors, but his summary generally agrees with Garland's rendering. Stouch says they rode in at noon. (*Ind. Commiss. Annual Reports, 1897*, p. 82.)

[25] Sheridan, Wyoming, is about sixty-five miles south of Lame Deer; Rosebud, Montana, is about sixty-five miles to the north.

condition to put them off the reservation as he should have done. He was forced to parley.

Meanwhile an Indian interpreter standing near had heard every word, and the few Indians working about the agency gradually, noiselessly and without haste slipped away to spread the alarm — "Our dreaded enemies, the white ranchers, are upon us."

Captain Stouch glanced often down the valley. In anticipation of something like this, he had telegraphed to Fort Custer for troops, and they should have arrived the day before.[26] He said again and again to the mob, "Go back, get out your warrants, and bring them to me and I will serve them, but you must get off the reservation. You are a menace. You are not here in due process of law."[27]

After a long pow-wow the sheriff yielded so far as to agree to go back, provided four deputies[28] should be allowed to remain "to quiet the crowd at the inquest." Captain Stouch finally agreed to this, "Though I don't see the good of it. They can do nothing."

Just in the final passages of this one-sided altercation, an officer of the United States cavalry, with shining white helmet and vividly blue uniform, came riding across the valley from the west. The agency employees were ready to burst into a cheer. The rider was Captain Robert D. Read, and his troops were not far behind. He rode up and reported to the agent, and his coming silenced the loud-mouthed boastings of the mob.[29]

Captain Read grasped the situation, and when his troops came streaming out of the valley a little later old White Bull felt his heart "grow glad." "The soldiers are my friends," he said. Captain Read was ready to escort the mob to the limits of the reservation and it should have been done, but Captain Stouch being a man of amiable disposition was not ready for such measures.

------

[26] Garland is in error. A detachment of one officer and ten men of the Second Infantry was permanently stationed at Camp Merritt, near the agency, but this force was deemed insufficient. To provide further security Stouch had asked the commander to telegraph Fort Custer for two troops of cavalry, and Troops A and K of the Tenth (Negro) under Captain Robert D. Read, Jr., arrived at Lame Deer on the evening of May 27, i. e., the day before the mob arrived. (*Ind. Commiss. Annual Reports, 1897*, pp. 80–82.) Read had gone on the morning of May 28 to the Tongue River vicinity to investigate the murder. Stouch had sent a courier to recall him, fearing the whites might attempt rash action, and anxiously awaited Read's return.

Camp Merritt was established in 1890, and became a subpost of Fort Keogh eight years later. (Francis Paul Prucha, *A Guide to the Military Posts of the United States, 1789–1895*, p. 91.) A few days after the arrival of Read and his troops, they were joined by others from Fort Custer and Fort Keogh, bringing the number of soldiers stationed there to 11 officers and 243 men. (Returns from U.S. Military Posts, 1800–1916, Camp Merritt, May and June, 1897.)

[27] On May 29 Stouch handed Deputy William D. Smith a note which said: "Under section 2152, Revised Statutes, United States, it is my duty as Indian Agent to 'procure the arrest and trial of all Indians accused of committing any crime, offense....'" (*Ind. Commiss. Annual Reports, 1897*, p. 84.)

[28] The deputies were William D. Smith, Matt Winter, and two others.

[29] Garland dramatizes this scene. Stouch recorded simply: "Captain Read with two troops of cavalry arrived just before the departure of the sheriff and his party." (*Ind. Commiss. Annual Reports, 1897*, p. 82.)

The crowd rode away, and then the Indians began to come back and resume their places about the agency.

At six o'clock White Bull and six of his headmen came to meet the agent, who again stated the accusation of the whites and said, "You must find these three men. The white men hold your band responsible and you must look hard and find these bad men of your band and bring them to me. The law of the white man must be obeyed. If my son should do wrong, I would give him up to the law. You must do the same." There was a long silence after he finished.

Among those who sat before him was an old man named Badger, a small man with a red-brown complexion and a fine profile. He was a quiet man of almost timid manners. When his turn came to shake hands with the agent he said, "I will try to find these men. I will look hard, and I will bring them in even if one of them is my own son."[30] Others said the same and one by one they withdrew.

White Bull then called a council[31] of his people to meet next day and early in the morning the headmen of the band were seated in a circle on the ground ready to listen to reports from those who sought to find out the murderers. White Bull, White Shield, Bull Thigh, Standing Elk, Badger, and White Hawk were conspicuous figures in the council, while just behind them sat a larger circle of young men mounted on their horses. All were most excited. The coming of the soldiers, the presence of the "cowboys," as they called the deputies, alarmed and bewildered them, but they had no wish to fight. White Bull was especially anxious to avoid trouble.

Soon after the council opened Little Whirlwind [David Stanley],[32] the son of Badger, appeared and his coming called out low words of astonishment. He was in full dress, completely armed and had his war paint on. Instantly every man who looked upon him said, "He is the man." The war paint, the gun, the dress and his actions proclaimed him. He entered without a word and took his seat beside White Bull. Bull Thigh took a seat directly before Little Whirlwind and the three men conversed in low voices for some time. The old man seemed to plead with Whirlwind. The horsemen crowded closer, and the people sat with eyes fixed upon the son and his father, whose face

---

[30] The *New York Times*, June 14, 1897, attributed the statement to White Bull. Stouch, like Garland, attributes it to Badger. (*Ind. Commiss. Annual Reports, 1897*, p. 82.)

[31] Stouch did not record the proceedings at the council. However, his summary of White Bull's report agrees with Garland's rendering. (*Ind. Commiss. Annual Reports, 1897*, p. 82.)

[32] Garland refers to the son of Badger by several names, including Little Whirlwind, Whirlwind, Little Whirlwind's Voice, and David Stanley. The *New York Times* on June 13 and 14, 1897, also referred to him by these names. However, apparently both Garland and the newspaper did not realize that there were *two* Indians at the agency by the same name. The man whose case is chronicled by Garland should not be confused with the Little Whirlwind discussed in the introduction to this essay. This man, of no relation to Badger, was the one found guilty of second-degree murder and sentenced to life imprisonment at the state penitentiary at Deer Lodge. Badger's son (David Stanley) was convicted as an accomplice, receiving only a ten-year sentence, but later admitted that he was the sole murderer in 1899, when he died in prison. (See introduction to this essay for additional details.)

betrayed great excitement. He had asked the headmen to find out from his son who was with him when he killed the man. "He is my son but I know nothing," he said. Little Whirlwind had been at school for a short time but could speak very little English. He was a rather good-looking young man but erratic in his habit. He had belonged to the Indian troop at Camp Keogh[33] and had been discharged for unsoundness of mind. He was not on good terms with his father and was known to be moody and flighty. His Indian name literally interpreted means "Little Whirlwind's Voice."

The three men conversed for some time trying hard to get him to tell who was with him. At last old White Bull rose and stepped into the middle of the circle. "Whirlwind's Voice is the man who killed the white man," he cried. "He did it alone. No one helped him, he says. Now you headmen, I want you to go down with me and tell the agent. You young men," he cried raising his voice and glancing round at the circle of young horsemen, "I want you to shake hands with Whirlwind's Voice and say good-bye to him and go home. You must have nothing more to do with him. Keep away from him. We don't want one man to give trouble to the whole tribe."

Bull Thigh then arose and said, "Whirlwind's Voice wants me to say to you that he wants you all to go home and get dinner and when you get through to let him know, and when the cowboys come, he will fight them."

White Bull was very much disturbed. He was afraid that if he went alone to tell the agent he would be held as a witness. Spotted Elk was also afraid of this, but at last they rose and went down to the agent, and White Bull drew the agent aside and told him that "Stanley" as the white folks called him, was the man. The spartan old father Badger waited outside the door. White Bull also said that Stanley wanted to fight.

"You go back and tell him he can't fight. You tell your men also that one man is not enough. I want three. White men say three men did it. Go back and find the others."

White Bull presently went back to make the demand of his headmen but Little Whirlwind persisted in saying, "There are no others. I alone did it. My folks don't treat me right. I am unhappy and I want to die. I will not go to jail. I will fight."

White Bull again reported to the agent and said, "He alone did it. There are no others."[34]

At about 3 o'clock the word ran around. "The Whirlwind's Voice is on the hill." People ran out and looked up at the hills to the east and there on one of the highest peaks[35] the accused man crouched beside his horse, his

---

[33] In April of 1891, recruiting began at Fort Keogh for Company I (Indian) of the Twenty-second Infantry, with the hope of recruiting a total of fifty-five. The company reached a strength of thirty-two in March of 1893, only to be discharged in the next two months. Whirlwind's (Stanley's) name does not appear on the records. (Returns from Regular Army Infantry Regiments, June 1821–December 1916, Fort Keogh, April, 1891–March, 1893.)

[34] Stouch did not record White Bull's second visit to the agency.

[35] This peak is located about one-half mile east of the agency.

rifle in his lap, his bridle reins looped around his arm. Beyond him a half-mile distant a group of horsemen crowned a lower hill.[36] Across the valley were nearly two hundred other mounted men and women on foot waiting to see the battle. It was a tense moment. Captain Read had moved on to Tongue River with the troops in order to meet and question the settlers drawn together by the coroner's inquest, leaving the agency for the time without garrison. A courier had been dispatched in the morning to bring him back, but he had not returned.[37] The four deputies were at hand, and the Cheyennes expected to see them try to take Whirlwind prisoner.

They seized this moment to send an alarming message to the settlers telling them to flee for their lives, that the Indians had risen. This lying note was written in the agent's office by one of the deputies and in a few hours the stampede became general and the wildest tales were telegraphd all over the land. The "out-break" had come at last and the Indians were to be exterminated.[38]

Just when the agent was sending a message to Little Whirlwind, Captain Read and his troops again rode into the yard. Again the blue uniforms brought a sense of security to the agency. No one feared the Indians — the fear was that reckless whites would precipitate battle.

The accused man was no longer alone. His wife was with him, whether to see her husband ride to his death or to prevent it will not be known. Perhaps she was even then singing a war song.[39]

Captain Read being uninformed of the situation said, "I will take him if you want it done."

"No," said the agent, "we must avoid all blood-shed. We must not excite the people by any violence."

Then one of the deputies[40] spoke up with a brave show, "I'll take him if you'll guarantee to keep the other Indians away."

"I don't want any fighting and I will guarantee nothing," said the agent sharply.

While this was going on, old She Bear came rushing down the hill, a courier for Little Whirlwind. He was breathless with excitement, "Whirlwind's Voice he say, he don't want to fight soldiers, he want fight cow-boys. He don't want fight towards agency, he 'fraid he hurt women and children."

---

[36]This hill is about one-half mile north of the peak upon which Whirlwind stood.

[37]Read left the agency at 9:00 that morning for the Barringer Ranch, and returned about 3:30 in the afternoon. At 1:00 Stouch sent a courier to Rosebud with a telegram to Brigadier General James F. Wade. (Stouch to Brigadier General James F. Wade, May 28, 1897, Tongue River Reservation Consolidated File 45572.)

[38]The Miles City *Yellowstone* on May 28, offered the following comment on the predicted war: "While the situation may have the appearance of being immediately dangerous for the settlers, they feel perfectly able to cope with the enemy and win."

[39]From Stouch's account of a similar incident in 1891, Whirlwind's wife was probably urging him to fight. (*Ind. Commiss. Annual Reports, 1897*, p. 83.)

[40]This was William D. Smith. (*New York Times*, June 14, 1897.)

"Go back and tell him he shan't fight anybody," answered the agent.[41]

Captain Read went into camp. The agent sent word to the spectators on the hills to go home, and the employees of the agency went about their duties as usual. The Cheyennes who were building fence and painting the barn went calmly back to work. The audience on the hills dispersed slowly until at last no sign of excitement remained in all the valley.

Meanwhile Little Whirlwind's Voice and his wife and babe stood on the rounded summit of the hill expecting each moment to see the "cow-boys" charge up the slope. At last when no one came, when the crowds disappeared from the hills, and all was quiet, these tragic figures also disappeared, and the danger point was passed.

That night the agent in consultation with Captain Read determined to order the deputies off the reservation for the reason that they irritated the people and hindered him in his search for the murderers. They went, darkly imprecating. This action of the agent was telegraphed the governor of the state,[42] and the agent was accused of shielding the murderers and of preventing their arrest, although no warrant had been issued. He was accused of defying the state law by these mob law representatives.[43]

Captain Read sent word to the settlers to return to their homes,[44] that there was no danger and had been none. And the agent next day again sent for the patient and zealous Chief White Bull and called upon him and all Cheyennes to help them find and deliver Whirlwind into the hands of the law. Old Badger did not know where his son was, and White Bull had not seen him since the night before. They all joined in the search, but it was not until the following morning that Red Bird[45] came to the Captain's window and said, "Whirlwind is in Black Eagle's Camp."

---

[41] Stouch feared that such a fight would make Stanley a hero to the young, excitable Cheyennes. (*Ind. Commiss. Annual Reports, 1897*, p. 83.)

[42] Lieutenant Governor Archibald E. Spriggs was acting governor at the time in the temporary absence of Robert B. Smith, governor of Montana, 1897–1899. (Billings *Weekly Times*, June 10, 1897.)

[43] On May 31 Sheriff Gibb and four deputies returned with a warrant charging Stouch with obstructing officers. The agent gave him a recognizance to appear in court when called. Gibb then demanded Stanley, but Stouch refused to surrender the Indian and asked the sheriff to leave. Gibb departed, leaving four deputies, whom Stouch ordered off the reservation. On June 4 Captain Read and a detachment of soldiers escorted Stanley to Rosebud. (Billings *Times*, June 10, 1897.) Gibb returned on June 9 with warrants for five other Cheyennes. Stouch arrested Yellow Hair and Sam Crow on June 11, and Spotted Hawk, Little Whirlwind (not Stanley), and Shoulder Blade on June 25. (*Ind. Commiss. Annual Reports, 1897*, pp. 82, 84, 87.)

[44] On May 30 Read sent letters to several of the local ranchers stating that Stouch was trying to obtain the names of all persons involved in the murder, and asking those who lived on the reservation borders to "keep cool and be patient." (Read to Snyder, Thompson, Brown, and O'Connell, May 30, 1897, Tongue River Reservation Consolidated File 45572.)

[45] Red Bird was Stanley's uncle. Stouch said that word of Stanley's whereabouts came by "two Indians." (*Ind. Commiss. Annual Reports, 1897*, p. 84.)

The agent and two interpreters[46] started at once for the place, which was sixteen miles away. He went unarmed, but Red Bird had his rifle. He came upon the fugitive in a teepee drinking some coffee. There were many young men well mounted and armed all about him, but the agent sent word that he wanted to talk with Little Whirlwind. At first he refused saying, "I don't want to talk. I did not do the killing. Why should I be made to talk?"

At last he came into the agent's presence mounted and armed. He was in terrible tension, like a man ready to die in hand-to-hand conflict. His face was set and his eyes restless and desperate. At last he yielded so far as to say, "I will talk with you at White Bull's Camp. I will not talk here."[47]

"Very well, you go first and I will follow."

"No, you go ahead," said Whirlwind.

The agent decided quickly that the best way was to show no distrust. He turned his team and rode down the road with the desperate man behind. Red Bird rode close beside the Whirlwind, his keen eyes watching him. He was ready to brain the Whirlwind at the first hostile motion.

They rode thus for a mile or two with the Whirlwind just behind. Suddenly he signaled for the wagon to stop. He wanted the baby which his wife was carrying on her back to be put into the wagon. This was done and then the Whirlwind said, "Go on."

When they neared the teepee where his mother was staying, he signaled the Captain to stop. "I will talk with you here," he said, "but I will talk with no one but Black Eagle and you."

"Very well," replied the agent. "But leave your gun."

Whirlwind shook his head, "No."

"But you see I am unarmed," persisted the agent. "My hands are empty. You are not afraid of an old man like me."

At last he yielded his gun to Spotted Elk, and they withdrew to one side. There the agent said to him, "You must come with me."

"I have done nothing. What will you do with me?"

"I will put you in jail[48] till your time of trial comes off. If you didn't kill the man you will go free then."

"I will not go to jail. I will fight."

"No, you can't fight; you must go with me."

He denied the charge again and again and said, "Tomorrow I will go. Send Black Eagle with me. He can keep hold of me all the time."

"No, you must go with me."

The poor fellow then plead to have the going put as far off as possible.

---

[46] Stouch went to the Indian camp in a wagon driven by his son accompanied by Badger, Red Bird, and two interpreters. (*Ind. Commiss. Annual Reports, 1897*, p. 84.)

[47] Stanley would not talk until he got to the agency and only in the presence of Badger and Black Eagle — not just Black Eagle as Garland says. Stouch arrested Stanley late on May 31. (*Ind. Commiss. Annual Reports, 1897*, p. 85.)

[48] The jail was at Camp Merritt.

He asked to see his mother before he went, and the agent consented. While he was in the teepee it began to rain, and every Indian disappeared. They were not so much excited but they feared a wetting.

At the end of a few moments the Captain called out, "Ready, Stanley."

He yielded at last to the inevitable, and as he passed the tents of his people he began singing his death song, a weird wailing chant which chilled the blood of every one who heard it. He knew he was leaving his kindred forever. He was putting himself into the hands of relentless enemies. The hideous grins of the white loafers gathered on the station walk at Miles City were not one grain more civilized than the scowl with which he faced them.[49] Little Whirlwind had at least the dignity of a wolf at bay.

Thus ended a typical Indian scare. A simple murder case magnified by hate and greed and the foment of uneasy consciences into the uprising of the Indians. Whirlwind was a poor undisciplined savage man and should be punished — but not content with his death, the Christian patriots of the surrounding white settlements must hold the whole Cheyenne people responsible and devote themselves to "wiping out the tribe." And men whose main possessions are a gun, a broncho, and a bottle of whiskey become leaders in a movement to defy the federal authority of the reservation and intimidate the agent.

It is well under the circumstances that the whole nation can have something to say about the invasion of the Cheyenne territory by a mob of interested ranch men, rustlers, husky men and local political candidates for county offices. If a bloody struggle had been precipitated that day, it would have been due to these whites and not to the Cheyennes. This is not the end.[50] These settlers are determined to keep the scare alive until their selfish ends are carried out. They make no secret of their purposes. They are bending all energy to effect Captain Stouch's removal, and woe to the Cheyennes if these plans are successful and a pliant political appointee put into Lame Deer Agency.[51]

---

[49] On June 6 Sheriff Gibb took Stanley from Rosebud to Miles City for incarceration. (*Ind. Commiss. Annual Reports, 1897,* p. 86.)

[50] The publicity given the Cheyenne "outbreak" brought government attention to the reservation's problems and hastened the settlement of the boundary question. On July 1, 1898, Congress appointed James McLaughlin to investigate the situation. McLaughlin recommended that Congress extend the Tongue River Reservation to furnish the Cheyennes with ample water and grazing lands, that it purchase this land and that of the settlers, that it order the north and south boundaries of the reservation to be fenced, that it spend $28,000 for cattle, and that it erect several new buildings at the agency. (*Ind. Commiss. Annual Reports, 1899,* pp. 137–138.) In May of 1900 Congress appropriated $171,615 for these purposes, thus settling the matter. (*Ind. Commiss. Annual Reports, 1900,* pp. 170–171.)

[51] Garland suggests that Stouch had made enemies who sought his removal as agent. However, on June 17 the Billings *Times* stated that Stouch had received more criticism than he deserved: "The blame for the occasional frictions between settlers and the Indians should be attributed to the Indian Department. . . ." Nevertheless, U.S. Indian agent J. C. Clifford replaced Stouch on November 16, 1897, and Stouch became agent to the Crow Indians. (*Ind. Commiss. Annual Reports, 1898,* p. 199; *Oklahoma Portrait and Biographical Record,* p. 381.) Special Indian agent A. C. Hawley, sent to investigate the incident, reported to the commissioner of Indian affairs that he supported Stouch's suggestions for boundary clarification and noted that "Stouch is a kind hearted, able, honest agent. . . ." (Hawley to Commissioner of Indian Affairs, June 15, 1897, Tongue River Reservation Consolidated File 45572.)

It is the self-interest and local barbarism of the whites which keep the Indian continually alarmed, suspicious and revengeful. A few days ago a settler came to the agent and reported hearing three shots in the hills.[52] He had been searching for traces of slaughtered cattle and admitted that he could find no evidence of it. "I [am] sure they were killing my cattle," he said. "I'm going to round up in a few days, and if I find any gone I'll know the Indians did it." Upon such evidence the Indians are convicted! If a steer strays away or falls into an arroyo or a calf is killed by wolves or a cow dies of old age, the loss is laid to the Indians and false charges of depredation and violence spread over the state to embitter good men who do not know the facts in the case. The settlers are remorseless, vindictive, and accept every lying report with eagerness and joy.

There is but one thing to do and that is to fence in these reservations. Keep the whites off the Indian's land and the Indian on his own land. It should be perfectly plain that this land is the Indians' and that no scheming of greedy ranchmen and pliant politicians can ever take it from them. Then these murders will cease and the Indian lay aside his knife and gun. Till then he has need to be as well armed as the white rustler — his neighbor.

HAMLIN GARLAND

Lame Deer — July 20/97.

---

[52]On July 10 several Indians, thought to be Cheyennes, supposedly fired into the home of Matt Winter, a rancher whose claim joined that of Badger's, the father of David Stanley. Winter had been one of the deputies at the agency, and it was speculated that he "would soon die at the hands of the Indians." (St. Louis *Globe-Democrat*, July 14, 1897; Billings *Gazette*, July 16, 1897.) Actually, the Indians had been at least seven hundred yards from Winter's house, and were on the reservation side of Otter Creek hunting turtles. (Read to Norvell and Norvell to Acting Adjutant General, July 25, 1897, Tongue River Reservation Consolidated File 45572.)

Background

The battle of the Little Bighorn on June 25, 1876, was a major turning point in the Sioux War because it outraged the public and made the army more determined than ever to subdue the Indians. The most noted battle in the Indian wars of the West, it has had a myriad of interpretations, many of which are controversial, to say the least. By the time Garland wrote the piece below, few accounts of the event from the Indian's vantage point had come before the public. Garland offers it without interpretation. The accuracy of Two Moon's facts is left for the historians to decide.

The significance of the piece lies in what it represents in terms of Garland's later works. The rationale of Two Moon concerning the Indians' attempts to move beyond the white man's reach becomes that of Sitting Bull in "The Silent Eaters," and the activities of Two Moon on the day of the battle are remarkably like those of Iapi in the later work.

More important, however, are the Indian perspective and the rhetoric. It is through the former that Garland later gave successful fictional form to "The Silent Eaters" and through the latter that he developed a successful style for the piece. Here he manages to capture both the perspective and the flavor of the language. Nowhere else, except in "The Silent Eaters," does he do that. Thus the work could be said to represent his apprenticeship for his most successful piece of fiction about the American Indian.[1]

---

[1] For a reproduction of Garland's original field notes on this subject, see the Introductory Survey in this book.

10. General Custer's Last Fight as Seen by Two Moon[2]

As we topped the low, pine-clad ridge and looked into the hot, dry valley, Wolf Voice, my Cheyenne interpreter, pointed at a little log cabin, toward the green line of alders wherein the Rosebud ran, and said:

"His house — Two Moon."[3]

As we drew near we came to a puzzling fork in the road. The left branch skirted a corner of a wire fence, the right turned into a field. We started to the left, but the waving of a blanket in the hands of a man at the cabin door directed us to the right. As we drew nearer we perceived Two Moon spreading blankets in the scant shade of his low cabin. Some young Cheyennes were grinding a sickle. A couple of children were playing about the little log stables. The barnyard and buildings were like those of a white settler on the new and arid sod. It was all barren and unlovely — the home of poverty.

As we dismounted at the door Two Moon came out to meet us with hand outstretched. "How?" he said, with the heartiest, long-drawn note of welcome. He motioned us to be seated on the blankets which he had spread for us upon seeing our approach. Nothing could exceed the dignity and sincerity of his greeting.

As we took seats he brought out tobacco and a pipe. He was a tall old man, of a fine, clear brown complexion, big-chested, erect, and martial of bearing. His smiling face was broadly benignant, and his manners were courteous and manly.

While he cut his tobacco Wolf Voice interpreted my wishes to him. I said, "Two Moon, I have come to hear your story of the Custer battle, for they tell me you were a chief there. After you tell me the story, I want to take some photographs of you. I want you to signal with a blanket as the great chiefs used to do in fight."

Wolf Voice[4] made this known to him, delivering also a message from the agents, and at every pause Two Moon uttered deep-voiced notes of comprehension. "Ai," "A-ah," "Hoh," — these sounds are commonly called "grunts," but they were low, long-drawn expulsions of breath, very expressive.

---

[2] Reprinted from *McClure's,* 11 (September, 1898): 443–448.

[3] For background on Two Moon, see Essay 8, note 11.

[4] Wolf Voice was Garland's interpreter during his visit to the Northern Cheyenne.

[159]

Then a long silence intervened. The old man mused. It required time to go from the silence of the hot valley, the shadow of his little cabin, and the wire fence of his pasture, back to the days of his youth. When he began to speak, it was with great deliberation. His face became each moment graver and his eyes more introspective.

"Two Moon does not like to talk about the days of fighting; but since you are to make a book, and the agent says you are a friend to Grinnell,[5] I will tell you about it — the truth. It is now a long time ago, and my words do not come quickly.

"That spring [1876][6] I was camped on Powder River with fifty lodges of my people — Cheyennes. The place is near what is now Fort McKenney [sic].[7] One morning soldiers charged my camp.[8] They were in command of Three Fingers [Colonel McKenzie].[9] We were surprised and scattered, leaving our ponies. The soldiers ran all our horses off. That night the soldiers slept, leaving the horses one side; so we crept up and stole them back again, and then we went away.

"We traveled far, and one day we met a big camp of Sioux at Charcoal Butte. We camped with the Sioux, and had a good time, plenty grass, plenty game, good water. Crazy Horse[10] was head chief of the camp. Sitting Bull[11] was camped a little ways below, on the Little Missouri River.

---

[5] George Bird Grinnell (1849–1938) in 1876 became editor of *Forest and Stream* and in 1880 president of the Forest and Stream Publishing Company. Grinnell lived with the Indians during his early expeditions to the West, and in the early 1890's he was voted head chief of the Blackfeet by the entire tribe. In 1895 he was appointed Commissioner to the Blackfeet and Belknap Indians and was asked to intercede in a bitter land controversy among the Sioux on the Standing Rock Reservation. Among his better known works are *Blackfoot Lodge Tales* (1892), *The Fighting Cheyennes* (1915), *When Buffalo Ran* (1920), and *By Cheyenne Campfires* (1926). (*The National Cyclopaedia of American Biography*, 30: 278.)

[6] Bracketed interpolations such as this one have been retained as they originally appeared in *McClure's*. While some may have been supplied by Garland, it is likely that most of them came from the pen of a *McClure's* editor.

[7] The site of this battle is in modern Powder River County, four miles northeast of Moorhead, Montana. It is some distance from Fort McKinney, which, at the time of the interview, was located three miles west of Buffalo, Wyoming. (Robert G. Ferris, ed., *Soldier and Brave*, pp. 200, 385.)

[8] This was March 17, 1876.

[9] The editor of *McClure's* is mistaken here. Colonel Joseph J. Reynolds was in command of the six troops of the Second and Third Cavalry. Colonel Ronald S. Mackenzie destroyed Dull Knife's camp on the Red Fork of the Powder River in November of 1876. (Ferris, ed., *Soldier and Brave*, pp. 200, 364.) Two Moon's account of the Powder River battle seems accurate.

[10] Crazy Horse was an Oglala Sioux who went on the warpath in 1875. He joined in the defeat of Custer and surrendered in the spring of 1877. Later that year, he was shot by guards during an escape attempt. (Frederick Webb Hodge, ed., *Handbook of American Indians North of Mexico*, Pt. 1, p. 359.)

[11] Sitting Bull (1834–1890) was leader of the Hunkpapa Sioux. He was on the warpath against Indians and whites from 1869 to 1876. He participated in the Custer fight, after which he escaped to Canada. He surrendered in 1881 and was confined at Fort Randall until 1883. Upon release he lived on the Standing Rock Reservation and steadily resisted government policy regarding the Sioux. He was influential in bringing the Ghost Dance to the reservation. Sitting Bull was killed by Indian police in 1890. (*The National Cyclopaedia of American Biography*, 13:454.)

Two Moon, the dignified Northern Cheyenne warrior inter-
viewed by Garland in 1897, asserted that the Cheyenne and
Sioux had been surprised by Custer's troops and were com-
pelled to fight.

"Crazy Horse said to me, 'I'm glad you are come. We are going to fight
the white man again.'

"The camp was already full of wounded men, women, and children.

"I said to Crazy Horse, 'All right. I am ready to fight. I have fought
already. My people have been killed, my horses stolen; I am satisfied to fight.' "

Here the old man paused a moment, and his face took on a lofty and
somber expression.

"I believed at that time the Great Spirits had made Sioux, put them there,"
— he drew a circle to the right — "and white men and Cheyennes here," —
indicating two places to the left — "expecting them to fight. The Great Spirits
I thought liked to see the fight; it was to them all the same like playing. So I
thought then about fighting." As he said this, he made me feel for one moment
the power of a sardonic god whose drama was the wars of men.

"About May, when the grass was tall and the horses strong, we broke
camp and started across the country to the mouth of the Tongue River. Then
Sitting Bull and Crazy Horse and all went up the Rosebud. There we had a

big fight with General Crook,[12] and whipped him.[13] Many soldiers were killed — few Indians. It was a great fight, much smoke and dust.

"From there we all went over the divide, and camped in the valley of Little Horn. Everybody thought, 'Now we are out of the white man's country. He can live there, we will live here.' After a few days, one morning when I was in camp north of Sitting Bull, a Sioux messenger rode up and said, 'Let everybody paint up, cook, and get ready for a big dance.'[14]

"Cheyennes then went to work to cook, cut up tobacco, and get ready. We all thought to dance all day. We were very glad to think we were far away from the white man.

"I went to water my horses at the creek, and washed them off with cool water, then took a swim myself. I came back to the camp afoot. When I got near my lodge, I looked up the Little Horn towards Sitting Bull's camp. I saw a great dust rising. It looked like a whirlwind. Soon Sioux horseman came rushing into camp shouting: 'Soldiers come! Plenty white soldiers.'

"I ran into my lodge, and said to my brother-in-law, 'Get your horses: the white man is coming. Everybody run for horses.'

"Outside, far up the valley, I heard a battle cry, *Hay-ay, hay-ay!* I heard shooting, too, this way [clapping his hands very fast]. I couldn't see any Indians. Everybody was getting horses and saddles. After I had caught my horse, a Sioux warrior came again and said, 'Many soldiers are coming.'

"Then he said to the women, 'Get out of the way, we are going to have hard fight.'

"I said, 'All right, I am ready.'

"I got on my horse, and rode out into my camp. I called out to the people all running about: 'I am Two Moon, your chief. Don't run away. Stay and fight. You must stay and fight the white soldiers. I shall stay even if I am to be killed.'

"I rode swiftly toward Sitting Bull's camp. There I saw the white soldiers fighting in a line [Reno's men].[15] Indians covered the flat. They began to drive the soldiers all mixed up — Sioux, then soldiers, then more Sioux, and all shooting. The air was full of smoke and dust. I saw the soldiers fall back and drop into the river-bed like buffalo fleeing. They had no time to look for a crossing.

---

[12] George Crook (1829–1890) was born in Dayton, Ohio, and graduated from West Point in 1852. He served in the West in the 1850s. In 1866 he was commissioned lieutenant-colonel and assigned to Idaho. He was commander of the Department of Platte in 1875 and went against the Sioux and Cheyenne in 1876. They were defeated by troops under his command. (*The National Cyclopaedia of American Biography,* 4:70.)

[13] This battle occurred on June 17, 1876. General Crook with 1,774 troops met 1,500 warriors under Crazy Horse. Crook drove the Indians from the field, but had to retreat for supplies and reinforcements. (Ferris, ed., *Soldier and Brave,* p. 200.)

[14] This was June 25, 1876.

[15] Major Marcus A. Reno engaged the Indians in the valley of the Little Bighorn and then retreated across the river and took a stand on some high ground, where his command spent the night of June 25. About the time he retreated, the attack on Custer began four miles away. The soldiers that Reno's men met on the hill were troops under the command of Captain Frederick W. Benteen. (Edgar I. Stewart, *Custer's Luck,* pp. 350ff., 379–380.)

The Sioux chased them up the hill, where they met more soldiers in wagons, and then messengers came saying more soldiers were going to kill the women, and the Sioux turned back. Chief Gall[16] was there fighting, Crazy Horse also.

"I then rode toward my camp, and stopped squaws from carrying off lodges. While I was sitting on my horse I saw flags come up over the hill to the east like that [he raised his finger-tips]. Then the soldiers rose all at once, all on horses, like this [he put his fingers behind each other to indicate that Custer appeared marching in columns of fours]. They formed into three bunches [squadrons] with a little ways between. Then a bugle sounded, and they all got off horses, and some soldiers led the horses back over the hill.

"Then the Sioux rode up the ridge on all sides, riding very fast. The Cheyennes went up the left way. Then the shooting was quick, quick. Pop — pop — pop very fast. Some of the soldiers were down on their knees, some standing. Officers all in front. The smoke was like a great cloud, and everywhere the Sioux went the dust rose like smoke. We circled all round him — swirling like water round a stone. We shoot, we ride fast, we shoot again. Soldiers drop, and horses fall on them. Soldiers in line drop, but one man rides up and down the line — all the time shouting. He rode a sorrel horse with white face and white fore-legs. I don't know who he was. He was a brave man.[17]

"Indians keep swirling round and round, and the soldiers killed only a few. Many soldiers fell. At last all horses killed but five. Once in a while some man would break out and run toward the river, but he would fall. At last about a hundred men and five horsemen stood on the hill all bunched together. All along the bugler kept blowing his commands. He was very brave too. Then a chief was killed. I hear it was Long Hair [Custer], I don't know; and then the five horsemen and the bunch of men, may be so forty, started toward the river. The man on the sorrel horse led them, shouting all the time. He wore a buckskin shirt, and had long black hair and mustache. He fought hard with a big knife. His men were all covered with white dust. I couldn't tell whether they were officers or not. One man all alone ran far down toward the river, then round up over the hill. I thought he was going to escape, but a Sioux fired and hit him in the head. He was the last man. He wore braid on his arms [sergeant].

"All the soldiers were now killed, and the bodies were stripped. After that no one could tell which were officers. The bodies were left where they fell. We had no dance that night. We were sorrowful.

"Next day four Sioux chiefs and two Cheyennes and I, Two Moon, went upon the battlefield to count the dead. One man carried a little bundle of sticks.

---

[16] Gall (1840–1894), chief of the Hunkpapa and a lieutenant of Sitting Bull, led the Sioux in the battle of Little Bighorn. He fled to Canada with Sitting Bull, but, with Crow Chief, left him in 1880. He surrendered in 1881 and was sent to the Standing Rock Reservation. Later, he denounced Sitting Bull and led his people in adopting white ways. He was influential in securing the treaty of 1889 that divided the Sioux lands into separate reservations and ceded others to the U.S. (Hodge, ed., *Handbook of American Indians North of Mexico*, Pt. 1, p. 482.)

[17] The identity of this man is uncertain. Evidence indicates that he could have been one of several officers. (Stewart, *Custer's Luck*, pp. 460–461.)

When we came to dead men, we took a little stick and gave it to another man, so we counted the dead. There were 388.[18] There were thirty-nine Sioux and seven Cheyennes killed, and about a hundred wounded.

"Some white soldiers were cut with knives, to make sure they were dead; and the war women had mangled some.[19] Most of them were left just where they fell. We came to the man with big mustache; he lay down the hills towards the river. The Indians did not take his buckskin shirt. The Sioux said, 'That is a big chief. That is Long Hair.' I don't know. I had never seen him. The man on the white-faced horse was the bravest man.

"That day as the sun was getting low our young men came up the Little Horn riding hard. Many white soldiers were coming in a big boat, and when we looked we could see the smoke rising.[20] I called my people together, and we hurried up the Little Horn, into Rotten Grass Valley. We camped there three days, and then rode swiftly back over our old trail to the east. Sitting Bull went back into the Rosebud and down the Yellowstone, and away to the north. I did not see him again."

The old man paused and filled his pipe. His story was done. His mind came back to his poor people on the barren land where the rain seldom falls.

"That was a long time ago. I am now old, and my mind has changed. I would rather see my people living in houses and singing and dancing. You have talked with me about fighting, and I have told you of the time long ago. All that is past. I think of these things now: First, that our reservation shall be fenced and the white settlers kept out and our young men kept in. Then there will be no trouble. Second, I want to see my people raising cattle and making butter. Last, I want to see my people going to school to learn the white man's way. That is all.'

There was something placid and powerful in the lines of the chief's broad brow, and his gestures were dramatic and noble in sweep. His extended arm, his musing eyes, his deep voice combined to express a meditative solemnity profoundly impressive. There was no anger in his voice, and no reminiscent ferocity. All that was strong and fine and distinctive in the Cheyenne character came out in the old man's talk. He seemed the leader and the thoughtful man he really is — patient under injustice, courteous even to his enemies.

----

[18] Two Moon's count is too high. According to Ferris, Custer lost 220 men and Reno and Benteen lost 47. (*Soldier and Brave*, p. 186.)

[19] In the old days, women went to war with the Cheyenne, sometimes fighting and sometimes counting coup on the enemy. (George Bird Grinnell, *The Cheyenne Indians,* 2: 157.) However, the proximity of the Indian camps in this instance explains the presence of the women. When General Alfred H. Terry's troops arrived at the site of the deserted Indian camp, they found a number of beheaded and mutilated bodies and three heads hanging from a lodgepole. The bodies of most of the men on the battle site were mutilated. Apparently, the women killed the wounded by hitting them in the head with axes. (Stewart, *Custer's Luck,* pp. 466, 469–470.)

[20] The Indians retreated before the advance of troops under the command of Generals Alfred H. Terry and John Gibbon. The steamboat was the *Far West,* which General Terry was to meet at the mouth of the Little Bighorn. (Stewart, *Custer's Luck,* p. 478.)

Background on
The Red Man's Present Needs

Garland's own introduction clearly states his intent in "The Red Man's Present Needs" and establishes his authority to speak out on the subject. He seems to realize that, in many ways, the article is a culmination of his work on the American Indian.

Appearing during his most productive period of writing on the Indian — in fact, near the end of his career in the field — "The Red Man's Present Needs" makes summary criticism of most of the evils of the native's condition which Garland had attacked thematically in his fiction. These were evils perpetrated not only by the government and the missionaries, but by American society, in general, as well.

The tone of this essay is bitter, often biting. Nowhere else in his writing on the Indian does Garland deliver such point-blank criticism in such clear and concise English sentences. As a result, "The Red Man's Present Needs" stands in the minds of many as his best, and most effective, piece of nonfiction about the American Indian.

11. The Red Man's Present Needs[1]

Garland's Introductory Note

(In my wanderings over the Rocky Mountain States, I have happened upon some twelve or fifteen Indian reservations. This unofficial inspection, made for fictional purposes, I now wish to turn to practical account in aid of a clearer understanding of the present conditions of the nation's wards.[2] I am not to be taken as the representative of any organization whatsoever, and I have never held, and never sought, and do not intend to seek, any position under the government. Perhaps this freedom from departmental bias may lend a certain value to my statement of what I saw and what I think should be done. A part of what follows is necessarily critical, but its main intent is constructive. I do not doubt the good intention of the Indian Department; on the contrary, I believe its head[3] to be sincerely anxious to clear the service of its abuses. What is here written is intended to aid rather than embarrass the Commissioner in getting rid of his inheritance of foolish policies.)

*   *   *

It is necessary at the start to clear away the common misapprehension that "one Indian is precisely like another." This is not true. On the contrary,

---

[1] Reprinted from *North American Review,* 174 (April, 1902): 476–488.

[2] In *Cherokee Nation v. Georgia* (1831), the Supreme Court compared the relationship of the tribe to the United States to "that of a ward to his guardian." After that date, the theory of "wardship" was used by both those who committed illegal acts against Indians and those who sought to protect their rights. According to Angie Debo, it was "loosely used even by reputable writers unaware of its technical meaning." (Debo, *A History of the Indians of the United States,* pp. 301–302.) Cohen finds ten distinct connotations of the term *ward* as it has been applied to the American Indian. Failure to distinguish among these senses has resulted in a great amount of confusion. (Cohen, *Handbook of Federal Indian Law,* pp. 169–173.) Garland, who was familiar with the reform literature of the day, was most likely familiar with such works as George W. Manypenny's *Our Indian Wards* (1880). Note that Garland elaborates upon the concept of wardship in more detail in the last paragraphs of this essay.

[3] William A. Jones served as Indian commissioner from 1897 to 1905. Although he has received little attention from historians, it should be noted that he served all but one year of his tenure as Commissioner under E. A. Hitchcock, who as Secretary of the Interior, was widely known for his attack on corruption among public officials. It was during Jones' administration that legislation was obtained and executed to provide for allotment of lands to the Five Civilized Tribes, among others.

there are very wide divergencies of habit among the native tribes now living in America. Red men living side by side are as widely separated in speech and in manner as the Turk and the German. There are, indeed, two or three distinct races of Americans included under the term "Indian," speaking many languages quite distinct and irrelatable.

The second point to be grasped is this: There are no Indians living as nomads or hunters to-day. If the reader will examine a map of the United States Indian Department, he will find scattered all over the West, minute, irregular patches of yellow, ranging from a thumb-nail's breadth to that of a silver quarter. These are the "corrals," or open-air prisons, into which the original owners of the continent have been impounded by the white race.[4] Most of these reservations are in the arid parts of the great Rocky Mountain Plateau; a few are in timbered regions of older States, like Wisconsin and Minnesota. Speaking generally, we may say these lands are relatively the most worthless to be found in the State or Territory whose boundaries enclose the red man's home, and were set aside for his use because he would cumber the earth less there than elsewhere. Furthermore, scarcely a single one of these minute spots is safe to the red people. Every acre of land is being scrutinized, and plans for securing even these miserable plots are being matured.[5]

It will appear, even from a glance at this map, that to understand the "Indian problem," is to understand the climate, soil and surroundings of each one of fifty reservations, in a dozen States, hundreds, even thousands of miles apart, and to take into account the peculiarities of as many differing tribes of men. A rule which would apply perfectly to the Cheyennes of Oklahoma would not in the least apply to the Cheyennes of Montana, but might aid the Wichitas, Kiowas, or Fort Sill Apaches,[6] not because the latter tribes are similar in habit, but because their soil, surroundings, and climate are practically the same.

The Sioux, Crows, Northern Cheyennes, Blackfeet, Gros Ventres, and Assiniboines, occupying respectively the Standing Rock reservation in Dakota, and the Crow, Tongue River, Fort Peck, Fort Belknap and Blackfeet reservations in Montana, are all in an arid climate and confronted with the problem of irrigation.

---

[4] In 1900 in the U.S., 78,372,000 acres of land were under the jurisdiction of the Bureau of Indian Affairs. (*Statistical Abstract of U.S.,* p. 202.)

[5] When the Dawes Act was passed in 1887, American Indians were still in possession of about 139,000,000 acres of land. When allotting ceased under provisions of the Indian Reorganization Act in 1934, Indians were in possession of 48,000,000. (Fontana, "Historical Foundations," p. 38.) Nor does the story end there. Between 1948 and 1957, the Indians lost over two and one half million additional acres. (Commission on the Rights, Liberties, and Responsibilities of the American Indian, *The Indian: America's Unfinished Business,* p. 219.)

[6] These tribes occupied lands in southwestern Oklahoma. The Wichitas were north of the Washita River in present Caddo County, the Kiowa were on the same reservation as the Comanche, and the Fort Sill Apache were Geronimo's band, captured in 1886 and later sent to Fort Sill.

The Blackfeet, also a hunting race, have a land even less adapted to the raising of corn and wheat; for their reservation lies high on the eastern slope of the continental divide, and frosts blast both the growing and the ripening crop. They have, however, a good grass country and can be made self-supporting as herders. The Fort Peck reservation, in eastern Montana, on the upper Missouri, like the land at Standing Rock, Dakota, is upland prairie, with meagre streams and poor timber, a dry bleak land, fit only for stock-raising, except along the bottoms, where irrigation is possible.

The Crows are a little better off. They have abundant water from two beautiful streams, which take their rise in the Big Horn mountains; and they have put through some fairly successful irrigating ditches. They have also owned for several years herds of cattle; a cut in rations would not leave them helpless. The Northern Cheyennes, their neighbors, are in a rougher country, a very arid country, with only a few feeble streams, but they have plenty of timber and good grazing lands. Their chief needs are cattle, and a fence to keep out the cattle-men.

The Sioux, the Blackfeet, and the Northern Cheyennes live practically the same life. They have small, badly-ventilated log or frame hovels of one or two rooms, into which they closely crowd during cold weather. In summer, they supplement these miserable shacks by canvas tepees and lodges, under which they do their cooking, and in which they sleep. Their home life has lost all its old-time picturesqueness, without acquiring even the comfort of the settler in a dug-out. Consumption is very common among them, because of their unsanitary housing during cold weather.

They dress in a sad mixture of good old buckskin garments and shoddy clothing, sold by the traders or issued by the government. They are, of course, miserably poor, with very little to do but sit and smoke and wait for ration day. To till the ground is practically useless, and their herds are too small to furnish them support. They are not allowed to leave the reservation to hunt or to seek work, and so they live like reconcentrados.[7] Their ration, which the government by an easy shift now calls a charity, feeds them for a week or ten days, and they go hungry till the next ration day comes round. From three to seven days are taken up with going after rations. These words also apply to the Jicarilla Apaches, and to a part of the Southern Utes. Chief Charley's followers[8] have lands along Pine River, which they irrigate. On some of these reservations lands are allotted, either actually or nominally, though the people make less account of it than the agent reports.

The visitor among the Southern Cheyennes, Arapahoes, Kiowas, and Fort Sill Apaches, will find conditions quite other than those of the North. The climate is mild and the land very productive. Corn, cotton, fruit of all kinds, and wheat can be grown. The winters are short, and water and timber fairly abundant. With the exception of the Yakima and Flathead reservations, those

---

[7] This term, popular during the Cuban Revolution of 1895–1898, referred particularly to rural population which had been reconcentrated in or about towns for the convenience of political or military administration.

[8] Here Garland refers to the Southern Utes. A picture of members of this tribe appears in Essay 1 of this book. For background on Charles Buckskin, or Chief Charlie, see Essay 1, note 18.

in Oklahoma are the only really habitable Indian lands I have visited.[9] Manifestly, a regulation which would do good in Oklahoma might work incalculable harm in Dakota and Montana. To cut rations among the Southern Cheyennes would prove only a temporary hardship; but a cut in rations among the Blackfeet or Sioux might result in actual starvation and death, or at least in slaughter of the small flocks of cattle which they have begun to cherish. These wide differences cannot be too often brought to departmental notice.

Upon close study, each tribe, whether Sioux, or Navajo, or Hopi, will be found to be divided, like a white village, into two parties, the radicals and the conservatives — those who are willing to change, to walk the white man's way; and those who are deeply, sullenly skeptical of all civilizing measures, clinging tenaciously to the traditions and the lore of their race. These men are often the strongest and bravest of their tribe, the most dignified and the most intellectual. They represent the spirit that will break but will not bow. And, broadly speaking, they are in the majority. Though in rags, their spirits are unbroken; from the point of view of their sympathizers, they are patriots.

There is much to admire in this unconquerable pride. I count it a virtue in that Northern chief who said: "I will not clean the spittoons of the white man's civilization."[10] Hatred of tyranny is a distinctly American attribute, and one that deserves honorable consideration on the part of the department. Only those who are besotted with the wine of our cruel and uneasy civilization will condemn rankly and contemptuously the love of liberty, no matter whether in the heart of a brown man or of a red man. There should be some way to conserve and turn to account the lofty pride of the Sioux and the Cheyenne. When they lose their self-respect, they will sink to vagabondage and beggary; to break them is to destroy them. Science has come to our aid; we understand as never before the constitution of a red man's mind. The philosophy of evolution has broadened our conception of the universe, and in our dealings with primitive men religious bigotry and race hatred should no longer enter. The greedy man, on the one hand, and the fanatic, on the other, have too long confused the situation for the Indian.

The allotment of lands in severalty which began in land-lust and is being carried to the bitter end by those who believe a Stone Age man can be developed into a citizen of the United States in a single generation, is in violent antagonism to every wish and innate desire of the red man, and has failed of expected results, even among the Southern Cheyennes, where the land is rich and climate mild, because it presents a sombre phase of civilized life.[11]

The attempt to make the Sioux a greedy land-owner, content to live the lonely life of the poor Western rancher, cut off from daily association with his fellows, is to me uselessly painful. If we would convert the primitive man to our ways, we must make our ways alluring.

---

[9] The Yakima Reservation is in south-central Oregon, west of the Cascade range; the Flatheads lived near St. Ignatius, northwest of Missoula, in western Montana.

[10] Garland used this statement in 1897 to culminate a moving speech by Rushing Bear in an unpublished story, "Rushing Bear and the Commission."

[11] Allotment had disastrous results from the loss of lands indicated in note 5 to psychological stress resulting from isolation on allotments. An analysis of the results of allotment to the Five Civilized Tribes is the subject of a study by Angie Debo, *And Still the Waters Run.*

We should not forget that the red man is a sociable animal, and that his life, so far from being silent and sombre, has always been full of song and rich in social interchange. All his duties — even his hunting — have always been performed in company with his fellows. He is a villager, never a solitary. He dreads solitude, and one of the old-time tribal punishments was to be thrust outside the camping circle. The life of every member of the tribe is open to comment. He confides every secret to his group of lodge-men. He shares his food, his tepee, with his fellows. It is this gregariousness of habit, this love of his kind, and this deep-seated dread of loneliness, which make the Sioux and the Cheyenne so reluctant to adopt the Dawes land theories.[12] They cling to the lodge for the reason that it can be easily moved, and is cheap.

Naturally, those who were resolute to make the Indian a solitary took little thought of this deep-seated mental characteristic, being confident that resolute whacking would jar his brain-cells into conformity with those of a white man of the same age. With them the red hunter is not a man peculiar to his environment; he is merely a bad boy who obstinately goes wrong. That he loves running water, that he needs to be near wood for his fires, that he shrinks from the bleak, wind-swept prairies, are considerations of small account to them; but a man with many years experience among the Cheyennes said to me: "It is hard to make progress under the present system."[13]

In the desire to make better Indians, and to make the transition from their old life to the new as easy as may be, to lessen rather than to add to the weight of their suffering, I offer the following suggestions:

First. Group the families of each tribe on the water courses of its reservation, in little settlements of four or five families, with their lands outlying, instead of forcibly scattering them over the bleak and barren uplands. The Standing Rock Sioux, Northern Cheyennes, and Assiniboines of Forts Peck and Belknap, could all be so colonized, and water drawn in from the streams upon their gardens,* while their cattle range in common. Why should not

---

*The farmer at Poplar Creek[14] two years ago showed me a garden of nearly one hundred acres which he had set aside in lots to some sixty or eighty men; and, though the season's water had been very meagre, he had been able to supply these families, through their own labor, with potatoes for the winter. He did more. He demonstrated that these people, with water for their lands, could be self-supporting in three years by means of a ditch costing not more than $50,000.

---

[12] Henry Laurens Dawes (1816–1903) of Massachusetts was elected to the Senate in 1875. His impact on Indian affairs was great. He was author of the General Allotment Act of 1887 and was chairman of the Senate Committee on Indian Affairs. He retired from the Senate in 1892. In 1895, he became chairman of the Dawes Commission to the Five Civilized Tribes, which successfully treated with them to do away with tribal government and to allot lands. (*The National Cyclopaedia of American Biography,* 4:321.)

[13] The identity of this person is unknown. However, it was probably Stouch or Seger.

[14] This was at the Fort Peck Reservation in Montana.

the Southern Cheyennes and Arapahoes, already on allotments along the streams, be allowed to draw together in villages if they please? The Northern Cheyennes, now in full possession of their streams, should retain these water rights in common.[15] Individual occupancy of lots and individual ownership of products is all that is necessary to their colonization on the arable and irrigable land. Cattle of gentle breed should be given to them as the beginning of individual herds. The red man's feeling, that the earth is for the use of all men, is right; he has always distinguished between the ownership of things and the ownership of land and water. It is possible to refine him without teaching him to be either greedy or stingy, just as we can emphasize the return to individual labor without forcing him to live as if in solitary confinement. I confess I have no sympathy with those who would make the red man suffer needlessly to fit their notion of discipline. As a boy, I hated the solitary labor of the Western farm, and I would not condemn even a convict to such life as is involved in a lonely cabin on the plains.

Second. Each reservation should be divided into districts, not too large, and a really competent man employed to personally teach the red men how to plow, sow, and reap. This essential part of the service is sadly inefficient. The "farmers" of the various agencies I have visited, are either ignorant or slothful, or they are so burdened with duties around the agency corrals, that they are hardly ever of marked use to the red man.[16] The present working of the Civil Service has led to a vicious habit of "transferring" a bad or weak man from post to post. Furthermore, the employees in many cases are hold-overs, men who sought the service as a refuge and who remain in it because they are unfitted for other life. I am willing to admit, however, in justice to the department, that the pay is too small to secure the services of a really capable man, unless he assumes double duty, as among the Southern Cheyennes, where the farmers serve as sub-agents, or school superintendents, and have little time to give to field work. Part of the useless travel in this work of superintending would be removed by settlement in groups as above outlined, but an increase in the number of industrial teachers must be given before adequate instruction can be assured. The government would save money in the end.

Life at most of the Indian agencies is not a joyous thing to contemplate.[17] The buildings are bare, bleak barracks. The boarding-houses are vile, and

---

[15] Control of their water rights was a recent development for the Northern Cheyennes. (See Essay 9, note 49, for details.)

[16] Garland may be recalling here, in part, what he learned from the Southern Ute agent in 1895. In his annual report for the previous year, David F. Day had written that "political agents and political farmers are the crowning curse of the Indian service." (*Ind. Commiss. Annual Report, 1894,* p. 129.)

[17] These same observations about life at an Indian agency appear as well in one of Garland's unpublished pieces, "The Indian Agency." The author had also incorporated them into *The Captain of the Gray-Horse Troop.* In the novel, Captain Curtis realizes that the loneliness and isolation of the job would make a lesser man come to find the Indians a symbol of his loneliness and begin to hate them. (Hamlin Garland, *The Captain of the Gray-Horse Troop,* p. 138.)

amusements are few. It is not wonderful that refined natures shudder and flee at first glance. Only the chain of necessity keeps the average employee to his post. The Indian soon becomes a burden, a nuisance. Duties are mechanically performed, and each man permits his hand to fall short rather than to over-reach his exact duty. The effect of such service is not precisely inspiring to the Indian. The only ways to change this service are these — raise the standard of wages and make life pleasanter for those who isolate themselves to teach.

Third. A vigorous, wholesome woman is needed in each district as matron. She ought not to be the wife of the farmer; her first duty should be the welfare of her wards, and she should have a genuine sympathy for them. As I go among the red people, the lack of a matron of this character seems the most crying omission of all. I have never seen this work properly done. It is, indeed, a sort of higher education. The women need to be taught by example how to cook and sew, how to keep house, how to bridge the chasm between the tepee fire and the cook-stove. The red people are like children[18] in all these things; they cannot go beyond their teacher; they can only follow. If their "farmer" is ignorant and a loafer, and their matron slothful and ill-humored, they are involved in these vices. They are like children, also, in that each effort is quite sincere, though fitful. They are easily discouraged. They can reason, they do reason, and they want to do the right thing; but the mental habits fixed by thousands of years of a simpler life are hard to overcome. The man or woman called to teach them should be patient and a leader. It is not true to say that this work is being done in the schools. Working in "relays" in the laundry or kitchen of a boarding-house is quite different from taking care of a home after marriage. The field matron is needed to supplement the instruction in the schools.

Fourth. Wherever a tribe has a peculiar natural appetite[19] for an art — as canoe-building, weaving, basket-making, or pottery-baking — the depart-ment should send among them a teacher capable of rescuing perishing forms and symbols, and able also to develop new forms built upon the old. The Jicarilla Apaches, for example, are fine basket-makers. This art, in place of being ignored or positively discouraged, as at present, should be at once seized as a means of benefiting the tribe. The growth of grass, willows or other material necessary for it should be cultivated and a market opened on just terms. *The value of such an art in maintaining the self-respect of a tribe cannot*

---

[18] Garland's choice of term is unfortunate here, for it leads the reader to a too-hasty conclusion that the author is perpetuating the common misconception that the Indians were simple, child-like folk. He instead intends only a comparison: the Indian, as he sets about learning to do things as the white man does them, is like the child who begins school; he can learn only as well as he is taught.

[19] Mainly through conversations with Ernest Thompson Seton, Garland arrived at the conclusion that the Indian was "an animal adapted to a certain environment." The implication here is that the environment of a tribe created in it "a peculiar natural appetite" for certain arts.

be over-estimated. The Rev. W. C. Roe,[20] a missionary at Seger's Colony,[21] Oklahoma, is of the sort I can commend. He is employing this month seventy men and women making bead-work, tepees, bows and arrows, moccasins, and ornamental pouches — and what he has done can be duplicated by the agents and missionaries of other tribes. The Navajo blankets and silver-ware, the Hopi and Tewan pottery, the Chippewa canoes, are all in demand, and the art of making them should be fostered. Life on most of the reservations is a grim contention against wind and sun and bare brown earth. Each condition should be minutely studied, and every favoring law seized upon. Whenever an industry can be developed along inherited aptitudes, it should be done.

John Seger, who has been for many years a friend and teacher among the Arapahoes and Southern Cheyennes, pleads for an Old Folks' Home near his school, where the old people could spend the rest of their lives in peace near their grandchildren. They will not last long, but we cannot afford to let them suffer. Under Seger's plan a great part of their food would be raised in a garden, and they could be employed to teach their native arts to the young people. The licensed trader is a survival of the old rule and should be abolished. His monopoly is intolerable. Under the single restriction that no liquor should be sold, competing stores should be welcomed on each reservation, in order that the red man may sell his product to better advantage, as well as supply his needs at the lowest possible cost.

Fifth. Schools should be established in each "farm district," which should be at once boarding and industrial schools, like those at Colony and Red Moon, Oklahoma,[22] and these schools should displace all sectarian and non-reservation schools whatsoever, and all forcible transportation of pupils to Eastern schools should instantly cease. The theory that to civilize the red man it is necessary to disrupt families and to smother natural emotions by teaching the child to abhor his parents, is so monstrous and so unchristian that its failure was foretold by every teacher who understood the law of heredity. The school should raise the parents with the child. Instruction should be most elementary, as it is at Seger, at Darlington, and at Red Moon, among the Southern Cheyennes. In these schools, the child is taught to grapple with the conditions of life on his own reservation. He is taught how to mend a harness and put it on a horse, not how to make a wagon; how to plant potatoes, not how to conjugate a Latin verb. After he has acquired the power to read and

---

[20] Walter C. Roe received the doctor of divinity degree from Williams College. He served as missionary of the Reformed Church of America to the Southern Cheyenne-Arapaho from 1897 to 1913. (Richard H. Harper, "The Missionary Work of the Reformed (Dutch) Church in America: In Oklahoma," p. 256.)

[21] Seger's Colony was a sub-agency, manual boarding school, and farm for the Southern Cheyenne and Arapaho. It was run by John Homer Seger, who established it. (See the Introductory Survey for a discussion of Garland's visit there in 1900.)

[22] Red Moon was a sub-agency of the Cheyenne-Arapaho Agency at Darlington. Garland visited Red Moon in 1900.

write and speak colloquially (which the Carlisle[23] Indians I have met seldom do), he is taught the value of money, and sufficient arithmetic to enable him to transact the business of a herder or farmer. But admirable as this is, there are other possibilities. Wherever white and red are mingled as settlers, I would educate them in the little red school-house together, and this can soon be done in some parts of Oklahoma. In any case, the education should arm the child for his battle for life and should not alienate him from his people. "Honor thy father and thy mother," is a command which the red children implicitly obey, until they are taught that everything their poor old parents do is vile.

Sixth. The missionaries in the field should be given to understand that they have no more rights in the premises than any other visitor, and that their attempt to regulate the amusements and the daily life of the red man is without sanction of federal authority. Many of the missionaries I have met are devoted souls, but I would not care to live where they had power to define what recreations were proper and what were not. Their view of "profane" songs and pleasures is absurdly narrow and (to put it mildly) inelastic. They do not represent the culture and scholarship of our day; and while I appreciate their motives and their sacrifices, I cannot but observe that they are often an embarrassment to the agent and sad examples of narrow piety.[24] In the interest of their own influence, I would urge all Eastern Missionary Societies to at once impress upon their representatives on the reservations the wisdom of assisting in the preservation and development of the native arts of the tribe with which they are associated. This they can do with very little money, by inducing all the old men and women (who are the fast fading representatives of these arts) to instruct their sons and daughters, nieces or grandchildren, in silver-smithing, basket-making, blanket-weaving, or whatever form of work they know best. The parent society could also form itself into an agency for the sale of wares, being careful to keep the advice of accredited authorities on art in order that the product may not lose vogue by becoming cheap and characterless. Mr. and Mrs. Roe, of Seger's Colony, Oklahoma, are examples of missionaries with larger aims than merely making converts. Mr. Roe's influence is not due to his preaching of dogma, but to his kindliness and helpfulness as a man and brother.

This industrial side of the Indian problem fits in just now with the revival of handicraft so strikingly general throughout the nation, and it may be that in it lies a very considerable means of aiding the red man, as he painfully crosses the gulf between his old warrior life and his life as a cattle-herder and

---

[23] Carlisle was established at Carlisle, Pennsylvania, in 1879 under the direction of General R. H. Pratt for the purpose of educating Indian youth. Its purpose, according to Pratt was "to teach English and give a primary education and a knowledge of some common and practical industry and means of self-support among civilized people." (Frederick Webb Hodge, ed., *Handbook of American Indians North of Mexico,* Pt. 1, p. 207.) Carlisle was officially closed on July 16, 1918. (William Heuman, *The Indians of Carlisle,* p. 123.)

[24] Garland's bitter attack on the missionaries here and in subsequent passages is understandable in light of his personal philosophy. To attack institutions, even organized religion, was a part of his reformist tendency. His embracing of Darwinian philosophy, as indicated in note 19 above, as well as his exploration of psychic phenomena, made his personal philosophy "unorthodox" in light of the views of most religious sects of his day.

gardener. He cannot be cut off from all his past; progress is not of that nature; it proceeds by slow displacement, by gradual accretion. Above all, the red man must feel that he is worth while, that he is a man among men — different, but not despicable because different. We should try to make him an admirable red man, as Booker Washington is trying to make the negro an admirable black man.

Seventh. Wherever a red man takes his allotment, he should be considered a citizen, free to come and go as he pleases, subject to the same general laws as his white neighbor. He should be allowed to visit other reservations and inter-marry with other tribes; he will never inter-marry to any extent with the whites; he ought not to do so if he could.[25] Under this new condition, the agent will no longer be the commander, but the friend, the adviser, the attorney; his authority will depend on his judgment, his tact, his helpfulness.

The present condition of the allottee is an anomalous one; he is neither man, brute, nor neighbor. He is told by the Commissioner that he is free to do as other men; but when he seeks to leave the reservation he is ordered back by the agent.[26] He is forbidden to visit in numbers exceeding five or ten; he is ordered not to dance, and admonished to wear his hair short. He is told that he must not use paint on his face, and a hundred other useless indignities and restrictions are put upon him;* and, if he protests, he is told that so long as

---

*The general effect of the legislation suggested by those who would convert the man of the Stone Age into a "Christian citizen" is something like this: "You, Whiteshield, will at once leave your pleasant camp in the grove beside the Washita and take yourself to your homequarter. You will at once give up the tepee and all your skin clothing. You will put off your moccasins and take to brogans. You will build a hut and live therein. You will have your hair cut short, and give up painting your face. You will cease all singing and dancing. Every form and symbol of the past is vile — put them away. You will send your children to school — even the little ones of five must go. Smoking is expensive, and leads to dreaming — stop it. To do bead-work or basket-weaving is heathen; your wife must abandon that. You will instantly begin to raise pigs and chickens, and work hard every day, because it is good to work. In order that you may know how sweet it is to live the life of the white farmer, you may go to church on Sunday and hear a man talk in words which you do not understand, and sing songs which white people sing when they have nothing better to do." This reads like caricature, but I assure the reader it is only a condensation of the suggestions made in my hearing by kindly people who believed themselves to be Christians.

---

[25] The reader should beware of accusing Garland of racism in this passage. He is apparently concerned that in the process of taking up the white man's ways the Indian might be destroyed. An active debate over whether the Indian was "vanishing" was being conducted in the popular magazines and journals of the day.

[26] There was never any statutory authority for confining Indians on reservations; administrators simply used the concept of "wardship" to justify the practice. It was given official sanction in a policy statement in 1890: "The Indian not being considered a citizen of the United States, but a ward of the nation, he can not even leave the reservation without permission." (Cohen, *Handbook of Federal Indian Law,* pp. 176–177.)

he eats the rations of the government he must obey the agent; and yet these rations are not only his necessity, they are his due. I have sometimes felt that the red man is the most patient and long-suffering creature in the world. Those who cry out against "pauperizing" him by means of rations have little comprehension of the barren lands he inhabits, and the necessity and the justice of his allowance.

The allottee should be made a citizen in truth, subject to punishment when he goes wrong, free to dress as he pleases and live as he pleases, so far as forceful change is concerned. He should be encouraged to live better, to dress in keeping with his fortunes. Religious bias should no longer control him. His rights as a man should be respected. I have no sympathy with those who would "break" the head man and discredit every native amusement, turning the tribe into a settlement of joyless hypocrites. The zealots who preach this are themselves losing power in the world. What sort of village would that be where sombre fanatics could regulate the amusements and the education of the citizens? A people must have play; and, until the young red men and women come naturally to enjoy baseball and the Virginia reel, the government is in cruel business when attempting to force relinquishment of native songs, games and dances.

Finally. The question of abolition of reservations comes up, and is advocated by those who would teach the red man to farm, as you teach a puppy to swim by flinging it into the river. "Let them sink, or paddle and keep afloat," they say, but to let down the bars on some of the reservations would be to submerge the tribe utterly and render it homeless. The reservation is still an "isle of safety" to the Northwest tribes.

Moreover, we must never forget that what is true of one reservation is not true of another. In Oklahoma, the settlers and the Cheyennes and Arapahoes are about to mingle peaceably, for the reason that "the horseman with a gun," the cattle-man, is passing away, and the peace-loving farmer is taking his place.[27] "I do not fear the man in the fields with his plow," said a Cheyenne to me; "but the man on the horse who rides and shoots, him I fear." In this remark is much enlightenment. Wherever the lands are generally arable, and the settlers are bent above plows and spades, where peaceful homes are being established and district schools built, there the lines of the reservation can safely give way. But to let the predatory cattle-men in on the reservation of the Northwest is to open the gate to trouble and corruption. The Cheyenne range should be fenced rather than leased or laid open to outside stock.

The cow-boy is a picturesque citizen, but he does not make for sweetness and light. He is not as lawless as he once was, but he is not even now an inspiration to a race struggling to acquire sobriety and thrift. Nevertheless, he has been for forty years the chief exemplar of the white man's civilization — so far as the red men were aware. Our agents have been mainly unmarried

---

[27] On June 1, 1900, 14,573 of the 59,324 white settlers in Oklahoma derived their principal source of income from livestock, while the remainder derived their income from hay and grain, vegetable, fruit, dairy, tobacco, cotton, and other farm products. (*Twelfth Census of the United States, Taken in the Year 1900,* Volume V, Part 1, p. 26.)

men, living as in a barrack, offering little in the way of domesticity to the eyes of the tribes they ruled. They were not all corrupt, but they were sojourners; they made no homes among the Indians. The female teachers and most missionaries are also solitaries, with repellent notions of man's duty to God and their own duties to the redskins. Speaking generally, it is safe to say that the red men and the red women have had very slender opportunity to learn of the ways in which the industrious, peaceful, kindly American farmer and his family live. The Ute, the Cheyenne and the Crow came in contact only with the ragged, filthy fringe of our civilization.

But the cow-boy, the "scout," the lawless trapper, the "lonesome men," are passing away. As a novelist, I am sorry to see them go; as a well-wisher of the red men, and as a believer in decent speech, sobriety and kindly living, I am glad of the cowboy's diminishing hoof-beats. He carries with him something fine, but his room is better than his presence when all is said and done. The ranchers of Oklahoma to-day are farmers, as they should be, paying for their grass and building homes for their wives and children — men who realize that protection lies in law, not in violence; they will make it a point to dwell in peace with their red neighbors.

Therefore, I would abolish the reservation line in Oklahoma, but I would retain it for the present in Montana. Instead of trying to "break the power of the chiefs," I would use them to influence others less able. The agent can do much to discredit a head man, but he cannot rob him of any genuine influence he may have, for among the red men of a reservation, as among white people in a community, there are those who are natural leaders, who are orators, with the power to convince and lead.

There are not wanting those who say cynically: "Why take all this trouble? There are only a couple of hundred thousand of the redskins; let 'em die!" To such words we reply: As a nation, we can't afford to rest under the stigma of inhuman cruelty. These red men are on our conscience and cannot by any easy shift be put away. They are survivals in our midst of the Stone Age; they are not to blame for their inelasticity of habit; moreover, they have many admirable qualities. We are answerable for them, just as we are answerable for the black man's future. As the dominant race, we have dispossessed them; we have pushed them to the last ditch — which will be their grave, unless we lay aside greed and religious prejudice and go to them as men and brothers, and help them to understand themselves and their problems; and only when we give our best to these red brethren of ours, do we justify ourselves as the dominant race of the Western continent.

Background

In recent years some of the better known journals of literary criticism have published pieces dealing with American writers' treatment of the American Indian. The critics usually refer to Albert Keiser's The Indian in American Literature *as the ultimate source. Very little attention has been given to "The Redman as Material," which is the first substantial statement on the subject by a well-known writer.*

In light of what modern pro-Indian writing and Indian history produced in this century have told us about the native American, Garland's criticism of earlier writers is still sound. But this essay is more than literary criticism. It is a moral indictment of writers who have helped shape public opinion of the Indians, and it is an indictment of the falsity of that opinion.

The subdued tone and the well-placed barbs of sarcasm make this one of Garland's more effective pieces of writing about the American Indian.

12. The Red Man as Material[1]

A very large part of the ferocity of the American Aborigine has arisen from the exigencies of new world literature. As they say in Missouri, he was "nacherly obleeged" to be devilish. Even the explorers could not endure to tamely report him peaceful nor the missionary recognize him as virtuous, for to do so were to make exploring altogether too easy and conversion of no avail.

When a man starts out to find a savage and terrible tribe he generally succeeds — in his book — and so the primitive races have ever been represented on their diabolic rather than on their human side. From the beginning they were "material."

Explorers cannot win glory by describing battles with sheep; they must set down the natives as treacherous, blood-thirsty tigers. Ah, that word "treacherous"! If ever there was an over-worked word this is the one. If a native in a tight place promises to be good and be kicked about the corners of his own land — and afterwards repents and kills the man who trampled him, he is a "treacherous devil," but if a white hunter similarly deceives his captors he is a diplomat.

You see, the explorer, the missionary, and the fictionist are each and every one working for a public, and their readers don't want a gentle, humane, pastoral, and peaceful native; they want a being whom it is a hardihood to discover, a danger to convert, and a glory to slaughter. And so, from Captain John Smith to Jack London, the red people of America have always had to take it.[2]

---

[1] Reprinted from *Booklover's Magazine*, 2 (August, 1903): 196–198.

[2] John Smith (1580–1631), in *The Generall Historie of Virginia, New-England, and the Summer Isles* (1624), gives numerous examples of Indian "treachery" and an extended treatment of a massacre on March 22, 1622, in which he describes the Indians as "beasts" and "hell-hounds" and their work as "butchery." (John Smith, *The Generall Historie of Virginia*, pp. 144–145.)
Jack London (1876–1916) is not known best for his stories about Indians. However, several of the tales in his early collections deal with Indians and Eskimos. For instance, Indian characters appear in "The Wisdom of the Trail," "The Wife of a King," and "An Odyssey of the North," which were published in *The Son of the Wolf* (1900), and in "Nam-Bok the Unvoracious" and "Keesh, the Son of Keesh," which were published in *Children of the Frost* (1902). Garland might have found many things objectionable in these stories, such as the frequent appearance of the pronouns *ye, thou,* and *thee* in the dialogue of the Indians. Certainly statements such as the following, which appears near the beginning of "The Wisdom of the Trail," must have been most distasteful to Garland: "The aboriginal mind is slow to generalize, and many facts, repeated often, are required to compass an understanding." (Jack London, *The Son of the Wolf,* p. 145.)

To the pilgrim fathers the savage was a child of the Devil. To the tender-foot Hollander, who settled New York, he was a vile cumberer of the earth which he longed to possess. To the Scotch Irishman, who settled Kentucky, he was a ferocious beast to be hunted. And to Cooper, Simms, Bird, Webber,[3] and a thousand others who followed them — the Cherokee or the Sioux was "the enemy" who furnished the hero an opportunity to display his valor.

Under these conditions you must not expect to gain any very clear notion of what a red family is like — for this "fiend" has no family: he is merely stalking the woods to capture "heroines" and clip locks of hair from temples of handsome young heroes. Occasionally he thrills a council, or in captivity makes a lofty appeal in language which only Ossian or Webster[4] could have uttered off-hand; but these moments of comparative magnanimity only confuse the situation — they do not tell us what the redman really is when he is at home with his children.

You would not expect a truthful picture of an Englishman from a French romancer in time of warfare. What can we hope to learn of the Winnebagoes from those who go out against them with guns or a rival creed?

Furthermore, while the redman was spared the pain of reading about himself in these various reports, recitals, novels, plays, and pleas, he was under the appalling disadvantage of not being able to state to the world his own case.

---

[3]James Fenimore Cooper's best-known novels dealing with Indians are the so-called "Leatherstocking Tales": *The Pioneers* (1823), *The Last of the Mohicans* (1826), *The Prairie* (1827), *The Pathfinder* (1840), and *The Deerslayer* (1841). Other well-known novels include *The Wept of Wish Ton-Wish* (1829), *The Chainbearer* (1845), and *Ravensnest; or The Redskins* (1846). (*The National Cyclopaedia of American Biography,* 1:398.)

William Gilmore Simms was a native of South Carolina. His fictional works dealing with the Indians were *The Yemassee* (1835), a novel, and *The Wigwam and the Cabin* (1845), a collection of tales. (*The National Cyclopaedia of American Biography,* 6:204.)

Delaware native Robert Montgomery Bird's best-known Indian novel is *Nick of the Woods; or The Jibbenainosay* (1837). (*The National Cyclopaedia of American Biography,* 7:183.) Apparently an avid reader of Western literature and history, Bird developed a disdainful attitude toward the Indian, as his preface to the Revised Edition shows: "The purposes of the author, in his book, confined him to real Indians. He drew them as, in his judgment, they existed — and as, according to all observation, they still exist wherever not softened by cultivation — ignorant, violent, debased, brutal. . . . " (Robert Montgomery Bird, *Nick of the Woods,* pp. 17, 32.)

Prolific novelist and adventurer Charles Wilkins Webber's major Indian works were *Old Hicks the Guide; or Adventures in the Comanche Country in Search of a Gold Mine* (1848), *The Gold Mine of the Gila: A Sequel to Old Hicks the Guide* (1849), and *The Prairie Scout, or, Agatone the Renegade* (1852). (*The National Cyclopaedia of American Biography,* 4:355.)

[4]Ossian was a legendary Gaelic hero and poet, the son of Fingal, a third century hero of Gaelic literature. James Macpherson claimed to have collected and translated Ossian's poems, publishing them as *Fingal* (1762) and *Temora* (1763). The Ossian poems are one of the best-known literary hoaxes.

Daniel Webster of New Hampshire, and later Massachusetts, spent forty years in politics. He was elected to the Senate in 1830. A great orator, he reached his apex when he stood against states' rights and nullification in his famous debates with Robert Y. Hayne. (*Concise Dictionary of American Biography,* 1162–1163.)

Black Hawk, Sitting Bull, and Cetewajo[5] should have had their own novelists — and then some of those "massacres" would have gone down to posterity as battles, and some of those "raids" would have been chronicled as "peaceful migrations which the uneasy consciences of white settlers magnified into well-merited revenges." To these red fictionists the white man would have yielded quite as thrilling material as the so-called "frog-eating Frenchmen"[6] has from time immemorial given to the English romanticist.

It is curious to observe that even a friendly fictionist like Cooper is forced, from the very necessities of his tale, to traduce the other tribes while ennobling the one he happens to know[7] — and this is a characteristic of many excellent books written since. It is necessary that the romance of adventure have an "enemy," and in order that the reader shall be blinded to the barbarism — the useless cruelty of the hero and his forces — the enemy is painted in the blackest colors so that the gentle soul who reads may say with a sigh at the end of a bloody chapter (wherein the native village is laid in ruin) — "Oh, well, they were so savage it's better so!"

Think of the disasters that would come to the fictionist should the sympathy of the reader go out toward the man hunted!

A very considerable exercise of the imagination is required for us to get even a Frenchman's point of view — how much more is required of the novelist who sets out to give the redman's conception of life and duty. Cooper honestly tried it, and he succeeded a great deal better than some of his latter-day critics seem to understand. But the kind of novel which he elected to write defeated him — he was forced to be superficial and unjust to the Miamis in order to exalt his hero and the friendly Delawares.

---

[5] Black Hawk, a Sauk chief, aided the British during the War of 1812 by raiding the border settlements. A treaty in 1804 with the Sauk and Fox had relinquished title to all lands of those Indians east of the Mississippi, and the majority of them under Keokuk moved after the War of 1812. Black Hawk refused and sought the aid of the Winnebago, Potawatomi, and Kickapoo against the Anglos. Subsequent deterioration of relations led to the opening of the Black Hawk War in May, 1832. Black Hawk was defeated, imprisoned and then sent west, where he settled on the Des Moines River. He died there in 1838. (Frederick Webb Hodge, ed., *Handbook of American Indians North of Mexico*, Pt. 1, pp. 150–152.)

For information on Sitting Bull, see Essay 10, note 10.

Cetewayo was a Zulu chief who rebelled against British rule in 1878. He was captured the next year and imprisoned until 1882, when the British attempted, but failed, to reinstate him as chief. While Cetewayo certainly had something in common with the Indian chiefs in regard to his relations to the whites, Garland's reference to him in an essay on the American Indian is out of place. (*Webster's Biographical Dictionary*, p. 274.)

[6] "Frog-Eater," "Frog," and "Froggy" were English slang expressions for Frenchmen, coming into popular use about 1860. The term originally applied only to Parisians. (Eric Partridge, *A Dictionary of Slang and Unconventional English*, 2:303.)

[7] Cooper generally held the "noble savage" concept of the Indian. However, in *The Last of the Mohicans*, for instance, he "enobles" Chingachgook and Uncas but presents Magua, the renegade Huron, as a fiend, and has him in one scene dash out an infant's brains and hand the quivering remains to its mother.

Many of those who came after Cooper lacked even his kindly interest in one particular tribe, and for the most part you will find in all this ruck of gory fiction only "the painted, treacherous, whooping, gliding, gleaming-eyed — antagonist." He is the mark for the dead-shot, the "wily" big game for "Tim, the trailer," the terror of the lovely maiden with an old-English way of speech — always he is "material."

All this would be harmless enough if the reader only understood that the novelist doesn't know anything about "Injuns," and couldn't use his knowledge if he did — but the gentle reader is a part of a great public, and reading this kind of thing leads to false notions of human life. Such fiction has helped to make the English-speaking peoples the most ruthless conquerors the world has ever seen, ruthless in the sense that they displace and destroy with large-hearted, joyous self-sufficiency, blotting out all manners, customs, religions, and governments which happen to differ from their own.

All this is done with supposed altruistic intentions — at least their proclamations are to that high effect; but it is all a matter of trade and commerce; and while I do not like to malign my own profession, I fear that if a real story of a kindly redman would pay better than a false story of a very horrid redman, we would all be doing our best, in every possible way, to furnish our readers *that* kind of material.

We're all human, even the novelist and his Indian, all parts of common humanity. We spring from the same good brown earth, and return thereto with an equal awe of "the great mystery." I hope Black Hawk's happy hunting ground exists, and that the white man will never find it.

Background on
The Final Council of the Creek Nation

The Creeks are a Muskhogean tribe which once, during historical times, occupied the greater part of what is now Alabama and Georgia. They were removed to Indian Territory during the 1830s. At that time they numbered between 15,000 and 20,000, many of whom were mixed bloods.[1]

They were a slave-holding tribe who followed agricultural pursuits. During the Civil War, the Creek Nation split its sympathy between the two sides. A treaty in 1866 provided for the emancipation of the Creek slaves and their adoption into the tribe.

The Five Civilized Tribes patterned their national system of government after that of the United States. Each tribe was organized as an independent nation within the Indian Territory. In 1874 the federal government consolidated its agencies into the Union Agency to assist these tribes in matters involving the United States.

The Creek Nation had a two-house legislature consisting of a House of Kings (their equivalent of a Senate) and a House of Warriors (their equivalent of a House of Representatives). The earliest written law governing the Creek Nation was dated 1817. Members were elected, as were other public officials, including the Principal Chief and Second Principal Chief. Their capital was Okmulgee. The capitol building was erected in 1878 and contained legislative chambers, offices for the chief executive, treasurer, auditor, superintendent of schools, and the various committees of the National Council, as well as chambers for the supreme court of the nation. The building, which has become a museum, stands in Block 139 of the city of Okmulgee, Oklahoma.

The Curtis Act of 1898 provided for allotment of land in severalty to the Creeks and for the dissolution of the tribal government. That government was to cease on March 6, 1906; thus the annual session of the Creek Council in 1905, the one Garland attended, was the last.

At that time there were 49 Creek towns, three of which — Arkansas, North Fork, and Canadian — were populated by freedmen. These Creek citizens had representation in the Council, a fact which Garland often comments upon. In 1904, there were 9,905 Creeks by blood — the majority of whom were mixed bloods — and 5,473 freedmen to whom allotments had been made.[2]

To Garland, as to Chief Pleasant Porter whom he interviewed, the cessation of the tribal affairs of the Creeks epitomizes a further stage in the development of Indian affairs: the dissolution of an Indian nation and the bestowing of U.S. citizenship upon its members.

---

[1] Frederick Webb Hodge, ed., *Handbook of American Indians North of Mexico*, Pt. 1, p. 364.

[2] Hodge, *Handbook of American Indians North of Mexico*, Pt. 1, p. 364.

13. The Final Council of the Creek Nation[3]

The Capitol building of the Creeks is located in the striving, but prosaic little Western town, which bears the name Okmulgee.[4] The name is old and some little part of the town is old, but for the most part, it is like any other prairie town. In its very midst, occupying what would be the Courthouse Square in an Illinois or Missouri county seat, stands a very plain, stone building, surrounded by a rough, stone wall — a building which typifies the passing order as the new brick blocks and ice-cream parlors on the corner announce the coming of the new. This gray structure, embowered in maple, is the Council House of the Creek Nation, a nation about to disappear.[5]

As I entered this building, I passed between groups of men, dark as negroes, and so far as many of them are concerned, of the negro physiognomy, for the Creeks have many negroes and halfbreeds among them. It was plain to see, here and there, how the red man's blood had warmed the black skin of the African into bronze or something lighter.

The interior of the building still more definitely and drearily typed the passing of tribal supremacy. The walls were in decay, and paper flapped from

---

[3] Item 437, Hamlin Garland Collection, University of Southern California Library, Los Angeles, published by permission of the University of Southern California Library and Constance Garland Doyle and Isabel Garland Lord. This document edited in a slightly different manner appeared in *Journal of the West*, 10 (July, 1971), 511–520, and is reprinted here with permission of *Journal of the West*.

[4] The Okmulgee were a branch of the Hitchiti, a Muskhogean tribe that became amalgamated with the Creeks. They settled along the great bend of the Chattahoochee River in the early eighteenth century. One hundred years later, they were on the Flint River in Georgia. Upon removal to the West, they reestablished themselves in the northeastern part of the Creek Nation. Pleasant Porter, chief in 1905, was from this group. (John R. Swanton, *The Indians of the Southeastern United States*, p. 168.) The town of Okmulgee became the county seat of Okmulgee County, Oklahoma.

[5] With the cessation of tribal relations, the Creeks became citizens of the United States, subject to its laws. The Council, as a law-making body, had no authority.

the ceiling and the grimy stairway (which parted like a gangway of a steamer) led to a desolate hall above. On the left of this hall, a square, bare room, not unlike an ordinary Western court-room, was the meeting place of the "House of Warriors," while on the right, a room half the size, and quite as bare, served as the chamber for the "House of Kings."[6] I walked lonesomely about, finding no one who spoke English or who could inform me whether the Council was to hold a session that evening or not, and when I returned to the street and inquired of the white citizens, no one seemed to know, and no one seemed to care.

After my supper at the most pretentious hotel in the village, I returned to the street in search of further information concerning the Council. The evening was warm with a splendid moon overhead, and as I strolled past the Council House, I heard singing; a chorus of voices that arrested my steps instantly.[7] The sound came from the House of Warriors· and was a chant, carried fòrward by men's voices alone — a splendid, rolling, deep-throated, manly chant, with the falling cadences which mark all the Indian music.[8]

I hastened at once to re-enter the building, and in the eastern room where the moon-light helped out the dim light of lamps, I found a dozen or two dark-skinned men, sitting in absolute immobility, yet singing together in singular solemnity. Their song was dignified and sad of quality, with the peculiar tone and time of the red man, touched by something which belongs to the black man. An elderly "citizen" with Indian profile, a bald man, of rather fine presence, occupied a seat at the flat table with his eyes fixed upon a small book which he held in his hand. Beside him, sat a younger man in whom it would be difficult to discover any trace of Indian blood.

They sang on and on endlessly, but the singing interested me very much. It was a peculiar blending of Christian hymns, negro melodies and the solemn

---

[6]The Council House, a two-story structure, has seven rooms on the ground floor, one of those being a large entry with doors and stairs at the north and south ends. The southeast part originally housed the Committee on Foreign Relations, and the southwest room originally was used by the Judiciary Committee. The upper floor has five rooms, with a large hall running through the center. The northeast room, originally the House of Warriors, is about twenty-by-sixty feet. Modern-day Creeks and various organizations still use this as a meeting room. The northwest part has three small rooms, which originally housed the Supreme Court. The room next to the court room was originally called the Mekko room (*Mekko Hlakko* was the term for the Principal Chief). The southwest room originally housed the House of Kings. (Jefferson Berryhill, *Indian-Pioneer History,* 15:29–30.)

[7]Alice M. Robertson states that she and her father attended the evening services which marked the council in session in the newly constructed Council House in 1878. They went at dusk when the bell was rung at the Council House to the House of Warriors, the "Tustenukkulkee" Hall, where hymns were sung and prayers were offered in the Creek language. (Alice M. Robertson, "The Creek Indian Council in Session," p. 897.)

[8]This and Garland's later generalizations regarding American Indian music have some substance; it is true that tribal melodic contours typically incorporate a pulsating quality, male tonal dominance, and pentatonic, descending melodies. Yet within these basic pan-Indian characteristics, there is considerable variation between tribes and within tribal repertoires. Furthermore, quite different song structures are sometimes exhibited, such as the pyramiding, rise-and-fall melodies and elusive tonality of native Pueblo music. (Gertrude Prokosh Kurath, "American Indian Peoples, Arts of, II. Music," in *New Encyclopedia Britannica* v. 1: pp. 663–667.)

and wild chanting of red warriors. They sang in unison or followed each other with a kind of natural harmonic adjustment. Each song started on a high key (as is usual among the red people) but fell now and again to tones that were like the moaning of the wind. The light from the kerosene lamps was too dim for me to see the faces clearly, but one or two of the younger men seated near me were fine types of the Creek. There were also a few women of the "guess" type. There was something sadly impressive to me in the sight of these people thus sitting and singing Christian hymns to the passing echoes of their war songs, while outside, the commonplace little town was listening to a cheap band, and smart business men were planning how to boom their town and sell their lots.[9]

I succeeded in finding someone who knew that the Creeks were holding regular sessions in the Council House from nine in the morning till three in the afternoon. Accordingly, I was early on hand and, being told to enter and make myself at home, I took a seat in one corner of the House of Warriors. Very soon the members began to drop in. There were a considerable number of negros,[10] and whether by pre-arrangement or not, they all passed into one corner of the room, to the right of the speaker's desk. The chairs were the ordinary bar-room chairs of a hotel and were arranged in three sections, about thirty on each side and as many more directly in front of the speaker. Two small deal tables were placed on either side of the platform on which were zinc pails, filled with water. The windows were uncurtained and spittoons were abundant.

Soon the hall was comfortably filled and I had gained a very good conception of the membership. There were fewer negroes than I had been led to expect, and on the left of the speaker, near where I sat, the fullblood Creeks now grouped.[11] Some of these were young, handsome, smiling, well dressed, and well barbered. But back against the wall, a row of six or eight older men sat, quietly — somberly. They were powerful-looking fellows and quite evidently, the conservative members of the body. Two or three looked like Japanese; one of them could easily pass for a famous Japanese general.

---

[9] Before allotment began, the United States set aside townsites which were platted between 1899 and 1903, at which time sales began on "a cash deposit and deferred payment plan." Payments were not completed until 1915, those in the Creek Nation amounting to $924,689.84. In 1903, a Congressional act allowed individuals to plat and sell townsites at their own expense. The result of transactions involved in both types of townsites was often fraud, the most serious of which occurred in the Creek Nation. (Angie Debo, *And Still the Waters Run*, pp. 48, 75–76, 120ff., 203–205.)

[10] The number of blacks in the legislature is not too surprising, since they comprised about one third of the Creek Nation's population. In the last quarter of the nineteenth century, there were several well-known legislators among the Creek freedmen, including such men as Scipio Sango, Jessie Franklin, Monday Durant, John Kernel, and Simon Brown.

[11] Since the Civil War, the fullblood Creek had formed a political unit, which, allied with the blacks, usually stood in opposition to the mixed bloods. Creek politics had nearly resulted in civil war during what was called "The Green Peach War" in 1882, in which the fullbloods took part. They opposed allotment, and after it came, they were unable to adjust, not understanding such things as deeds, leases, and taxes. (Angie Debo, *The Road to Disappearance*, pp. 249ff., 376.)

The clerk[12] looked as though he might be a quarter-blood and the secretary,[13] a bright looking young woman, dressed in navy blue, might have been half Creek, half Japanese. She was very much at home and very lady-like and attended to her duties with an air of dainty precision. She sat between the clerk and the presiding officer. The chairman,[14] quite evidently a Creek, was of a type very difficult to understand. There must have been some white blood in him, and possibly a touch of negro. He was lame, bowlegged and walked with a cane, but seemed to be a man of considerable ability.

A hump-backed, small man opened the services with prayer, and the clerk read the minutes in a formal, alternating patchwork of Creek and Western English. He was rapid, business-like, and had evidently formulated his manner upon that of the reading clerk in the lower house at Washington. His voice was rather nasal, and the Creek words followed each other very rapidly, with a crackling effect.

The first order of business was the report of the various committees, and I was interested to observe the character of the men in charge. The educational committee was represented by a big, good-looking full-blood Indian,[15] who might have been a college graduate. The report of the Judiciary Committee was made by a big plump negro with shining jovial face,[16] and during his speech, a dog scratched at the door, seeking entrance, and when the sergeant at arms went to see who was there, the dog came in and I was glad to see nearly everyone break into smiles at this interruption. The chairman was so interested in the knowing air and assured step of the dog, that he quite forgot what the big negro was saying. They had hardly recovered from this diversion, when a very small yellow man, with a black moustache, entered, walked sedately forward and laid his broad, limp hat directly in front of the chairman, partly covering the record book of the Council. This amused the secretary, but seemed to be taken as a matter of course by everyone else.

The session immediately took on the appearance of a town meeting in some rude Western community. Affairs moved slowly; no one seemed in haste; the chairman and the clerk and the secretary went off into meditation, and there were long pauses when nothing came to mind. Once when the chairman of the Judiciary Committee went forward to the desk, another member subtracted his chair and substituted another with a lower and less comfortable back. Somebody warned him of this nefarious proceeding, and, looking around, he caught the offender in the act. However, he seemed to understand that it

---

[12] Garland has personages confused here. The clerk of the House of Warriors was a woman, Mildred McIntosh Childers. The person he designates as the clerk was more likely the door-keeper, a member of the Light Horse, i.e., the Indian Police.

[13] Mildred McIntosh Childers was the only woman to hold the position of clerk of the House of Warriors. (*Foreman Transcripts,* 2:309–311; *Creek-National Council,* Document 33949.)

[14] Alex Davis was speaker of the House of Warriors. (*Ibid.*)

[15] This was perhaps Chessie McIntosh, who was the superintendent of schools for the Creek Nation. (*Purcell Register,* October 13, 1905.)

[16] The identity of this man is unknown.

was all "in the game" and smiled back with a gesture which seemed to say, "I'll get even with you some time."

One by one they rose to speak on the various questions which slowly came up, and one of the most noticeable features of their eloquence lay in the use of the hands. In all the fullbloods I could detect survivals of the sign language.[17] Their hands were slim, beautifully modeled, and very expressive. They spoke quietly and often with humor. All were colloquial. Even when most impassioned they remained quiet, a suppressed quiet. They all chewed tobacco in the Southern fashion, and spittoons were a necessity at the beginning of every speech.

One man, a small thin man with tousled hair, secured the attention of the chairman. His neck was encircled with a silk handkerchief; gold rings were in his ears; and his clothing was cheap and ill-fitting, but no sooner was he on his feet with his hands in the air, than he seemed a man transformed. He was the natural orator. In fact, they all spoke exceedingly well. As to the manner of their speech, I cannot say; it was all "Creek" to me, but I doubt whether it would affect a New York councilman as having much weight. Their business is only that of winding up the affairs of the Nation, and doubtless their discussions were upon cattle leases, coal lands, fraudulent allotments,[18] and so on. They all spoke fluently and in rather staccato fashion without drawling or the use of gutterals. Even the negroes produced the same clear, clean-cut effect. The measured speech of the old time warrior is heard but seldom.

From the House of Warriors I passed to the House of Kings, and at first glance the types and the distributions of white, black, and red blood seemed about the same. But the presiding officer[19] in this case looked like a chieftain from one of the hill tribes of Asia. His moustache was thin, grey and very long, and his whiskers sparse and set low on the chin like those of a mandarin.

---

[17]Although traces of sign language may be found among all tribes in North America, sign language as a system of communication was most commonly used by the Plains Indians. (Garrick Mallery, *Sign Language Among North American Indians Compared With That Among Other Peoples and Deaf Mutes,* p. 316.) At the time Garland visited the Creek Council house, he had just come from Weatherford, Oklahoma, where he had spent several weeks with John Seger, who used sign language exclusively among his Cheyenne and Arapaho friends. (Garland, *Companions on the Trail,* pp. 313–314.)

[18]Chief Pleasant Porter spoke on such matters as fraudulent allotments and allotment progress in his address at the opening of the annual council on October 13, 1905. When enrollment was completed, there were to be 19,868 receiving allotments. (*Purcell Register,* October 13, November 3, 1905; *Indian Journal,* March 9, 1906; J. B. Campbell, comp., *Campbell's Abstract of Creek Indian Census Cards and Index.*) The act which had provided for allotment of land to the Creeks had placed control of agricultural leases in the hands of the Department of the Interior. Nevertheless, frauds occurred, and litigation concerning leases continued for years. The Creek country also had rich deposits of coal and, it was later discovered, of oil. Among the Creeks, mineral rights were allotted with the land. (Debo, *And Still the Waters Run,* pp. 35, 141, 212–213, 335–336.)

[19]The presiding officer in the House of Kings was President James Smith, known as the "Mekkulkee." (*Foreman Transcripts,* 2: 309–311; *Creek-National Council,* Document 33949.)

The clerk resembled an old New England deacon, or a statesman of the Charles Sumner type, badly sunburned.[20]

Some of these "Kings," which by the way means chief men or head men, also wore rings in their ears. Several of the members at my left looked like white men and could hardly be detected from any other Western settlers, except the lines of their noses. They were all touched with a hawk's bill. One of these, a big and handsome fellow, turned to me with a sigh of weariness, after a long speech, and said: "All this talk, talk, and nothin' to say," which I suspect was very largely true.

A little deal table, supported a zinc water-pail and zinc "gourd"; a small stove also gave evidence of a desire on the part of the Kings to be comfortable and was much in use. The clerk's desk was a long pine table, painted blue, and covered with oil cloth.

The setting and the general effect of even this renowned body was that of a town meeting, only the speakers were more patient with each other. No man was interrupted; no man's speech was cut short; no one seemed in haste; and so far as I could discover, no one seemed in ill-temper.

One of the questions which they were discussing, was the old, old question, "What right has the public to make a road through your land when the law says the road shall be made along the section line?" And two or three spoke at great length and with considerable eloquence upon this burning question. Among the others was a very old, very grizzled, and very picturesque colored man, who might have gone upon the stage without the change of a line, as "Uncle Tom." They listened to him patiently and I listened, or rather watched, absorbedly, for it was profoundly interesting to me to see in his gestures the effect of a lifetime among the people who resort to signs to illustrate or to fill out their speech.

I observed also that the presiding officers assumed all their prerogatives and talked even more freely than the chairmen of white councils. However, they had the grace never to interrupt, and never to belittle those who spoke from the floor. Even when there was "nothing doing," as my seat mate said, they remained gravely patient and every man had a chance. Jokes were frequent, but some of the fullbloods never laughed, although a faint gleam of light came into their eyes to signify that they had heard and understood, but that it was not their habit to *ha ha.*

The men speaking here were different beings in their appearance, at least, from those who sat outside on the grocery steps silently watching the white man build his brick blocks to submerge their Council House. Here they were still masters. Here they lived in the past. Perhaps these old men, with their backs to the wall, are dreaming of the day when they were lords of the plain.[21]

---

[20] The clerk of the House of Kings was Sam Grayson. (*Ibid.*) Garland is probably comparing his hefty physical appearance with that of Sumner, whom Garland would have known through his biography of U. S. Grant.

[21] Garland's metaphor is not quite appropriate here. The Creeks were in no way considered Plains Indians.

Perhaps the man making this long and deeply, quietly passionate speech is advocating a migration to Mexico, in order that the tribal laws and traditions may be maintained.[22]

Without doubt, if I could have understood their speech, I would have been able to detect, now and then, some reference to the past, some illustration taken from their immemorial traditions. But from all this I was debarred, and I softly tip-toed out.

Chief Porter[23] had his office on the first floor, in a bare and dusty room, but there was nothing prosaic about him. He was a big man, too big, he complained to me, "I find I am getting too heavy; it grows on me." He was distinctly Indian, and at first sight not prepossessing, but the longer I talked with him the more deeply he impressed me. He surprised me by his quickness of mind, and by the pace and poetry of his diction. Of course we fell to talking upon the Creek character and history, and everything he said was precise and illuminating. He knew the story of his people, and he knew American history, and rose to poetic solemnity in discussing the inevitable disappearance of the tribal government.

He confessed to being sixty-five years of age, and smiled as he said, "I thought I was an old man at forty-five." When I spoke of having visited the Council House, he seemed pleased, but added sadly, "Of course, we have no legislation to enact for the future. All we have to do now is to put our house in order for the new tenant. There is much detail in the way of transferring the various contracts which we have made, and I doubt if we can settle all these matters before the first of March. A Commission will need to be appointed from among us to represent the Creek Government after March 6th."[24]

Without any hint on my part as to my feelings, he added, "Yes, we are in decay. My nation is about to disappear. But no nation and no people endures forever. The life of the greatest nations is, after all, but a small span of history," and he conveyed to me in other fine and lofty words, the attitude of

---

[22]Throughout the 1890s and the early years of this century, many fullblood members of the Creek, as well as of the other Civilized Tribes, entertained various utopian schemes to emigrate to Mexico, where they hoped to recapture their old ways of living. Some of the schemes were promoted by those who would practice fraud on the Indians by offering to trade them land, which they did not have, in Mexico for their allotments. For emigration plans and schemes among the Creeks, see the following: *Perkins Journal,* February 5, 1904; *Daily Oklahoman,* April 4, 1905; *Indian Journal,* January 24, 1908; *Lexington Leader,* October 16, 1908.

[23]Pleasant Porter (1840–1907), the seventh and last elected chief of the Creek Nation, was born at Coweta, Indian Territory. His father was a white man. Through wide reading, Porter became one of the best informed Indians in the territory, beginning his political career as clerk of the National Council. He served in the Council for twelve years, one term as president of the House of Kings. (Hodge, ed., *Handbook of American Indians North of Mexico,* Pt. 2, pp. 287–288.) He ran in 1899 on a platform of compromise with the Dawes Commission, which was attempting to settle Creek national affairs and make ready their transition to citizenship in the United States. Porter died just before the new state of Oklahoma joined the Union. (Debo, *The Road to Disappearance,* p. 376.)

[24]Provisions were made for a delegation to carry on tribal governmental business and activities until statehood in 1907. (*Indian Journal,* March 6, 1906.)

Chief Pleasant Porter, whom Garland interviewed, exemplifies the Creek Tribe's high degree of assimilation into Anglo culture.

the chief who, while not content to see his people's traditions disappear, is, after all, resigned to the inevitable laws of civilized society.

Nothing that I have seen in the Creek Nation has been so revealing, so significant of the changes in progress, as this quaint and curious legislature, sitting in their decaying building, while to the ring of the trowel and the tap of the carpenter's hammer, white men are building a new, alien, and inexorable civilization around them.[25]

---

[25] The Anglo society was not quite as "alien" to most of the Creeks as Garland would have the reader think. The Creeks had modern railroad transportation and telegraph and telephone service among their modes of communication. Their towns were much like their counterparts in the adjoining states (Garland admits this in his opening paragraph). Muskogee, their principal town, was the economic and cultural hub of the Creek Nation. Its opera houses billed performances by some of the best stage performers of the day. For the most part, the Creeks by this time had been Anglicized.

PART III
Reference Materials

References

MAJOR REPOSITORIES AND LIBRARIES

Indian Archives Division, Oklahoma Historical Society, Oklahoma City
National Archives, Washington, D.C.
University of Arizona Library, Tucson
University of Arkansas Library, Fayetteville
University of Arkansas at Little Rock Library, Little Rock
University of Southern California Library, Los Angeles

FEDERAL AND STATE RECORDS

Annual Report of the Commissioner of Indian Affairs to the Secretary of the Interior for the Year 1879. Washington: Government Printing Office, 1879.

Annual Report of the Commissioner of Indian Affairs to the Secretary of the Interior for the Year 1887. Washington: Government Printing Office, 1887.

Annual Report of the Commissioner of Indian Affairs to the Secretary of the Interior. Washington: Government Printing Office, 1892.

Annual Report of the Commissioner of Indian Affairs, 1894. Washington: Government Printing Office, 1895.

Annual Report of the Secretary of the Interior for the Fiscal Year Ended June 30, 1895 [Report of the Commissioner of Indian Affairs]. Washington: Government Printing Office, 1896.

Annual Report of the Secretary of the Interior for the Fiscal Year Ended June 30, 1896 [Report of the Commissioner of Indian Affairs]. Washington: Government Printing Office, 1897.

Annual Reports of the Department of the Interior for the Fiscal Year Ended June 30, 1897 [Report of the Commissioner of Indian Affairs]. Washington: Government Printing Office, 1897.

Annual Reports of the Department of the Interior for the Fiscal Year Ended June 30, 1898 [Report of the Commissioner of Indian Affairs]. Washington: Government Printing Office, 1898.

Annual Reports of the Department of the Interior for the Fiscal Year Ended June 30, 1899 [Report of the Commissioner of Indian Affairs, Part I]. Washington: Government Printing Office, 1899.

Annual Reports of the Department of the Interior for the Fiscal Year Ended June 30, 1900 [Report of the Commissioner of Indian Affairs]. Washington: Government Printing Office, 1900.

Annual Reports of the Department of the Interior for the Fiscal Year Ended June 30, 1901 [Report of the Commissioner of Indian Affairs, Part I]. Washington: Government Printing Office, 1902.

Official Register of the United States, Containing a List of the Officers and Employees in the Civil, Military, and Naval Service, Together With a List of Vessels Belonging to the United States, July 1, 1897, Volume I. Washington: Government Printing Office, 1897.

Returns from Regular Army Infantry Regiments, June 1821–December 1916. Microcopy M665, Roll 230, National Archives Microfilm Publications.

Returns of the United States Military Posts, 1800–1916. Microcopy M617, Roll 773, National Archives Microfilm Publications.

Statistical Abstract of the U.S. Washington: U.S. Department of Commerce, Social and Economic Statistics Administration, Bureau of the Census, 1974.

Twelfth Census of the United States, Taken in the Year 1900, Volume V, Part I. Washington: U.S. Census Office, 1902.

UNPUBLISHED MATERIALS

Arvidson, Lloyd A. "A Bibliography of the Published Writings of Hamlin Garland." Unpublished Master's Thesis. University of Southern California, Los Angeles, 1952.

Creek-National Council. Records of the Creek Nation, Indian Archives Division, Oklahoma Historical Society, Oklahoma City.

District Court Records, Seventh Judicial District, Miles City, Montana.

Foreman Transcripts. Indian Archives Division, Oklahoma Historical Society, Oklahoma City.

Tongue River Reservation Consolidated File 44572. Records of the Adjutant General's Office, Records Group 94, National Archives.

U.S. Department of the Interior. "Rosters and Lists of Indian Names," Item 460b, Hamlin Garland Collection, University of Southern California Library, Los Angeles.

NEWSPAPERS

Daily Oklahoman (Oklahoma City, Oklahoma Territory)

Gazette (Billings, Montana)

Globe-Democrat (St. Louis, Missouri)

Indian Journal (Eufaula, Creek Nation)

Lexington Leader (Oklahoma Territory)

New York Times

Perkins Journal (Oklahoma Territory)

Purcell Register (Chickasaw Nation)

Times (Billings, Montana)

Weekly Times (Billings, Montana)

Yellowstone (Miles City, Montana)

GARLAND MANUSCRIPTS

The following Hamlin Garland manuscripts are in the Hamlin Garland Collection in t'.e University of Southern California Library, Los Angeles.

"Among the Southern Utes," Item 434.

"Colorado, Ouray, 1896," Item 48.

"A Day at Isleta," Item 435.

"A Day at Zuni," Item 436.

"The Final Council of the Creek Nation," Item 437.

"Glimpses of the Navajo Indians," Item 441.

"The Harvest Dance Among the Accomans," Item 442.

"The Jicarilla Apaches," Item 448.

"The Most Mysterious People in America," Item 449.

"Notes on the Cheyenne Country and Lame Deer," Item 450.

"Notes and Hints, 1892–1897," Item 34.

"A Typical Indian Scare: The Cheyenne Trouble," Item 459.

BOOKS AND ARTICLES

Arvidson, Lloyd A., ed. and comp. *Hamlin Garland: Centennial Tributes and a Checklist of the Hamlin Garland Papers in the University of Southern California Library*. Los Angeles: The University of Southern California Library, 1962.

Bailey, Lynn R. "Thomas Varker Keam: Tusayan Trader." *Arizoniana* 2 (Winter 1961): 15–19.

Berryhill, Jefferson. *Indian-Pioneer History*. Oklahoma City: Indian Archives Division, Oklahoma Historical Society.

Bird, Robert Montgomery. *Nick of the Woods; or, The Jibbenainosay*. Curtis Dahl, ed. New Haven: College & University Press, 1967.

Bloom, Lansing B., ed. "Bourke on the Southwest, XIII." *New Mexico Historical Review* 13 (April 1938): 192–209.

Bourke, John G. *The Snake-Dance of the Moquis of Arizona*. New York: Charles Scribner's Sons, 1884.

Campbell, J. B., comp. *Campbell's Abstracts of Creek Indian Census Cards and Index*. Muskogee, Oklahoma: Muskogee Phoenix Job Printing Company, 1915.

Cohen, Felix S. *Handbook of Federal Indian Law*. Washington: Government Printing Office, 1942.

Commission on the Rights, Liberties, and Responsibilities of the American Indian. *The Indian: America's Unfinished Business,* William A. Brophy and Sophie D. Aberle, comps. Norman: University of Oklahoma Press, 1966.

Concise Dictionary of American Biography. New York: Charles Scribner's Sons, 1964.

Debo, Angie. *And Still the Waters Run*. Princeton: Princeton University Press, 1972.

————. *A History of the Indians of the United States*. Norman: University of Oklahoma Press, 1970.

————. *The Road to Disappearance*. Norman: University of Oklahoma Press, 1941.

Dozier, Edward P. *The Pueblo Indians of North America*. New York: Holt, Rinehart and Winston, Inc., 1970.

Dutton, Bertha P., ed. *Indians of the Southwest*. Santa Fe: Southwestern Association of Indian Affairs, Inc., 1963.

Eggan, Fred. *Social Organization of the Western Pueblos.* Chicago: The University of Chicago Press, 1950.

Ferris, Robert G., ed. *Soldier and Brave: Historical Places Associated with Indian Affairs and the Indian Wars of the Trans-Mississippi West.* Washington: National Park Service, 1971.

Fontana, Bernard L. "Historical Foundations," in *Indians of Arizona: A Contemporary Perspective,* Thomas Weaver, ed. Tucson: University of Arizona Press, 1974.

Forrest, Earle R. *Missions and Pueblos of the Old Southwest.* Cleveland: The Arthur H. Clark Company, 1929.

Garland, Hamlin. "Among the Moki Indians." *Harper's Weekly* 40 (August 15, 1896): 801–807.

————. *The Captain of the Gray-Horse Troop.* New York: Harper & Brothers, 1902.

————. *A Daughter of the Middle Border.* New York: The Macmillan Company, 1921.

————. "General Custer's Last Fight as Seen by Two Moon." *McClure's* 11 (September 1898): 443–448.

————. "The Red Man's Present Needs." *North American Review* 174 (April 1902): 476–488.

————. "The Redman as Material." *Booklover's Magazine* 2 (August 1903): 196–198.

————. *Roadside Meetings.* New York: The Macmillan Company, 1930.

————. "The Ute Lover." *Century* 58 (June 1899): 218–220.

Granger, Byrd H., ed. *Will C. Barnes' Arizona Place Names.* Tucson: University of Arizona Press, 1960.

Grinnell, George B. *The Cheyennes: Their History and Ways of Life.* Reprint edition. 2 volumes. New York: Cooper Square Publishers, Inc., 1962.

Harper, Richard H. "The Missionary Work of the Reformed (Dutch) Church in America: In Oklahoma." *The Chronicles of Oklahoma* 18 (September 1940): 252–265.

Heuman, William. *The Indians of Carlisle.* New York: Putnam, 1965.

Hodge, Frederick Webb, ed. *Handbook of American Indians North of Mexico.* 2 parts. Washington: Government Printing Office, 1907 and 1910.

Hoebel, E. Adamson. *The Cheyennes: Indians of the Great Plains.* New York: Henry Holt and Company, 1960.

Holloway, Jean. *Hamlin Garland: A Biography.* Austin: University of Texas Press, 1960.

Hough, Walter. *The Moki Snake Dance.* Chicago: Passenger Department, Santa Fe Route, 1899.

Irenholm, U. C. *The Shoshonis, Sentinels of the Rockies.* Norman: University of Oklahoma Press, 1964.

Kappler, Charles J., comp. and ed. *Indian Affairs: Laws and Treaties.* 5 volumes. Washington: Government Printing Office, 1903–1941.

Kluckhohn, Clyde, and Dorthea Leighton. *The Navaho.* rev. by Lucy H. Wales and Richard Kluckhohn. Garden City: Doubleday & Company, Inc., 1962.

Kurath, Gertrude Prokosh. "American Indian Peoples, Arts of, II. Music." *The New Encyclopedia Britannica.* 30 volumes. 15th edition. Chicago: William Benton, 1974.

La Farge, Oliver. *A Pictorial History of the American Indian.* New York: Crown Publishers, 1956.

Lange, Charles H., and Carroll L. Riley, eds., with the assistance of Elizabeth M. Lange. *The Southwestern Journals of Adolph F. Bandelier, 1883–1884*. Albuquerque: The University of New Mexico Press, 1970.

Littlefield, Daniel F., Jr., and Lonnie E. Underhill. "Renaming the American Indian: 1890–1913." *American Studies* 12 (Fall 1971): 33–45.

London, Jack. *The Son of the Wolf*. New York: Garrett Press, Inc., 1968.

Mallery, Garrick. *Sign Language Among North American Indians Compared With That Among Other Peoples and Deaf Mutes*, in J. W. Powell, *First Annual Report of the Bureau of Ethnology to the Secretary of the Smithsonian Institution, 1879–80*. Washington: Government Printing Office, 1881.

McNitt, Frank. *The Indian Traders*. Norman: University of Oklahoma Press, 1962.

Meyer, Roy W. "Hamlin Garland and the American Indian." *Western American Literature* 2 (Summer 1967): 109–125.

Morton, Robert H. *Territory of New Mexico Map*. Washington, D.C.: A. B. Graham Photo Lithographer, 1896.

National Cyclopaedia of American Biography, The. 49 volumes. Reprint edition. Ann Arbor: University Microfilms, 1967.

Partridge, Eric. *A Dictionary of Slang and Unconventional English*. 2 volumes. London: Routledge & Kegan Paul Ltd., 1970.

Portrait and Biographical Record of Oklahoma. Chicago: Chapman Publishing Company, 1901.

Prucha, Francis Paul. *A Guide to the Military Posts of the United States, 1789–1895*. Madison: State Historical Society of Wisconsin, 1964.

Reamer, Owen J. "Garland and the Indians." *New Mexico Quarterly* 34 (Autumn 1964): 257–280.

Robertson, Alice M. "The Creek Indian Council in Session." *The Chronicles of Oklahoma* 11 (September 1933): 895–898.

Rockwell, Wilson. *Utes: A Forgotten People*. Denver: Sage Books, 1956.

Roosevelt, Theodore. "The Hopi Snake Dance." *The Outlook* 105 (October 18, 1913): 565–573.

Sapir, Edward. *Southern Paiute, A Shoshonean Language*. Proceedings of the American Academy of Arts and Sciences 65 (June 1930).

Schoolcraft, Henry R. *Historical and Statistical Information Respecting the History, Condition and Prospects of the Indian Tribes of the United States*. Six parts. Reprint edition. New York: Paladin Press, 1969.

Schroeder, Albert H. "Rio Grande Ethnohistory" in Alfonso Ortiz, ed., *New Perspectives on the Pueblos*. Albuquerque: The University of New Mexico Press, 1972.

Smith, John. *The Generall Historie of Virginia, New-England, and the Summer Isles*. Ann Arbor: University Microfilms, Inc., 1966.

Stands In Timber, John, and Margot Liberty, with the assistance of Robert M. Utley. *Cheyenne Memories*. New Haven: Yale University Press, 1967.

Stewart, Edgar I. *Custer's Luck*. Norman: University of Oklahoma Press, 1955.

Stubbs, Stanley A. *Bird's-Eye View of the Pueblos*. Norman: University of Oklahoma Press, 1950.

Swanton, John R. *The Indians of the Southeastern United States*. New York: Greenwood Press, 1969.

Townsend, R. B. "Snake-Dancers of Mishongnovi." *Nineteenth Century* 55 (March 1904): 429–443.

Underhill, Lonnie E., ed. "Hamlin Garland and the Final Council of the Creek Nation." *Journal of the West* 10 (July 1971): 511–520.

Underhill, Lonnie E., and Daniel F. Littlefield, Jr., eds. "The Cheyenne 'Outbreak' of 1897 as Reported by Hamlin Garland." *Arizona and the West* 15 (Autumn 1973): 257–274.

——. "Hamlin Garland and the Navajos." *The Journal of Arizona History* 13 (Winter 1972): 275–285.

——. "Hamlin Garland at Isleta Pueblo." *Southwestern Historical Quarterly* 78 (July 1974): 45–68.

Webster's Biographical Dictionary. Springfield, Massachusetts: G. & C. Merriam Company, Publishers, 1972.

Bibliography of Garland's Writings on the American Indian

PUBLISHED WRITINGS

"Among the Moki Indians." *Harper's Weekly* 40 (August 15, 1896): 801–807.

"Among the Southern Utes," Item 434, Hamlin Garland Collection, University of Southern California Library, Los Angeles [Appeared in "Over Indian Trails" series].

Back-Trailers from the Middle Border. New York: The Macmillan Company, 1928.

"The Bad Medicine Man." *The Independent* 52 (December 6, 1900): 2899–2904.

"Big Moggasen." *The Independent* 52 (November 1, 1900): 2622–2624; reprinted in *The Book of the American Indian* (1923).

"The Blood Lust," in *The Book of the American Indian* (1923).

The Book of the American Indian. New York: Harper & Brothers, 1923.

"The Captain of the Gray-Horse Troop." *The Saturday Evening Post* 174 (December 14, 1901–March 29, 1902):

No.	No.
24 (Dec. 14, 1901): 3–5, 19.	33 (Feb. 15, 1902): 10–11, 14.
26 (Dec. 28, 1901): 6–8, 18.	34 (Feb. 22, 1902): 8–10, 20.
27 (Jan. 4, 1902): 12–13, 18.	35 (Mar. 1, 1902): 8–9.
28 (Jan. 11, 1902): 6–8.	36 (Mar. 8, 1902): 10–11.
29 (Jan. 18, 1902): 10–11, 18.	37 (Mar. 15, 1902): 10–11, 15.
30 (Jan. 25, 1902): 13–16.	38 (Mar. 22, 1902): 10–11.
31 (Feb. 1, 1902): 8–9, 18.	39 (Mar. 29, 1902): 10–11.
32 (Feb. 8, 1902): 8–9.	

The Captain of the Gray-Horse Troop. New York: Harper & Brothers, 1902.

Companions on the Trail. New York: The Macmillan Company, 1931.

A Daughter of the Middle Border. New York: The Macmillan Company, 1921.

"A Day at Isleta," Item 435, Hamlin Garland Collection, University of Southern California Library, Los Angeles [Possibly appeared in "Over Indian Trails" series].

"A Decree of Council," in *The Book of the American Indian* (1923).

"Drifting Crane." *Harper's Weekly* 34 (May 31, 1890): 421–422; reprinted in *Prairie Folks* (1893) and *Prairie Folks* (1899).

"The Faith of His Fathers." *Harper's Weekly* 47 (May 30, 1903): 892–893.

"General Custer's Last Fight as Seen by Two Moon." *McClure's* 11 (September 1898): 443–448.

[201]

"Glimpses of the Navajo Indians," Item 441, Hamlin Garland Collection, University of Southern California Library, Los Angeles [Appeared in "Over Indian Trails" series].

"The Harvest Dance among the Accomans," Item 442, Hamlin Garland Collection, University of Southern California Library, Los Angeles [Possibly appeared in "Over Indian Trails" series].

"Hippy, the Dare-Devil." *McClure's* 19 (September 1902): 474–480.

"Histoire de l'Indian Loup Hulant." trans. Mme. P. Chène. *Revue Politique et Littéraire* 71 (February 18–March 4, 1933): 103–107, 138–143.

"Houtan, le Courrier Rouge." trans. Mme. P. Chène. *Revue Politique et Littéraire* 75 (December 18, 1937): 777–778.

"The Human Side of the Redman." *Current Literature* 3 (November 28–December 2, 1927): 25–26, 41–42.

"The Iron Khiva." *Harper's Weekly* 47 (August 29, 1903): 1416–1419; reprinted in *The Book of the American Indian* (1923) and as "La Maison d'Ecole des Hommes Blancs," in *Revue Politique et Littéraire,* February, 1939.

"Joe, the Navajo Teamster." *The Youth's Companion* 71 (November 18, 1897): 579–580.

"Lone Wolf's Old Guard." *Harper's Weekly* 42 (May 2, 1903): 716–718; reprinted in *The Book of the American Indian* (1923).

"La Maison d'Ecole des Hommes Blancs." trans. Mme. P. Chène. *Revue Politique et Littéraire* 77 (February 1939): 56–60.

"The Most Mysterious People in America: The Cliff Dwellers and Pueblo People of Arizona." *Ladies' Home Journal* 8 (October 1896): 5–6.

"The New Medicine House." *Harper's Weekly* 46 (December 6, 1902): 36–37; reprinted in *The Book of the American Indian* (1923).

"Nistina." *Harper's Weekly* 47 (April 4, 1903): 544–545; reprinted in *The Book of the American Indian* (1923).

"Nuko's Revenge," in "Two Stories of Oklahoma." *Century* 68 (June 1904): 328–329.

"The Outlaw." *Harper's Weekly* 47 (June 13, 1903): 972–973; appeared as "The Story of Howling Wolf" in *The Book of the American Indian* (1923) and as "Historie de l'Indian Loup Hulant" in *Revue Politique et Littéraire* in February and March, 1933.

"The People of the Buffalo." *McClure's* 16 (December 1900): 153–159; appeared as "The Storm-Child" in *The Book of the American Indian* (1923).

Prairie Folks. Chicago: F. J. Schulte & Company, 1893.

Prairie Folks. New York: The Macmillan Company, 1899.

"The Red Man's Present Needs." *North American Review* 174 (April 1902): 476–488.

"A Red Man's View of Evolution," in "Two Stories of Oklahoma." *Century* 68 (June 1904): 328–329.

"Red Plowman." *Craftsman* 13 (November 1907): 180–182.

"The Redman as Material." *Booklovers' Magazine* 2 (August 1903): 196–198.

"The Remorse of Waumdisapa," in *The Book of the American Indian* (1923).

"Rising Wolf — Ghost Dancer." *McClure's* 12 (January 1899): 241–248; reprinted in *The Book of the American Indian* (1923).

"The Rivers Warning." *Frank Leslie's* 53 (January 1902): 297–304; reprinted in *The Book of the American Indian* (1923).

Roadside Meetings. New York: The Macmillan Company, 1930.

"The Silent Eaters," in *The Book of the American Indian* (1923).

"Sitting Bull's Defiance." *McClure's* 20 (November 1902): 35–40.

"The Spartan Mother." *Ladies' Home Journal* 22 (February 1905): 10, 50; reprinted as "Wahiah — A Spartan Mother," in *The Book of the American Indian* (1923).

"The Stony Knoll." *The Youth's Companion* 71 (December 18, 1897): 635.

"The Story of Howling Wolf," in *The Book of the American Indian* (1923).

The Trail of the Goldseekers. New York: The Macmillan Company, 1899.

"Two Stories of Oklahoma." *Century* 68 (June 1904): 328–329.

"The Ute Lover." *Century* 58 (June 1899): 218–220; reprinted in *The Trail of the Goldseekers* (1899).

"The White Weasel; A True Indian Story." *The Dearborn Independent* 27 (December 18, 1926): 4, 5, 27.

MANUSCRIPT MATERIAL

The following notes, nonfiction, fiction, poetry, and dramatic works are in the Hamlin Garland Collection in the University of Southern California Library, Los Angeles.

Notes

The following notes are arranged chronologically by Garland's trips to the West:

Notes on Walpi, 1895, in Item 47.

Notes on Zuni [1895], inserted in Item 43.

Notes on Laguna [1895], in Item 54–5.

Notes on Acoma [1895], in Item 54–5.

Notes on the Jicarilla Apaches [1896], in Item 48.

Notes on the Sioux [1897], in Item 49–3.

Notes on the Crow Reservation [1897], in Item 49–3.

Notes on the Northern Cheyenne [1897], in Item 49–3 and Item 49–2.

Notes on the Crow Reservation, Second Visit [1897], in Item 49–2.

Notes on the Flathead Reservation [1897], in Item 49–2.

Notes on the Nez Percé Reservation [1897], in Item 49–2.

Notes on the Yakima Reservation [1897], in Item 49–1.

Notes on the Blackfoot Reservation [1897], in Item 49–1.

Notes on the Fort Belknap Reservation [1897], in Item 49–1.

Notes on the Fort Peck Reservation [1897], in Item 49–1.

Notes on the Southern Cheyenne and Arapaho [1900], in Item 54–1.

Notes on the Navajo, 1899, in Item 54–1.

Notes on the Sioux [1900], in Item 54–2.

Notes on the Blackfoot Reservation [1900], in Item 54–3.

Notes on the Southern Cheyenne and Arapaho [1901], in Item 54–4.

Notes on Laguna [1901], in Item 54–6.

"Oklahoma, 1902. Ind. Ter. 1904," Item 56.

"Oklahoma, 1905," Item 60.

Notes on the Wind River Reservation, 1909, in Item 63–3.

Notes on the Crow Reservation, 1909, in Item 63–6.

Notes on the Flathead Reservation, 1913, in Item 63–9.

"Notes and hints" [1892–1897], Item 34.

Nonfiction

"Chief Charlevoy," Item 81.
"Chief Charlevoy," in "The Human Side of the Redman," Item 443.
"Companions on the Trail," Item 3.
"A Daughter of the Middle Border," Item 4.
"A Day at Isleta," Item 435.
"A Day at Zuni," Item 436.
"The Final Council of the Creek Nation," Item 437.
"Four Horns: Piegan," Item 438.
"General Custer's Last Fight as Seen by Two Moons," Item 439.
"The Gentle Side of the Red Man," Item 440.
"The Harvest Dance among the Accomans," Item 442.
"The Human Side of the Redman," Item 443.
"The Indian Agency," Item 444.
"Indian Humor," Item 445.
"Indian Names," Item 446.
"The Jicarilla Apaches," Item 448.
"The Most Mysterious People in America," Item 449.
"Notes on the Cheyenne Country and Lame Deer," Item 450.
"The Other Side of the Redman," in "Redman's Magic."
"The Red Man's Gift," in "The Human Side of the Redman."
"The Red Man's Present Needs," Item 452.
"Redman's Magic," Item 455.
"Roadside Meetings," Item 7.
"The Sacred Rock of the Cheyennes," Item 456.
Seger manuscript [introduced and, presumably, rewritten by Garland], Item 457.
"A Trip to Zuni," Item 458.
"A Typical Indian Scare: The Cheyenne Trouble," Item 459.

Fiction

"The Bad Medicine Man," Item 70.
"Big Moggasen," Item 71.
"The Faith of his Fathers," Item 97.
"Hippy," Item 110.
"Houtan — The Red Pioneer," Item 115.
"Leaders in the Trail," Item 128.
"Nistina," Item 147.
"The Padlock on the Trail," Item 451.
"Rising Wolf — Ghost Dancer," Item 166.
"The River's Warning," Item 167.
"Rushing Bear and the Commission," Item 169.
"The Seminole Strain," Item 170.
"The Silent Eaters," Item 172.
"The Sitting Bull's Visit," Item 174.
"A Spartan Mother," Item 177.

"The Storm Child," Item 182.
"The White Weasel," Item 192.
"Whiteman's Court," Item 193.

Poetry

"The Cheyenne Dance," Item 235.
"The Dance," in Item 63–9.
"The Indian," in Item 46.
"Signal Fires," Item 327.
"The Ute Lover," Item 344.

Dramatic Works

"The Red Pioneer" [Scenario for a silent film], Item 197b.
"The Storm Child" [First scene of a play], Item 212.
"Wamdesapa" [Libretto for an operetta], Item 216.

Index